MOUNTAIN
SUMMERS

MOUNTAIN SUMMERS

*Tales of hiking and exploration in the
White Mountains from 1878 to 1886
as seen through the eyes of women*

Foreword by
Laura and Guy Waterman

Edited by
Peter Rowan and June Hammond Rowan

GULFSIDE PRESS
GORHAM, NEW HAMPSHIRE

DEDICATION

This project is respectfully dedicated to:

Doug and Andrea Philbrook
and
Joe and Ann Kent

for it is they who are responsible for the procurement

and preservation of these precious chronicles.

CONTENTS

LIST OF ILLUSTRATIONS

FOREWORD

Mountains, the sea, the polar regions — those three mighty arenas in which humanity is humbled before the immensity, the terrifying power, the serene beauty, and the infinite subtlety of nature — mean many things to us, depending on our mood or perspective.

Of the mountains, one of the self-styled "middle-aged spinsters" in this book wrote to another during the winter of 1885:

The mountains give us what we take to them. . . .As a poet one may ascribe many things to the mountains and they may be very true things but they may not be all the truth, only one phase of it. . . .The mountains speak to us with our own voice . . .but, after all, they are only echoes.

Whether true or shadow reality, mountains convey to people all sorts of vivid experience: joy, discovery, adventure, beauty, terror, serenity, enriched relationships with their companions — or unabridged alienation from them. "What we take to them?" Perhaps. But life seems magnified, deepened, called up in voracious intensity among the high crags and deep coniferous forests of the mountains.

Thus for Reinhold Messner the mountains hold extreme physical and mental test; for John McPhee they hint long sweeps of geological events; for Lord Byron they induce transports of romantic ecstasy; for David Brower they marshall political crusade; for Lynn Hill they're a fitness center for the exercise of competitive gymnastics; for the Chinese or Indian sage they are holy places for contemplation of the mystery of The One.

Our little homespun mountains of New Hampshire invite just such a range of response, if on a level somewhat more pedestrian (neat word!) than the Alps or Himalayas. And much of that diversity of individual dialogue with mountains is found in the pages that follow.

Reader, when you set forth among these letters of (primarily) four strange, wonderful and mysterious women of the 1880s, you will find joy and adventure, friendship and unbridged gulfs, Victorian repressed inhibitions and Victorian mad release, uplifting spirit and anguished guilt, and at least one heart-breaking love story.

"Our own voice?" Perhaps. But read, and find out.

All four of these women were astonishingly strong climbers, full of vitality and adventurous spirit, ever ready to plunge into the thickest of krummholz thickets, routinely ascending then-much-rougher trails in a fraction of today's guidebook time, eagerly exploring every untrod ridge and valley. Said one of the local guides of the time:

Never seed ladies go like them, they never stopped to rest. . . . I reckon their party would tucker out any o' the men folks here about.

All their extraordinary performances were pulled off in a mood of playful, upbeat vivacity — and all in the uncompromising Victorian dress code of long and heavy skirts and stockings. Among other things you'll learn herein is how these ladies climbed trees for a better viewpoint without loss of modesty ("The getting up is very easy as the skirts come naturally after. A graceful descent is more difficult, as the same skirts are apt to remain above. . . .").

But this is not to conjure up a picture of brute Amazonian virility. These women also possessed a fine appreciation of mountain beauty, of quiet and stillness, of delicate shades of color and the details of forest greenery and tundra vegetation. Edith Cook writes a special note to Isabella Stone to tell her rapturously of a hushed moment with two deer at the edge of the woods at the base of Mount Jefferson. Marian Pychowska intersperses her accounts of diving through thickets or out onto dizzy crags with calmer moments of peace among the flowers and ferns and sunsets. Not just the quiet of the hills either: the violence of mountain storms also attracted their admiration and awe — and they didn't mind getting thoroughly wet in the process of observing them first-hand.

Nor were they undisciplined romantics in their assimilation of mountain beauty. The Pychowskas especially were knowledgeable on mountain flora and geology, submitting botanical notes to the journals and devoting many hours searching for alpine plants on the heights or for as many species of ferns as could be found in woods near their lodgings.

These letters also have much to say of friendship, of human relationships. Isabella's haunted blend of bold adventurousness and timid hypochondria evokes differing responses in the elder Pychowska's maternal but sometimes caustic advice, Marian's playful rallying, and Edith Cook's sensitive reassurance. For some readers, the most touching moments of all will be the heart-rending love affair so delicately left unrealized between Isabella and her "quiet, slow, plain, honest-hearted farmer, with a hidden appreciation of mountain beauties which my enthusiasm seemed to draw out." And the final unwritten act of this drama is possibly even more wrenching: Marian, the quintessential youth, the exuberant, the unquenchable, suddenly renouncing her mountain world to enter a convent and devote the final fifty-plus years of her long life to religious devotions of the sternest reclusive discipline. Romantic nineteenth century novel stuff!

Strange, wonderful, mysterious, these four such disparate and intriguing women from long ago. How fortunate posterity that Isabella chose to squirrel away her correspondence with her mountain-happy friends. Through a partially-revealed chain of events, those letters found their way to an auction where knowledgeable White Mountain historians snapped them up. Then, through the generosity of their final owners, Douglas and Andrea Philbrook and George ("Joe") and Ann Kent, plus the persistence, scholarship and perceptive comprehension of Peter Rowan and June Hammond Rowan, they made their halting way to print.

Here they are for us today. Return to a world where the White Mountains held the romance of discovery and quest; where Mount Garfield was known as Mount Hooket; where "the smokes" from loggers' forest fires routinely obscured summit views; where two men traversed the entire Presidential Range in one day, dined at an elegant hotel, and that evening walked back to their lodging 24 miles after dinner; where women in long skirts merrily thrust through thickets most would regard as impassable today; where tiny villages crackled with vitality and uproarious good times; where mountain gloom and mountain glory captured the hearts of four women so strange, so wonderful, so mysterious.

Laura and Guy Waterman

ACKNOWLEDGEMENTS

We would like to thank the following people and organizations who facilitated our research and helped make *Mountain Summers* possible:

Sybil Carey, Kacy Cuddy, Jessica Gill, Ellie Lang, Sister Mary Imelda Lytle, Alan McIntyre, Lex Paradis, Sister Mary Margaret Perry, Eric Pulliam, Rett Rowley, Sister Mary Grace Thul, Appalachian Mountain Club Library, Baker Library of Dartmouth College, Boston Public Library, Cincinnati Public Library, Firestone Library of Princeton University, Framingham Historical and Natural History Society, Framingham Public Library, Gorham Public Library, Hoboken Historical Museum, Hoboken Public Library, Mount Washington Observatory, New Hampshire Historical Society, Newark Public Library, Philbrook Farm Inn, Saint Dominic's Monastery, Seton Hall University Archives.

And, a very special thanks to Laura and Guy Waterman for their encouragement and assistance from the beginning to the end.

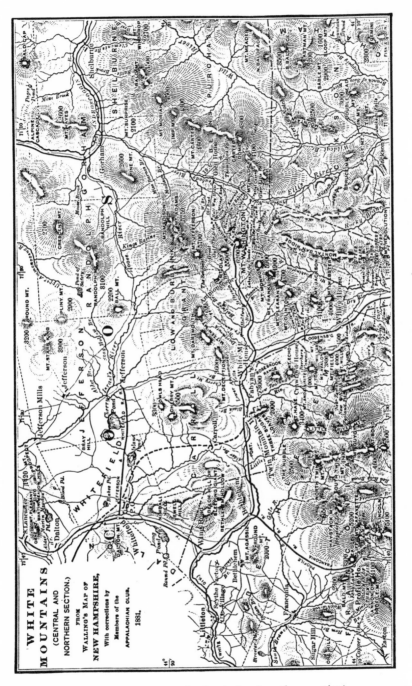

Map of the White Mountains (central and northern section)

xv

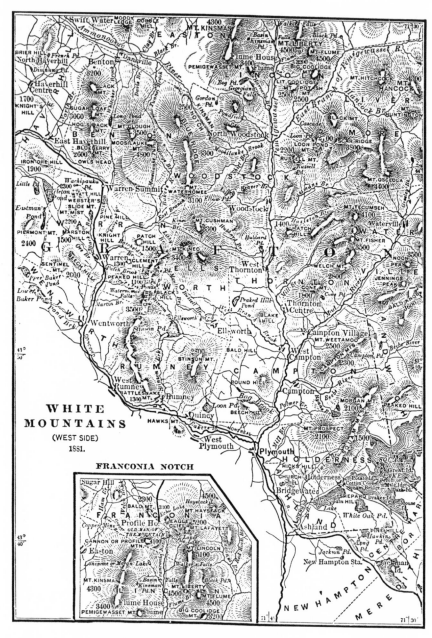

Map of the White Mountains (west side)

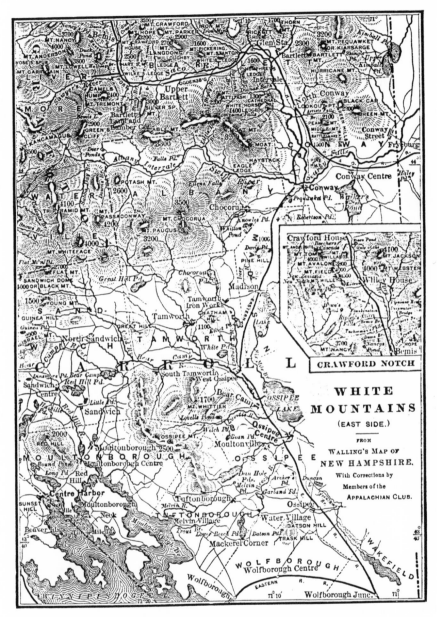

Map of the White Mountains (east side)

INTRODUCTION

The White Mountains of northern New England have long been a popular destination, and by the late nineteenth century the hotel and tourist trades were beginning to flourish in this region. People traveled by railroad and stagecoach to spend the summer, seeking rest and relaxation and the chance to experience for themselves the enchantment and beauty of the mountains that they had heard or read so much about.

It would not be an overstatement to say that a great deal has been written about the White Mountains. Even as early as 1911, Allen H. Bent, in the introduction to his *Bibliography of the White Mountains*, noted that more had been published about these mountains than any others except the Alps. Of all that has been recorded, however, very few personal narratives exist.

Mountain Summers is unique in that it is a collection of letters and diary entries written by women, offering a rare, first-hand account of exploration and adventures in the White Mountains from an uncommon female perspective. Captured within these chronicles are the early days of recreational hiking and trail building in the northeast, a saga of which these women were an integral part.

The primary correspondents in this collection are Marian Pychowska, Lucia Pychowska, Edith Cook and Isabella Stone. In addition, many other notable people appear throughout *Mountain Summers*. Among these figures are well-known White Mountain explorers, scientists, trail builders, guides, and innkeepers, each of whom contributed in their own way to the rich history of the area.

The women of *Mountain Summers* and their families frequented the White Mountains for many years, taking up residence at various boardinghouses usually for the full length of the summer season. From these hostelries, they explored their surroundings, botanized, surveyed new paths and trails, and composed beautiful letters to each other about their discoveries. Their excursions, which still would be considered adventurous, primarily took place in what is now the White Mountain National Forest; and since much of the landscape and many of the trail routes remain largely unchanged, today's hikers can retrace their steps.

The art of letter writing, on the other hand, has changed substantially, unfortunately lost in the advancement of technology. Letters written during the nineteenth century were often more eloquent and carefully prepared than those of today. This truth is apparent in the correspondences in *Mountain Summers*; extraordinary compositions with unmatched descriptions of the mountains, the spirited adventures of the characters, and life both at home and at the boardinghouses. The letters — positive, encouraging and inspiring — contain interesting aspects of the correspondents' personal philosophies which reveal their intellect and depth of education.

Friendship is a powerful theme of *Mountain Summers* as well. The letters gain force and energy as friendships grow stronger over the years, perhaps due to "...that knitting of friendly ties for which the mountains have so subtle a power." The result for the reader is an increasing sense of affection for the characters and identification with the mountains they loved so much.

It is noteworthy that these letters and diaries collectively fashion an excellent informal history of the early years of the Appalachian Mountain Club to which most of the characters belonged. The Appalachian Mountain Club was formed on January 8, 1876, for "the advancement of those who visit the mountains of New England and adjacent regions, whether for the purpose of scientific research or summer recreation." Today, it is the oldest continuously operating mountain club in the United States. At the second regular meeting of the club on March 8, 1876, it was voted to admit women to the membership.

Marian, Lucia, Edith and Isabella were without question unselfish, giving people deserving of praise for their voluntary efforts in the mountains. Appropriately, the Appalachian Mountain Club has established the Marian Pychowska Award to honor club members who have been exemplary of a high level of volunteerism and stewardship. In general, however, the true measure of achievement by these women and the specific details of their lives have largely been unknown. Much more is known about the men with whom they shared these experiences, for history has favored recording details about them. Fortunately, the letters and diaries in *Mountain Summers*, originally collected and preserved by Isabella Stone over one hundred fifteen years ago, have survived and provide significant insight into these remarkable people.

Mary Isabella Stone was born on January 24, 1850, in Concord, New Hampshire. She was the only child of Dr. Henry Orne Stone and Mary B. Low Stone. When Isabella was just a few months old, the Stone family moved to Massachusetts and settled in the town of Framingham. Isabella resided in Framingham until her death on September 28, 1921. She never married.

Isabella Stone

The Stone family first visited the White Mountains in 1863 and returned for many summer seasons thereafter. Isabella loved to hike and spent much of her mountain time out on excursions, scouting the area for potential trail locations, making note of those that needed to be improved, and publishing articles about her thorough surveys. She was a major force behind the development of trails in Franconia Notch and the Mount Moosilauke region of the western White Mountains. To a great extent, Isabella was responsible for the trails to Georgiana and Bridal Veil Falls, obtaining rights of way from property owners and urging the Appalachian Mountain Club, of which she was a member for forty-one years, to hire local woodsmen to work on improving these trails.

Isabella kept meticulous records of her undertakings and likewise carefully saved the correspondences that she received from her mountain friends. Her intimate friendship with the Cook and Pychowska families began when they met at the Goodnow House in Sugar Hill, New Hampshire in 1876.

The Cooks and the Pychowskas shared a stately residence on the Hudson River in Hoboken, New Jersey. Here Eugene Cook lived with his two sisters, Edith Walker Cook, and Lucia Duncan Cook Pychowska and her family. Lucia, Eugene, and Edith were the children of William Cook and Martha Elizabeth Duncan Walker Cook. He was an engineer and brigadier general of the New Jersey militia, and she was an author, poet, editor and translator well-known as a humanitarian with a passion for justice. Martha Cook was unsatisfied with a life of conventional social duties and so devoted herself to literary pursuits and educating her children. Her influence is apparent in the writings and scholarly achievements of her three children and her only grandchild, Marian Pychowska.

Lucia Duncan Cook Pychowska was the oldest of the Cook children and the only one who ever married. Her husband was Chevalier John Pychowski, a Polish aristocrat and celebrated concert musician. Lucia, frequently recognized as Madame Pychowska, has been portrayed as "a most restless, agile, lovable little lady, whose flashing thought and rapier repartee found a match only in her daughter." In addition to being a skilled pioneer in the outdoor pursuits of hiking and botany, Lucia was also a gifted poet, author, and translator. She published various works including a book, *Dante and Catholic Philosophy in the Thirteenth Century*, translated from French. She was the treasurer of the Ladies Benevolent Society of her church in Hoboken and gave much of her time to help the poor. Lucia died at the age of seventy-nine on August 5, 1905.

Lucia's younger sister, Edith Walker Cook, was an accomplished poet and author as well. She was best known, however, for her work as an artist, producing many landscape paintings and sketches of the White Mountains, most of which she gave away as gifts. Like her siblings and mother, she had a compassionate spirit and loathed injustice and oppression, which is apparent in her writing. Edith lived in Hoboken until her death on February 17, 1902, at sixty-three years of age.

Eugene Beauharnais Cook was, in part, named in honor of Napoleon's family with whom his parents were friends. He was born on May 19, 1830, in New York City and lived for almost eighty-five years, dying on March 15, 1915, at home in Hoboken. He was known as an honorable and brilliant man with a keen sense of humor. Besides being an avid hiker and trail builder, Eugene was a remarkably talented skater and has been referred to by some as the "Father of Figure Skating in America." Furthermore, he was a most capable violinist and a renowned chess authority. He possessed one of the world's largest chess libraries which is now housed at Princeton University. Eugene published a book entitled *American Chess-Nuts* in 1868, and following his death, a book, *The Chess Compositions of E. B. Cook*, was written as a tribute to his proficiency as a chess master.

Martha Marian Pychowska, commonly known as Marian, was born on October 22, 1859, in Newark, New Jersey. In 1878, when the letters in this collection begin, she was only eighteen years old, and her writing is exceptional for someone of this age. Even in her youth, she had profound insight and a palpable understanding of the world around her. Marian, like her mother, aunt, and uncle, became a most enthusiastic hiker, explorer, and author. Curiously, her father, who summered in the mountains with the family, did not share this interest in adventure, but rather pursued his music. In addition to exploring the mountains and publishing numerous articles recounting her own and her family's endeavors, Marian composed one of the earlier sketch maps of the Northern Presidential Range. In 1887, Marian relinquished the freedom of her mountain summers and likewise the liberty of corresponding with her dear friend Isabella. A devout Catholic, she chose to become a nun and entered the cloistered and seclusive Monastery of Saint Dominic in Newark. She eventually moved to Ohio where she was the founding Mother Superior at Saint Dominic's in Cincinnati. To this day, Mother Mary Saint Peter, as Marian was later known, remains most highly regarded by the Church. In fact, her character was of such great virtue and spiritual benevolence, many consider her to be a saint. Marian died in Cincinnati on May 24, 1942, at the age of eighty-two.

After spending a few summers in the Adirondack Mountains of New York, the Cooks and Pychowskas came in 1872 and 1873 to the northern White Mountains where their names are found among those in the guest register of the Philbrook Farm Inn in Shelburne, New Hampshire. They were subsequently engaged for several summer seasons in the western White Mountains before returning to the north in 1882 and taking up residence at the Ravine House in Randolph, New Hampshire. It was here, at the foot of the Northern Presidential Range, that the family chose to spend

Lucia Pychowska (left) and Marian Pychowska (right)

the rest of their mountain summers, establishing a headquarters for their explorations along with other spirited members of the community and the Appalachian Mountain Club.

The Cooks and Pychowskas were indeed most enthusiastic members of the Appalachian Mountain Club and when Eugene served as the club's Councillor of Exploration from 1883 to 1885, it was a duty which the whole family took seriously. While Eugene Cook has been credited with building more miles of hiking trails in the White Mountains than anyone else during the nineteenth century, the letters in *Mountain Summers* show that Marian, Lucia, and Edith deserve ample credit as well for they were often alongside Eugene and others, aiding them in exploring new routes, measuring distances, and putting up trail signs. They all published accounts of their pursuits, mostly in *Appalachia*, the journal of the Appalachian Mountain Club.

All their hard work aside, the Cooks and Pychowskas, like Isabella Stone, hiked and climbed for the love of being outdoors and the chance to admire the wonders of nature. They would often spend several hours on the top of a mountain contemplating and recording the details and splendor of the view.

For women, there was an extra challenge in reaching mountain summits, as social customs of the day dictated wearing long, full skirts and dresses even while hiking. These correspondences contain numerous references to the encumbrances of women's clothing as well as innovative ideas for adapting one's dress to outdoor pursuits while remaining in step with society's expectations. Various materials for hiking attire are recommended as being superior to others and suggestions are made for adjusting garments to make them more accommodating to the terrain. At times, however, it was simply easier to dismiss the gentlemen in the party in order not to embarrass the ladies, as when descending from a lofty tree-top vista.

It is also interesting that Marian, Lucia, Edith, and Isabella spent a good portion of their time hiking in the mountains without the company of men. Marian, in describing the particulars of one trip, wrote to Isabella with a seeming sense of pride, "We had it all our own way for there were no gentlemen in the party."

While the following pages clearly provide us with a unique and dynamic slice of life from an era long since past, it is remarkable how many of the characters' social and ethical concerns still confront people in the White Mountains more than a century later. Key issues, such as the impact of logging practices, trash discarded by hikers, the necessity and possible danger of building open fires in the backcountry, respect for local residents and their communities, and all that is inherent in the development of any region, arise throughout *Mountain Summers*. Perhaps certain aspects of history do not repeat themselves, but rather remain constant.

Peter Rowan and June Hammond Rowan
Randolph, NH

1878

"We scarcely wanted to bury ourselves in a ravine, if the mountains meant to be so handsome, but the brook and deeply moss-carpeted woods soon reconciled us."

Marian Pychowska writes to Isabella Stone.

Goodnow House[1]
Sugar Hill, N.H.
Tuesday, September 24, 1878

Dear Miss Stone,

I am going to take the liberty of amusing myself by giving you a little chronicle of our life since you left. I will also try to add whatever may interest you during the few days we still spend here. Friday my uncle and Mr. Sargent[2] went to Coppermine Brook, and reported beautiful falls. My aunt and I did not go with them because the day was lowery. Saturday the same two gentlemen took a buggy and accomplished Georgiana Falls and Lonesome Lake. Sunday was a splendid day and we prepared ourselves for Mt. Kinsman on Monday.

This proved to be the day of days, and the party, consisting of Mr. Spaulding[3], Mr. Sargent, my uncle, aunt, and self, started off jubilantly about quarter of nine. We were driven to the base of the mountain and

---

[1] A boardinghouse in Sugar Hill, NH. Built in 1875, little is known about the early history of the house. The name was changed to the Franconia Inn in 1892 and the operation was eventually enlarged to accommodate two hundred guests. It was destroyed by fire in 1907.

[2] Dr. George A. Sargent of Boston, MA, was an avid hiker and long-time partner and friend of the Cooks and Pychowskas. He spent many of his mountain summers staying at the Ravine House in Randolph, NH. Sargent eventually purchased a small farm of his own in Randolph that was situated beneath the brow of Lookout Ledge. Today a trail from the site of this farm to the ledge bears his name.

[3] Rev. Henry G. Spaulding of Dorchester, MA, was a founding member of the Appalachian Mountain Club. A spring at Edmand's Col on Mount Jefferson is named in his honor.

Goodnow House

began our climb at half past ten. The guidebook speaks of the smallness of the reward in comparison to the difficultly of ascent, but we did not find it so.

Our way up Slide Brook was pleasant climbing over smooth rocks and large boulders, by the side of the stream, which slides in a long succession of cascades over the polished ledges. When we came to the great slide, we left the brook and followed up over the loose stones, and then through some low spruce to the bare top. There we found a Coast Survey signal[4] like that on Sugar Hill. The distance can scarcely be more than three miles from where we left the road and our reward was a magnificent view. The atmosphere was very clear, although columns of smoke[5] were rising from the new Monday fires that threatened soon to obscure it. Mt. Lafayette cut off all our view of the White Mountains proper, but to the right we could see all the way to Chocorua, the Pemigewasset Valley as you know from Cannon, then a very fine view of Moosilauke. To the west,

---

[4] The United States Coast Survey, which was under the direction of the Treasury, was the most comprehensive organization doing precision surveying during this period. The signals mentioned above served as benchmarks in surveying.

[5] Smoke, or smokes, is mentioned throughout the letters and refers to clouds of smoke generated by immense logging operations. Farmers also contributed to the problem by burning their fields and expanding them by logging and burning the slash.

the long line of Green Mountains with Camel's Hump, Mansfield, Jay Peak, and the Willoughby Mountains. A little to the left of the last, we could see in the far distance a round blue mountain that we concluded was Owl's Head. I knew you would be glad to think that this point can be seen from the neighborhood of Sugar Hill, though the hill itself must be too low to bring it above the horizon.

From our beautiful top we looked down into a number of dear little ponds that Kinsman carries way up on his shoulders, places where the deer come to drink. We would very much have liked to visit one of these lakes on our way down, but time scarcely allowed. After more than an hour spent in looking at the view and eating our dinner, we started at a quarter to three, followed down the slide and the brook to the road. Our walk home was enlivened by the most inveterate punning on the part of the three gentlemen, although my uncle and Mr. Sargent had agreed the day before that they would leave it to Mr. Spaulding to make the puns, and then they would laugh sarcastically at them. This pact was soon broken, and the sarcastic laughter was left to my aunt and myself.

Mr. Spaulding left Goodnow's on Wednesday, Mr. Hinkley[6] and Mr. Sargent on Thursday, so that after Kinsman our next trip of importance was on Friday to the Coppermine Brook Falls[7]. We had been having a fire in the parlor for some days, but this morning was particularly cold, and the clouds swept low from the northwest. Our small family party of three set out after breakfast. As we left the road to turn up the stream, the clouds lifted a little, and we could see the flanks of Lafayette, Cannon and Kinsman white with frost. We scarcely wanted to bury ourselves in a ravine, if the mountains meant to be so handsome, but the brook and deeply moss-carpeted woods soon reconciled us.

As for the falls, Edith and I were charmed with their picturesque beauty. The shaft of water flows out sideways, and striking a projecting rock, dashes out in a spray to the ledge below. Behind the fall is a recess which runs up among the rocks further than we could see. Into this dripping mossy place we crawled, and looked out through the falling water, down the pine-clad ravine to the blue hills across the country. We also went to the top of the fall, and then returned to the foot to eat our dinner. We ate and shivered. The sun was excluded by the high bank, the air was chill, and our feet were so wet. However, we managed to be so jolly that none of us took cold. It was pleasant to start once more, and the exercise soon warmed us. As we came out to the road again, the clouds were off the mountains, the lesser ones were frost-crowned but the sun shone on

---

[6] C. H. Hinkley of Hanover, NH.
[7] Also known as Bridal Veil Falls.

Lafayette white with snow. Later the clouds came down again, and kept our snow for the next day.

For the last few days my aunt moved into an east room, so Friday night I slept with her, and we rose early to the dawn and sunrise. It was one of those cloudless dawns when the mountain lines are sharp against the glowing sky. As the light grew, the Franconia Valley shone with a thick frost, which diminished on the hillsides. The lowest that I actually saw the thermometer reach was thirty-seven degrees.

Monday my uncle and aunt came home, and Wednesday we followed them, leaving the remaining guests to finish their time out. And now we are beginning a new life, very good, very pleasant, but very different. We are all well except my mother, who does not get rid of her cold, caught during the frost weather. I must beg your pardon for my patchwork letter, but I know you will give it for the sake of our mountains that I tell about. Please remember us very kindly to Dr. and Mrs. Stone, and believe me,

> Yours very sincerely,
> Marian Pychowska

1879

"The stage route on the west bank of the river we had traversed before, but the road on the east bank had all the attraction of entire novelty. You will easily guess which way we chose."

Marian Pychowska writes to Isabella Stone.

Blair's House[1]
Campton, N.H.
July 26, 1879

Dear Miss Stone,

Your letter gave us much pleasure. It is very nice to know that we are missed in our summer haunts. They are still fresh in our minds as well as the companion who helped us to enjoy them. I have been waiting to answer you until I could sit down with a mind unburdened with other things so that I might enjoy to the full talking to you about the things that interest both of us. This sounds as if I had very important matters to attend to, but though they are unimportant they succeed in running away with the time. Beside the time I give to keep up my music etc. as usual, we have a friend with us this summer who suffers so much from her eyes as scarcely to be able to use them, and it is a pleasure to us to while away some of her long day by reading to her. She proposed a bargain to me when she came, of which the reading is the fulfillment of my part, while she took upon herself the task of teaching me in arithmetic and algebra. As she is an experienced teacher, I hope to have my mathematical ideas much simplified.

It was no accident that prevented our going to Sugar Hill, although I think we would all have liked it, but among other reasons, Campton was not so long a journey. Now that we are settled here (we three) everything is pleasant. My uncle and aunt expect to come August 1. The house is

---

[1] A boardinghouse where the Pychowskas and Cooks spent the summers of 1879 and 1880.

Blair's House

very comfortable, the table good, and the big attic room that my mother and I occupy has a lovely view from the window. The river valley with its beautifully wooded slopes is apparently closed in by Mounts Tecumseh and Welch, looking much as they do in the profile which I send. If you care to refer to your Appalachian map, you will find us on the west bank of the Pemigewasset nearly opposite the mouth of the Beebe River, with Round Hill just back of us. This hill is wooded but you will see on the map just to the north a small hill without a name. This is known to us as Taylor's Hill. It commands both the Pemigewasset and Mad River valleys. Looking at the Franconias on some of the clear, perfect days we have had this month, the local coloring of the distance, the shining sides of Cannon and Eagle Cliffs, have made it seem to be an easy day's walk to Franconia Notch, but I scarce think, even if we get that far, that we can pay you a visit. Many thanks for your invitation and many more for the kindness which prompted it. You say you have never seen this valley. How nice it would be if when the time comes for the home journey you took this road and gave us a little time on the way.

To return to our mountains. I am sure you will recognize our friends about the Notch, but I am not artist enough to give ideas of the Waterville Mountains which are very fine. My uncle will probably make a near acquaintance with some of them. Waterville itself is only fourteen miles from here. The mountains are seen in a great variety of ways from many points on the beautiful roads about the country, as well as from the hill tops. Beech Hill and Bald Hill are two of the latter easily accessible, while from Mt. Prospect, about four miles from here, the most extended view of all is obtained. There is a carriage road nearly to the top of this high, bald hill, and I must say, even if it sounds to you like treason, that the reward is as great as from Sugar Hill's self.

Beside the mountains I have outlined, Moosilauke rises grandly on its successive swells; Hooket[2], crooked as ever, comes in to the right of Flume; over the Mad River Valley may be seen Carrigain in the center of the wilderness, and over many other ridges rises Mt. Washington with the great spur that surmounts Tuckerman's Ravine. The day we saw this, the transparent air gave us not only the clear outline of the distant peak, but also its genuine rocky look and its white houses. Still to the right, to make up for the loss of Tripyramid which is hidden by Sandwich Dome, we saw other friends, visited from West Ossipee, Whiteface, Paugus (or part of it) and the tip of Chocorua, the unmistakable white peak. This is only half of the horizon sweep. For the rest, Squam and Winnipesaukee are spread out before you with all their beautiful winding bays and wooded islands, and then hills, mountains and valleys of lesser note bring you round to Moosilauke again. One little depression in the hills lets in the faint outline of Green Mountains, but not Camel's Hump!

We were prudent the day we went to Mt. Prospect, and made the distance behind a pair of horses, my father being with us. He enjoys himself much, though in his own way; composing. As he does not often leave his work to take a walk, I think he misses somewhat the extensive view he had before him last summer without the trouble of seeking it. Still, he likes the place here.

Our woods near are rich and beautiful. My mother and I have found about twenty different kinds of fern, but no maidenhair.

I will answer your questions. Although Blair's is nearer Campton Post Office or West Campton than Plymouth, there is more communication with the latter place. The Profile stages[3] bring and take our mail as they pass. The last we heard of Mr. Sargent, he with Mr. Hinkley and sister were to be at St. Albans, Vt. We cannot but sympathize in your sorrow for the changes at Goodnow's. You say nothing of the new railroad. Please give kind remembrances to your father and mother from my mother and self, and our best wishes for a pleasant summer. I hope you enjoy reading a guidebook letter! Later I may have more exciting things to relate.

> Yours truly,
> Marian Pychowska

---

[2] Known today as Mount Garfield.
[3] Stage coaches that travelled to and from the Profile House in Franconia Notch.

Lucia Pychowska writes to Isabella Stone.

Blair's House
Campton, N.H.
August 6, 1879

My dear Miss Stone,

I was indeed well pleased to receive your letter, not only for its interesting contents, but also as a proof of your kind remembrances and regard. Will you say to your parents that I am sorry not to be at Franconia, that I might improve my acquaintance with them both. My memories in that direction are more than pleasant and you must not think that you were ever a "clog", as we were only too glad to have you with us, and to bear you now in mind with such lovely backgrounds. I am sorry to learn that Mrs. Stone is not feeling even as well as she did last year, but trust that before the summer is over she may have regained at least her usual strength.

Professor Niles[4] writes to say there may be a meeting of "Appalachian Mountain Club"[5] at Waterville about August 20. If so, we shall attend it, as we have never yet been able to meet our fellow members and Waterville is only fifteen miles from where we now are.

When you read the "History of Poland", remember that it is only a popular work and by no means goes into the depths of things. The few little flings at the Jesuits, etc., are to be taken with the grain of allowance needful to make in the face of old prejudices, from which indeed few mortals are exempt. But it is the best short history of the country I have been able to find. It is picturesque and entertaining and gives some genuine idea of the Polish spirit and character, a peculiar one, hard to comprehend in this work-a-day world.

We saw in the *Echo*[6] an account of the excursion from your house to the top of Mt. Lafayette. The smokes have begun on this side of the mountains. Haying being nearly over, the farmers have time to turn their attention to the obscuration of the atmosphere. I must try and stir up the

---

[4] William H. Niles of Cambridge, MA, was a founding member of the Appalachian Mountain Club. He served as President (1879,1882) as well as Vice-President, Councillor of Natural History, and Councillor of Topography.

[5] The Appalachian Mountain Club (AMC) was formed on January 8, 1876, for "the advancement of those who visit the mountains of New England and adjacent regions, whether for the purpose of scientific research or summer recreation." Today, it is the oldest continuously operating mountain club in the United States. At the second regular meeting of the club on March 8, 1876, it was voted to admit women to the membership.

[6] *The White Mountain Echo and Tourists' Register* was a summer newspaper established in 1878 and published in Bethlehem, NH.

"Appalachians" on the subject. We have some lovely walks here, both short and long which I would like to show you. Trusting that some year again we may have an opportunity of pursuing our explorations together, I remain,

Very truly your friend,
Lucia D. Pychowska

＊ ＊ ＊ ＊ ＊ ＊ ＊ ＊ ＊ ＊ ＊ ＊

Lucia Pychowska writes to Isabella Stone.

Blair's House
Campton, N.H.
August 24, 1879

My dear Miss Stone,

Marian has received your very interesting and graphic letter, and will answer it ere long. Meantime, I write a line to say that in September there will be plenty of room in this establishment, a large number of guests leaving the first week in that month. We should be delighted to welcome you, and show you the neighborhood.

Last week, we attended the meeting of the Appalachian Club at Waterville. I furnished a paper on Baldcap Mountain (Shelburne), Marian one on ascents of Mt. Ingalls and Goose Eye, and my sister gave an account of the visit to Coppermine Brook Falls, made last September, also, a semi-comic, semi-serious squib in verse, entitled a "Warning to Travelers". The latter is to appear in some newspaper, but without any name or offensive allusion, as the editor of the *Echo* is a member of the Club, and he must not be affronted. We met Professor Niles, Professor Fay[7], and other pleasant members of the Club.

Of course Mr. Goodnow is right to make all he can out of his advantageous position, but I must say I always grieve over the enlargement of familiar haunts. They invariably lose a portion of their charm.

Will you remember me most kindly to Dr. and Mrs. Stone, and believe me,

Very truly your friend,
Lucia Pychowska

---

[7] Professor Charles E. Fay of Boston, MA, taught at Tufts University. Professor Fay chaired the preliminary meeting to organize the AMC and served, over a period of many years, as the club's President(1878,1893), Vice-President, Councillor of Art, Councillor of Explorations, Corresponding Secretary, and Trustee of Real Estate. He was also the first editor of *Appalachia* (the journal of the AMC), holding that position for nearly forty years. Fay was one of the first climbers to explore the Canadian Rockies and the Selkirk Mountains. Mt. Fay in Canada is named in his honor.

Marian Pychowska writes to Isabella Stone.

Blair's House
Campton, N.H.
September 7, 1879

Dear Miss Stone,

Your letter renewed our associations with Sugar Hill and its inhabitants most pleasantly, and I thank you very much for giving me such a full account of them. In return, I will try to give you an idea of what we have done in the way of excursions. There is nothing that gives me more pleasure to write about, when I feel my correspondent will not be bored by it.

In the first place, though, I must hope that the little plan of your visit here may be realized. If you come soon you will add to the Sugar Hill colony established at Blair's already, Mr. Hinkley and Mr. Sargent having been with us now a week. The former proposes to leave next Saturday, but the latter's stay is indefinite. Our household is now reduced to about eighteen, all pleasant and interesting. August gaiety has not entirely departed, our evenings being usually enlivened by a Virginia reel in which my mother and aunt and other older ladies take part, thereby adding much to our pleasure. As was the case last year at Goodnow's, the "September people" are more given to late hours than the "August people", for now they get fairly settled down in the evenings and discussion pays little regard to the passage of time.

My mother told you in her note something about our trip to Waterville, and how agreeable the Appalachians made themselves. The *Echo* of August 30, had a short account of the sessions merely incorrect in stating that the paper prepared by my aunt was also read by her. The burden of reading all the things we had arranged was laid on my mother, as member of the Club.

Wednesday, the beautiful day you speak of in your letter, and the day of the meeting, was followed by a morning very soon overcast and ending in showery rain. This was our chance for ascending Mt. Osceola. My uncle started early, as he intended to walk back to Blair's in the afternoon, and we three followed at our leisure. Several other parties from Greeley's[8] were on the path, and without being hampered with each other, we had pleasant little encounters along the way. Two of the gentlemen belonging to the Club and knowing the mountain well, joined us the last part of the way, and shortened it with pleasant conversation. You see if we could talk climbing the steepest part of Osceola, it cannot be a very rough walk, and it is indeed the easiest mountain for its height (4,400 feet)

---

[8] Greeley's Boardinghouse in Waterville Valley, NH. Merrill Greeley was the proprietor.

that I ever went up. The distance from Greeley's is four and one-sixth miles and the path, smooth and of a pleasant grade through stately forests. Though the air was thick and ever thickening with smoke and cloud, the view repaid us well. Besides our friends of the Presidential and Franconia Mountains, the great Pemigewasset forest was spread before us with Carrigain commanding its lesser summits. Of course the Green Mountains and other distant points were not visible, but what the smoke could not hide or disfigure, was the great ravine of Osceola, on whose edge we stood. Mt. Tripyramid showed its slide[9], about which we had heard so much discussion at the meeting, from top to bottom. As we had been receiving hospitality from one of the gentleman owning cottages at Waterville, the hotel being crammed, we could not well stay more than two nights, but our nice little plan of walking home on Friday was thwarted by the rain. We drove down to Campton Village with Mr. Greeley, and as it promised to clear then we walked from there.

You may remember hearing my mother speak last summer of a long cherished plan of visiting Pollard's Boardinghouse on the East Branch of the Pemigewasset River in North Woodstock. It was at last carried into execution last Monday. She and I drove up to Fox's[10] in the morning, and here our team left us. Six or seven miles separated us from our final destination, and so, having dined and looked about us, we started on our travels afoot. As it was exceedingly warm, we considered for some time which road was likely to afford us the most shade. The stage route on the west bank of the river we had traversed before, but the road on the east bank had all the attraction of entire novelty. You will easily guess which way we chose. Despite the smoke we had beautiful near views of Franconia Notch and Mt. Moosilauke, that from the North Woodstock bridge the most superb. At this bridge we had to cross the river and recross it again a little bit below "Tuttle's"[11] where the Pollard turnoff is. Another mile brought us to our journey's end about five o'clock, very glad to get freshened and washed before tea.

Pollard's is a very plain little house, but a convenient and quite comfortable place for those who love the true wilderness. It has a lovely situation in a charming piece of "interval" on the very edge of the great forest. Moosilauke and its immense shoulders lying to the west, across the valley the Coolidges shutting off Mt. Lafayette from the house, but not from other parts of the "interval". Up the East Branch the mountains look steep, and dark with pines, a most solemn wilderness, but the stream itself was the great charm to us. We went down to it at sunset, and watched it flow-

---

[9] A large rock slide that occurred in 1869.
[10] Fox's Boardinghouse in North Woodstock, NH. Isaac Fox was the proprietor.
[11] Tuttle's Boardinghouse in Woodstock, NH.

ing clear, strong, and wild over its great boulders. The following morning Mr. Pollard drove us home, the warm, thick weather preventing our proposed walk.

Last Saturday we did not allow to slip by unused, as you may imagine. My uncle had been waiting for such a day to go on Sandwich Dome (Black Mountain) and as it is a ten-mile ride to the base, an early start was necessary. Eight of us were at breakfast at half past six, and off a little after seven with our four-horse team. However we were not all bound for the Dome, Welch Mountain claiming half of us. My uncle, aunt, Miss Bailey and Mr. Sargent took the big mountain, while my mother and self with two more from the house were content with the little one. We had a jolly drive and then separated for the day. Our work was to ascend a remarkable twin peak of no great height, but composed of steep granite ledges as to give ample opportunity for rough climbing. The path was easily traced for sometime, but finally we lost it among the rocks, and tried to make the best of our way to the top without it. In accomplishing this, we had some gymnastics to perform, especially in crossing the broad sheets of worn granite whose sharp incline made every patch of grass or moss a precious support.

The outlook from the summit repaid us for all our scrambling, the mountain on which our friends had gone being one of its grandest features. You will sympathize with my pleasure when in sweeping the horizon to identify points I know, I recognized Camel's Hump, Vt., Mounts Lafayette and Liberty, Cannon, Kinsman, and Moosilauke were in line before us.

After some hours delightfully spent in rambling from one point to another we came down, this time with the path for our guide. It led us through some narrow passages between the cliffs which had so obstructed us in ascending. We returned to the house where the other party was to join us, and the good people there regaled us with apple pie and rich milk. Before our departure, they presented us with some beautiful feathers from their peacocks, which led to some amiable envy when the other party did come along to pick us up. They had much to tell of paths of Black Mountain and its grand view, but I think the *Echo* would make a more exciting story our of little scramble!

Please remember us to all friends at Goodnow's, and believe me,
                                    Yours sincerely,
                                    Marian Pychowska

Marian Pychowska writes to Isabella Stone.

Hoboken, N.J.
October 5, 1879

Dear Miss Stone,

I am very glad you stayed late at Goodnow's this year, and that the season displayed all of its beauties for your benefit. The account of your many excursions, especially your fourteen mile walk, shows me that your health must have improved very much since you wrote me in July.

While you were employing the favorable weather so well at Franconia, we Camptonites were busy too. Our last ten days were very full. Friday, the 19th, my mother, aunt, Mr. Sargent and self were driven part way to Waterville and climbed Mt. Weetamoo, the highest point of the Campton mountains. The day was very clear and bright and the view superb, but the wind was so cold that we were glad to get down behind a rock in a sunny place to eat our dinner. Mr. Blair's dog, "Towser", a handsome part Newfoundland, had been in the habit of taking smaller walks with us, and he was ready to follow the wagon any distance. On this day I write of, we supposed we had said good-bye to him when we left the wagon at the base of the mountain, but while we were resting on the pretty wood path after our first pull uphill, a dark object came bounding up the road and Towser joined us. Poor fellow! He had no lunch bag, and while we ate our dinner, he looked at us with longing eyes for contributions of doughnuts and maple sugar.

The top of Weetamoo is very picturesque with its fine rock and the growth of spruces, and mountain ash covered with scarlet berries. Going home, we let the map guide us by unfrequented roads, passing over the spurs of the Campton mountains, up hill and down dale, and having, beside their intrinsic beauty, the great charm of novelty.

On Saturday my uncle took the big walk he had been saving himself for. This was to the top of Tecumseh by way of Waterville, the distance being about thirty-five to thirty-eight miles. Sunday we talked over our plans for the last week and it was agreed the next thing in order was to do a piece of exploring work suggested to us by Professor Fay, the Councillor of Explorations of the "AMC". This was a nameless mountain[12], indicated on the map we both use, to the east of Mt. Kineo. The whole range including both these points used to be known as Carr's Mountain, but this name being now restricted to one part, and Kineo given to another, the eastern end was still open to an appellation.

Our mountain appears from Campton village as a dark, wooded mass, hiding Kineo and about 3,000 feet or less in height. Monday morn-

---

[12] Presumedly, the mountain referred to here is the still-nameless far eastern peak of Mount Kineo.

ing my uncle was sufficiently rested from his long tramp, so Mr. Blair drove us toward Ellsworth over the beautiful Cook's Hill Road from which the view of Franconia Notch and Waterville mountains is so surpassingly fine. At quarter past eleven, we left the wagon at a high farm and between then and a quarter past five we scoured the wooded crest from end to end. It was delightful to be in pathless woods once more and to struggle with as fine a growth of hobble bush (familiarly known as "shinhopple") as we have ever seen. From one point on the northern end of the ridges, through an opening in the trees, we got a splendid near view of Moosilauke with its great ravine, at its foot lying some high farms of Warren. From another point where a large spruce had opened an outlook in falling, we had the whole sweep from Cannon to Tripyramid, and White Mountains proper (the Presidential Range), their heads capped with cloud, coming in finely between the Twin Range and the great shoulders of Hancock and Carrigain. Although our mountain cannot be recommended as a view point, we enjoyed finding this fact for ourselves and we would like to call it after our chief, "Mt. Fay", as this gentleman has done so much exploring work in the neighborhood of Campton. Our drive home that evening was decidedly cool, but not to be compared to the temperature of that cold, windy Thursday night on which you wrote to me.

That afternoon three of us went to Beech Hill by a very rambling short cut on which I was guide. We had the pleasure of seeing the snowy head of Lafayette, but the wind blew through us so that we soon reluctantly left the top. In the morning my uncle had left on foot for Waterville, intending to ascend Mt. Weetamoo by the way. We were to join him Friday morning and all go up Tripyramid.

The thermometer in our cold north room was at forty-two degrees, if I remember rightly, as I dressed for this expedition. When we drove off a little after seven, the ground was still white with frost and the butternut trees were fast losing both nuts and leaves. Towser had apparently been satisfied with his trip to Mt. Fay and was not forthcoming for Tripyramid. I was bundled up worthy of my mother for this early drive, and our wraps were completed by Mr. Blair's buffalo robe. On the way we learned that Greeley's was closed for the season, and the family moved out to winter quarters near Campton Village, but when we arrived at Waterville, my uncle was waiting, having passed the night at one of the few other houses of the village. We started at once, the time being short and the work unknown.

For two miles we had a good path as far as Beckytown[13], an old deserted clearing on Norway Brook. From here the new Livermore path

---

[13] Beckytown was named for Rebekah Blanchard who lived at this remote homestead location with her husband years earlier.

continues across the wilderness to the White Mountain (Crawford) Notch, and we thought it possible that, with all the energy of the Watervillians for path making, there might be some branch leading off toward our destination. With this idea we followed the new trail about three-quarters of a mile until we saw it was useless to expect the desired branch. A good half hour had been lost when we returned on our steps to Beckytown. It was now half past eleven and much work to do, so we started up Norway Brook at a brisk pace, clambering over the fallen trees and rock debris, left even this far down by the great slide which took this course in 1869. Having read a description of the slide by Professor Fay in an old number of *Appalachia*[14] and heard the long discussions on this subject at the August meeting, we were prepared to recognize the points of interest. The celebrated "V" through which the stream runs is one of them.

Finally we reached the elbow where the mountain side that slid off met the brook, and having been well warmed up with our work, my uncle proposed that we should sit down in a shady place by the water and eat dinner. We soon began to feel much too cool, my aunt discovering that her foot was resting on a piece of ice which coated the stone by her. (We had the luxury of sucking pieces of ice on our way up.) A move was made to the sunny bank above and this was soon left to make the ascent of the slide proper. In this each one took his own time, the very "slidery" nature of the rock and gravel making it desirable not to have near neighbors. In about fifty minutes we four were all assembled at the top of this steep half mile, looking down on the silver threads of water running through the great mass of debris where we had eaten dinner. Opposite us was Sandwich Dome, and to the left, blue Lake Winnepesaukee. A few hundred feet above the slide brought us to the top of the south pyramid. The trees that used to cover it have kindly died and fallen away, so that, by dodging about, we obtained a very fine view. Mounts Passaconaway, Whiteface and Chocorua were old friends, with a beautiful bit of Swift River Intervale beside their feet. Kearsarge, Moat, Carter and the sea of ridges between bring the eyes around to the dome of Washington set up on its ravine ploughed plateau. Set in between the two other near pyramids are Carrigain, and Willey (perhaps). To the left lie the Franconias; Hooket a prominent feature.

We left the summit about three o'clock, preferring the woods to the slide until we neared the elbow, where we again took to it and traversed the two miles of stream and forest bank to Beckytown. The ice was still unmelted, and we had some lovely views of Osceola bathed in afternoon sunshine, with wild Norway Brook and some bright maples and birches

---

[14] The journal of the Appalachian Mountain Club. Conceived by Samuel H. Scudder in 1876, *Appalachia* is still being published today.

for our foreground. It was half past five when we got back to Greeley's and we bundled into our wraps and robes for the drive of fifteen or sixteen miles that separated us from friends, fire and supper. Mr. Blair got us home at eight o'clock. There I found your letter awaiting me.

Saturday afternoon we celebrated the anniversary of our visit to the Coppermine Brook Falls by taking a very lovely walk over Sunset Hill; this day having time to stop and enjoy all the beauties along the way. This was our farewell walk, except for my uncle, Sunday being lowering. Mr. Sargent left Monday, and we ourselves on Tuesday. For ten days we had been the sole inhabitants (in the boarder way) at Blair's, with the exception of a solitary artist, who came late to see the autumn color, and him we left in possession. Now I have told you the whole story and I wish you may enjoy reading as much as I have enjoyed writing it.

We have come home to solid duty, our minds stocked with pleasant recollections. You have these also, and then beside, the pleasure of having helped the aspiring young school teacher you wrote me about.

I hope Dr. and Mrs. Stone have recovered entirely from their ill attacks and that you all will feel better through the winter for your summer at Goodnow's. Another year I hope we may be more fortunate, and either have a visit from you or pay you one. There are so many walks you would enjoy at Campton. If you are so good as to write me sometimes during the winter, we can continue to talk of our pleasant remembrances, and plans for the future which may be enjoyed in prospect even if never realized.

Yours very sincerely,
Marian Pychowska

1880

"Leaving the path, we crossed a pasture, and then came out into a perfect paradise of ferns, great beds of maidenhair waving in the wind, and almost all the other kinds that we have found in these parts, all growing with the greatest luxuriance."

Lucia Pychowska writes to Isabella Stone.

Hoboken, N.J.
February 15, 1880

My dear Miss Stone,

Thanks for your letter received and for article[1] returned. I will endeavor to answer your questions categorically, as nearly as may be.

1st: By Mr. Chase's[2] path, the distance from Gates' Cottage[3], on the high road, to Dream Lake, is about two and a half miles, more or less.

2nd: The path is findable, with care, or was, it may be somewhat grown up now, but not exactly plain.

3rd: It does pass over the main front of Bald Cap Peak.

4th: We do mean to diverge a little from the path, toward the right, by reason of the steep ledges, but did not like to say it exactly in the paper read before the Club, as that might seem to cast a reflection upon Mr. Chase's path which we did not wish to do. You know, my brother always finds the easiest as well as the most direct way to reach any mountain point, and he generally took us to the right of the path until the crest was reached, when one falls naturally into the path again.

5th: It is about one mile and a half from Dream Lake to the true summit of Bald Cap Mountain, but there is no path, and the way is not easy to find, as what seems the summit from Dream Lake, is a mere eminence, all overgrown with trees, and affording no view over the Success wilderness and the country beyond.

---

[1] An article prepared for *Appalachia* on Bald Cap Mountain in Shelburne, NH.
[2] Mr. R. Stuart Chase of Haverhill, MA, was a founding member of the AMC.
[3] A boardinghouse in Shelburne, NH.

6th: The Dryad Falls branch comes into Mill Brook on the west side of the stream. That is, on the left hand as you look up the stream. Mill Brook has a general direction from the north toward the south.

7th: You leave the high road to go up Mill Brook either by Burbank's Mill on the west side of the stream or by a pathway leaving the road after you cross the bridge and going up the east bank to the so called "Bowls and Pitchers" or "Leonard's Bowls", a series of singular pot-holes at the falls on Mill Brook, about a mile from the high road.

8th: Lary's Flume is difficult to find from any description of the way, and the only direction that can be given is, to keep up Mill Brook until you strike it, a direction not easily followed as the lay of the land requires you often to leave the bed of the brook and take to the wood roads on either side of the stream, by which it is quite possible to miss the Flume. I do not think any more definite way can be laid down than that already given in the article.

Mr. Sargent has been recently quite out of health, and came down to New York to recoup. He passed a week of his time with us. We also had another visit from one of our Campton sojourners, Mr. Twombly of Boston. New York is so central, many pass through on the way south or west. Marian will write ere long. Will you present my best regards to Dr. and Mrs. Stone, and believe me,

Very truly yours,

Lucia D. Pychowska

* * * * * * * * * * * *

Marian Pychowska writes to Isabella Stone.

Hoboken, N.J.

April 4, 1880

Dear Miss Stone,

It is very kind of my mountain friend of 1878 to remember one all the way to Easter of 1880, especially as I have owed her a letter for two months. When my mother wrote to you, she was not able to find any meaning for the two French words you mentioned in your last letter. Many things must have occupied your mind since that time, and yet perhaps you would like to know what my uncle has been able to glean from the Academy Dictionary. He has been busy making extracts of chess interest from books in the Aster Library, so my mother asked him to look out the two mysterious words. The nearest we could come to "la vareuse", as it was not in the dictionary, was that it might be derived from Var, "le Varus des anciens", one of the southern departments of France, and applied to a person or thing belonging to that district. A French friend of ours has a vague idea that it means a shirt, perhaps some piece of local costume.

Indeed I do congratulate you on having become an "Ape"[4], as we used to delight to call them before we knew how nice they are. I hope you have been able to attend a meeting and that it was as pleasant as the Waterville one, but that means a great deal!

Among other pieces of work that my aunt has done since your visit, is a small picture of Dream Lake on Mt. Baldcap. It is the view described in our sketch of the mountain—the peaks of Adams and Madison framed by the lake and its wild shores. She painted it for another purpose, but when done, it struck her that, being a characteristic view of an unfrequented spot, it might interest the Club. She expects to send it through Professor Niles, so perhaps, in the course of time, you may see it in the Appalachian gallery!

Mr. Booth[5] is now in New York at the theater which used to belong to him, and the town is for once treating him as he deserves by crowding the house. My mother was in Brooklyn not long ago, and called on Mrs. Seymour, who spoke with much pleasure of your visit to her. Last Thursday as we were wandering through the exhibition of pictures at the Academy of Design, who should accost us but Mr. Spaulding. He was only down for a few days, and very busy. Probably you know they are now living in Springfield, where Bessie is free from her asthma.

Our early spring came to suit the early Easter of this year, and our daffodils, despite the cold and the snows of Passion and Holy Weeks, were true to their Dutch name of "Paas-flowers" and were in bloom on that day, bound to be a part of "the day that the Lord hath made".

Our summer arrangements are made, as far as possible and promise to be a repetition of last summer. We expect to go to Blair's, to occupy the same rooms and meet the same people. As you went home last year through the big Notch, you ought to patronize the Pemigewasset Valley this time, either going to or returning from Goodnow's.

I wish the little violets I send would keep their sweet perfume for you[6]. The clump of arbutus my aunt brought from Campton, has burst into beautiful white flowers. With kind remembrances to Dr. and Mrs. Stone, I am,

Yours sincerely,
Marian Pychowska

---

[4] A member of the Appalachian Mountain Club.

[5] Edwin Thomas Booth (1833-1893) was an actor and the brother of John Wilkes Booth, the actor who assassinated President Abraham Lincoln.

[6] Although their sweet perfume has long since passed, these dried violets are included in the collection of original letters.

Isabella Stone writes to Amos Merrill.

                                                     Framingham, Mass.
                                                     Saturday, June 5, 1880

Mr. Amos L. Merrill
Merrill House
Warren, New Hampshire
Dear Sir,

Having heard of your boardinghouse near the foot of Mt. Moosilauke, I write, both for myself and several friends, to inquire for particulars about your place and its attractions. If you will kindly take the trouble to answer the following questions, as I have left space for answers to each, and return these sheets to M. I. Stone, Framingham Centre, Mass., Post Office Box 112, you will confer a favor. If we should not be able to go to your house this summer, we might like to engage rooms in season next year.

1. Have you ever taken boarders afflicted with "Rose-Cold" or "Hay-Fever"?
   Never had but one.
2. Were they cured at your place?
   Were very much better while here.
3. Do passengers on Boston, Concord, and Montreal Railroad get out at Warren to go to your place?
   They do.
4. How far is it from the depot to your house?
   Between five and six miles.
5. Does one go by stage?
   (no answer)
6. If so, what is the price?
   (no answer)
7. Or do you meet them with a team?
   I do.
8. What price?
   Seventy-five cents.
9. Is your home situated on "Moosilauke Turnpike"?
   At the foot of it.
10. North or south of "Merrill Brook"? and how far from the Brook?
    North, about fifteen rods.
11. Or is your house situated on the road up Moosilauke Mountain which turns off a mile or two north of the village called "Warren Summit"?
    Am not on the Warren Summit side of the mountain.
12. How many boarders do you take?
    About twenty-five.

13. Price per week apiece for two in a room?
    Ladies five dollars, gentlemen six dollars.
14. Price per week for one in a room?
    (no answer)
    Price per day for transient boarders?
    One dollar.
15. Price in each case in June and September, when landlords usually lower their prices?
    (no answer)
16. Towards which point of the compass does your house fall?
    South.
17. In which direction from the house does one look for the best view?
    (no answer)
18. How far is your house from the top of the mountain?
    About five miles.
19. Do you drive boarders up in your own team?
    I do generally.
20. What do you charge apiece?
    Two dollars.
21. How long does it take to ride to the top from your house?
    Three hours.
22. Have you a picture of your house, on sheets of paper as many proprietors do have? If so, please send me one. Also a circular.
    Haven't either.
23. Do your chambers have closets?
    All of large rooms do.
24. Have you a good room up one flight of stairs, with a closet, the sun in the morning, for a gentleman and wife? How many windows and which direction do they look?
    (no answer)
25. Have you two such suitable rooms?
    (no answer)
26. Have you a single room on the same floor with these, with a closet, place for a fire and the morning sun?
    Have not.
    If not all these things, which of them does your best single room have?
    Have not got a room with accommodations for fire.
    Is it up one or two flights?
    One.
    Which way does the window look?
    (no answer)
    How many single rooms?
    (no answer)

27. Please send me the post office address of some persons who have spent one whole season or more at your place that we may write to them.
    (no answer)
28. Do you provide spring beds? Feather beds? Mattresses?
    Some of each kind. Mattresses not hair.

I have written my questions in this form so as to give you the least possible trouble in answering them. Please reply soon.

We have spent many summers in different parts of the White Mountains, enjoy fine scenery, and desire to have good country fare: milk, and berries, fresh vegetables, good meat once a day at least, and oatmeal. I presume you furnish these with good sweet bread and butter. One of us is an invalid, such one has Hay-Fever, so I have been particular in my inquiries, as we wish to know more about a place than a printed circular usually furnishes, before we all go to it, not wishing to travel about.

Respectfully yours,
M. I. Stone

* * * * * * * * * * * *

Amos Merrill writes to Isabella Stone.

Merrill House
Warren, N.H.
June 8, 1880

Dear Miss Stone,

Yours of the 5th received. I wish to explain a little about my house, as I think by your letter that your idea of it is a fashionable boardinghouse or Hotel which it is not so. I am a farmer and this house was built for that purpose fifty years ago. Since travel commenced to the mountains it has been built over with additions so I take about the number of boarders mentioned on your sheet. My rooms are good, but the house is old fashioned. I write this so you may not be disappointed if you should come here expecting more than you would find.

The scenery here is called good and the view from Moosilauke is called equal to that from Mt. Washington by many who have been to both places. My house is nearly surrounded by mountains. Moosilauke on the north, Mounts Kineo, Cushman, and Carr on the east and south. I have never had boarders in June. Some of them stay a while in September, but I do not make any difference in the price. My rooms facing the south and east are good size with good closets. Those to the east get the morning sun. I have some smaller rooms (not front, neat and comfortable for single persons). No closets to them.

I have front rooms not engaged and can accommodate you if you engage before someone else takes them.

I have never asked permission of any of my boarders to use their names for reference, but I do not think they will care. Henry M. Ordway of Lowell, Mass. has been here six or seven seasons in succession. Also Professor B. F. Clarke, Providence, R.I., Amos Sarned, Hartford, Conn., and James M. Nichols, Haverhill, Mass.

Hoping to hear from you soon I am yours truly,

Amos L. Merrill

P.S. No mosquitoes to trouble, but Potato Bugs in abundance.

* * * * * * * * * * * *

Mrs. H. M. Ordway writes to Isabella Stone.

Lowell, Mass.

June 15, 1880

Miss I. Stone,

In the absence of Mr. Ordway, I take the liberty to answer inquires in regard to the Merrill House. Having spent many summers there one can easily imagine that we ought to be qualified to judge of its "attractions", also of its "objections and inconveniences". It is true that we are constantly sending friends to that locality, but are first careful to know the tastes or fancy of the individual. It is not a desirable place for one who craves excitement, dress, luxuries for table, finely furnished rooms, or beds, or any "special natural wonders".

It is a long five-mile drive all the way ascending from Warren to the Merrill House. The place is very primitive but extremely neat, comfortable and homelike. The "Breezy Point House", which will accommodate fifty guests, is close by in a more commanding position and is kept by Mr. Burt Merrill, a cousin to Amos L. The attractions of the Merrill House are namely the elevated position of fifteen hundred feet above the level of the sea, dry, exhilarating air, pure water, and nearness to a chain of mountains which sweep in a semicircle down the Asquam-Shumauke Valley. It has numerous trout streams, immense forests, beautiful spruce and maple groves, a picturesque river filled with tiny cascades, ravines to explore, and mountain crests to surmount. In short, it is the coolest, quietest, and most restful place imaginable.

The facilities for obtaining food of the first quality are quite limited. Lamb is plenty and of fine quality. Quite fair chickens are furnished once a week. Raspberries, green peas, string beans, and beets are very abundant through August. Bread and butter, oatmeal, griddle cakes, doughnuts, fancy cake, pies, sauce, etc. are usually good. Beef and coffee are poor. Tea and chocolate can be procured any time. The table is always supplied without limit and with good country fare. The drives are too mountainous to be enjoyable. The only ride being up and down the mountain road, five miles either way.

Having spent summers at various points among the White Mountains for many years, principally at hotels, we are fully convinced that for pure, healthful air and water, fair living at an economical rate, and perfect recuperation, no place can excel the Merrill's.

Mr. Ordway will return to the city in a day or two and will be happy to give you other information desired.

Miss Phillips of the "Framingham High School" was a guest of the Merrill House last season.

Yours in haste,
Mrs. H. M. Ordway

* * * * * * * * * * * *

Benjamin Clarke writes to Isabella Stone.

Providence, R.I.
June 15, 1880

M. I. Stone,

Yours of the 14th is at hand and I am not a little perplexed to know what to say to you for there is such a diversity of tastes in respect to boarding places. What suits my family may not suit yours.

We enjoyed Mr. Merrill's house so well that we intend to go there again. But we spend a romping sort of life in the country, usually enjoy good health and making up our minds in the beginning to take things as they come and extract all the enjoyment possible out of every event. We manage to enjoy ourselves almost everywhere. Our sort of life kept us usually hungry so that we enjoyed Mr. Merrill's table very much. I do not suppose an epicure would have liked it so well. In regard to their attention to boarders, I should say they let us alone to do very much as we please and that was just exactly what we liked.

The attraction for us is the very roughness of the country; the deep and almost inaccessible gorges and trout brooks. Him who is anxious to keep his clothes whole I would not advise to visit those places which are the chief attractions for me. Riding would not be a chief feature of my enjoyment, for we are situated on the side of the mountain. In one direction you ascend the mountain which is uphill business. On the other you descend, which business is just about as much downhill for a mile or more and quite steep. After that the driving is pleasant. As for covered buggies for invalids, I cannot say much. Mr. Merrill always furnished me a careful driver for he always let me drive myself.

The walks about the immediate vicinity are very pleasant. For extended excursions you would be obliged either to go up or down the mountain or you would find rough paths. You would have pure air and water in any quantities. We experienced no difficulty or inconvenience from dampness. The drainage was not perfect, but I understand that it had much improved and was to be further improved by carrying the water from the kitchen farther from the house than last season.

I think everything about the food was neat and I am sure it was well cooked and the mention of chickens revives pleasant memories in my mind. During our stay we had strawberries and raspberries but we were too soon for most summer vegetables. We found no lack in respect to milk, cream and eggs though oatmeal we did not have. I have no doubt Mr. Merrill would furnish it if wanted. Ham is a staple.

In regard to beds, they are not so comfortable as mine at home, but we usually found ourselves so tired at night that we found no difficulty in sleeping. I think the room we occupied had a straw matting on the floor, but I think many of the rooms were not carpeted at all.

For me, it is a most enjoyable place. It might not be the same to you. I go away sometimes in the morning and spend the day among the trout brooks and return at night with wet feet and torn clothes. You might not enjoy that. I do.

Now if you should go to Mr. Merrill's you will find a very kind hearted family, but if it should prove to be a place which you could not enjoy, please do not blame me for recommending it for I have tried to present the facts to you just as they exist.

Yours truly,
Benjamin F. Clarke

* * * * * * * * * * * *

Marian Pychowska writes to Isabella Stone.

Blair's House
Campton, N.H.
July 1, 1880

My dear Miss Stone,

Perhaps today you are at "Goodnow's", or at least on the way there. I hope your battle with colds has come to an end, and that you will be able to begin at once to enjoy the country. You see we are settled at Campton. We have been here just a week today, having left home some days earlier than we intended. Our excursions, however, have been confined within the limits of the arbor in front of the house, and the grove behind it, and this because I have not been well, and my mother has not felt inclined to go alone. She seems to be beginning the summer with a better stock of health than for some years past, and I expect that in a few days we shall both be able to inspect our old haunts with renewed vigor.

With the exception of Friday and Monday, which, I should think, must have been warm through the whole region, the weather has been very pleasant and the atmosphere very clear. Last evening toward sunset, a beautiful shower swept across the mounts, and later the sun came out and shone on their green sides and on the remnants of the clouds. If you were at Sugar Hill, you must have had a fine performance there.

Mr. Blair has been making some improvements about the house, and adding a few new rooms, as it promises to be a crowded season. A party of eight cousins of ours, who made up their minds to join us in August, were unable to get rooms here. They are to be at a small house nearby until the 1st of September, when our house will probably thin out. As far as I can tell, you will find us here through September whenever you can come.

I think you will be pleased to hear, if you do not know it already, that the "Baldcap" is to be in the number of *Appalachia* now preparing. Also, Mr. Sweetser[7], the editor of *Osgood's Guide*, wrote to my mother for the papers on Shelburne, that he might make use of some of the information they contain in the new edition of the Guide that he is now bringing out.

I am glad you saw my aunt's sketch of "Dream Lake". One of the members of the Club, Mr. Chase (mentioned in the "Baldcap") was so well pleased with it, that he ordered a duplicate from her. He has made his plans to spend the summer at Gates' Cottage and will probably do much in the way of verifying and correcting old explorations, as well as gaining new information about that region.

The *Echo* explorer has not reached that side of the mountains yet. My mother has written to the *Echo* office and we shall probably see it all summer so if you have any extraordinary doings at Goodnow's, we shall know of them. I should not be very much surprised to read your name among those of "a party who made the ascent of Lafayette on horseback, and had one of the clearest views of the season".

I was very much pleased to get your photograph and like it well. The one I send in return[8] was taken eighteen months ago, but I do not think I have changed much since then! My mother joins me in kind remembrances to you, and to Dr. and Mrs. Stone. Hoping to get a glimpse of you this year, I remain sincerely your friend,

Marian Pychowska

---

[7] Moses F. Sweetser was the author of *The White Mountains, A Handbook for Travelers*, first published in 1876. This book was also called *Osgood's Guide* and was the most comprehensive White Mountain guidebook available at the time.

[8] This photograph was not found among the collection of original letters.

Marian Pychowska writes to Isabella Stone.

Blair's House
Campton, N.H.
August 8, 1880

Dear Miss Stone,

Today I must at least begin the letter that I have been wanting to write you ever since the Appalachian field meeting in Plymouth.

My uncle and aunt arrived here about the time that I received your last, and this week we have welcomed a large party of our cousins from Washington. They were unable to get rooms here, but are comfortably settled at a farm house a quarter of a mile or so away. Of course there will have to be a great deal of visiting back and forth until the first of September when they are to come here. Through this month our house will be, I suppose, as full as possible, and perhaps a little more so! But the crowd is composed of such pleasant people, that one does not feel inclined to complain.

A grand festivity was held here on Friday evening in return for one given at Sanborn's[9] a week ago. The programme began with "Punch and Judy", included two charades, and several comic things gotten up by the very clever young people in our house, and ended with ice cream and dancing at a very late hour. I think we can now say that effort is over for the season. Perhaps the next thing will be a picnic.

Our fellow boarders are not much given to walking, but occasionally a party of fifteen or twenty start off for some point of interest on foot. I hope you have seen the report of the new *Echo* exploration. The explorers must indeed have seen some very beautiful places.

In the *Echo* of July 31 was a full report of Professor Fay's paper, read by him at the meeting, giving an account of his walk from Warren to Thornton over Mt. Kineo. My mother and I enjoyed exceedingly meeting our Appalachian acquaintances of last year, and were well pleased with our new ones. Mr. Blair drove us down to Plymouth, and, as usual, we were the first on hand at the Normal School[10]. Mr. Warren, the principal, took us into the room hung around with beautiful maps of New Hampshire, and with these we entertained ourselves until Mr. Henck[11] made his appearance.

After a few words from Professor Cross[12], Colonel Higginson[13] read

---

[9] Sanborn's Boardinghouse in Campton Village, NH.
[10] A school that prepares secondary school graduates to become teachers.
[11] John B. Henck, Jr. of Boston, MA, was a founding member of the AMC. Henck served as Secretary from 1876 to 1878, and later as Vice-President.
[12] Charles R. Cross of Jamaica Plain, MA, was a founding member of the AMC and served as President in 1880.
[13] Colonel Thomas Wentworth Higginson of Cambridge, MA, was an avid explorer. He served as President of the AMC in 1885.

his charming paper, "An Ascent to Les Grands Mulets", then Mr. Warren called the attention of the Club to the beautiful stretch of country between Fryeburg and Bethel[14], with its wild mountains and many ponds. He spent part of his boyhood there, and did not think its beauties were appreciated.

Professor Fay's paper followed, and then Mr. Scott[15], the Councillor on Exploration, detailed a recent trip from the Swift River Valley to Waterville over Tripyramid. The explorations of both the last named gentlemen were made with a view to path making some time or other. Already there is a subscription on foot in some of the houses here for the West Thornton–Warren Path. Its object is to make Mt. Moosilauke more accessible from this valley.

Among other miscellanies at the end of the meeting, were brought into notice some very fine falls in the great ravine of Moosilauke, which have been nicely named by their visitor and describer, "the Plirades", in allusion to their number. Most of the persons present were looking forward to an excursion to Moosilauke as soon as the weather permitted. We wished we might be of this number.

Next day Professor Fay notified us that the long trip was postponed for a day, and that the short one, to Mt. Prospect was to occupy that afternoon. My mother and I set out for the point named in true Appalachian style, and as we drew near the place where the two roads, from Plymouth and from Campton, unite for the last ascent, we met the pedestrian portion of the Plymouth party. You can imagine how pleasant it was to talk over mutual mountain friends with Professors Fay and Pickering[16] and Mr. Scott as we climbed the hill. Soon the carriage party joined us, and the company spread themselves over the rocks to enjoy and discuss the view. Professor Niles was particularly kind and agreeable to us, and took us in charge, I think because we are friends of the Spauldings, whose brother-in-law he is.

I had my first sight of Appalachians at work. Mr. Edmands[17] pro-

---

[14] The Evans Notch region lies between Fryeburg and Bethel, Maine.

[15] Augustus E. Scott from Lexington, MA, was a founding member of the AMC. He served as President (1884,1888), Vice-President, and Councillor of Improvements.

[16] Edward C. Pickering was a Professor of Physics at the Massachusetts Institute of Technology. He is justly regarded as **the** founding father of the AMC and was elected the first President in 1876. He later served as Councillor of Topography and again as President in 1882.

[17] J. Rayner Edmands, of the Harvard University Observatory, was a founding member of the AMC. He served as President (1886), Vice-President, Councillor of Exploration, Councillor of Topography, and leader of scientific activities for the club. Edmands spent many summers building trails in the White Mountains, primarily in Randolph and Bretton Woods. In 1892 he built two camps, Cascade Camp and the Perch, on Mount Adams. The col between Mounts Jefferson and Adams, as well as a trail up Mount Eisenhower, bear his name today.

duced some instruments, among others a heliotrope[18], which was set so as to signal Professor Quimby[19] on Mt. Washington. One of the gentlemen was kind enough to give me a lesson in the use of the heliotrope and I was permitted to watch it and keep it rightly directed. We stayed till nearly six o'clock, enjoying the late afternoon light on the mountains, and the good company, and then left the assembly to wind our way home to a late tea.

This was not the only pleasure brought us by the meeting. Last week Colonel and Mrs. Higginson drove over from Plymouth to consult my mother as an authority on the ferns of this region. Imagine my mother's surprise at being regarded in such a light. The Colonel wished to show us a wonderful fern garden a short distance from Plymouth. My mother, my aunt and I went down last Saturday afternoon, and found the rest of the party, consisting of the Colonel and three very pleasant ladies. We were led by a lovely old disused road, which has degenerated into a cattle-path and a stream-bed, but is still shaded by old willows. Leaving the path, we crossed a pasture, and then came out into a perfect paradise of ferns, great beds of maidenhair waving in the wind, and almost all the other kinds that we have found in these parts, all growing with the greatest luxuriance. After a while I left the others to sit or ramble as they pleased, and wandered down into an attractive piece of wet ground. There I found a new kind of Aspidium, which makes number twenty-nine on our list.

About two weeks ago we revisited Bald Hill. It was a splendid day, with a cold northwest wind and great masses of cloud which made lovely shadows on the mountains of the Pemigewasset Forest. We could see a distant peak which seemed very like the top of Washington, but as the clouds were sweeping over it and we had no glass, we were not able to verify it. We are looking forward to another day there, with all necessary apparatus.

My mother is unusually strong and free from headache this year, and feels equal to taking real long walks. I am sorry you speak of not being able to do as much walking as last summer, but I hope to learn from your next letter that you have gained more rapidly than you expected.

Your original impression with regard to "Pollard's" was correct. It is a primitive place, and, I believe, chiefly patronized by those who are going into the wilderness. I think it would be delightful to spend a few days at Pollard's, even if only to smell the wilderness, but I don't know that I could recommend it to a delicate person as a place to spend a length of time at, on account of the fare. The Pollard family seem very obliging, but have a strong flavor of the back woods. It is the dream of my mother

---

[18] A group of mirrors arranged for reflecting sunlight from a distant point to an observation station.

[19] Professor Elihu T. Quimby of Hanover, NH, was a founding member of the AMC. Quimby is credited with designing the portable heliotrope.

and of myself to go there again and ascend Loon Pond Mountain.

My aunt's price for a picture the size of the "Dream Lake" is fifteen dollars if she retain the privilege of reproducing it, and somewhat more without that liberty.

My poor scrappy letter began on Sunday, is brought to an end on Wednesday, but owing to this delay I have the pleasure of announcing that the notice of the new path planned, which my mother posted in the entry, has been undersigned to the amount of eleven dollars. I hope I may have something very interesting to write you about when I answer the letter I look forward to receiving from you soon. With kind remembrance to Dr. and Mrs. Stone, and all old friends and acquaintances at Goodnow's, I am yours sincerely,

Marian Pychowska

* * * * * * * * * * * *

Marian Pychowska writes to Isabella Stone.

Blair's House
Campton, N.H.
September 5, 1880

Dear Miss Stone,

Mrs. Blair authorizes me to say that you could have a room here with two requisites, a closet and a fire, certainly, after the 15th, and probably before that date. Last week a good many left, but their places have been filled by others. The new comers only intend staying a short time, however, and by the third week I dare say our party will reign supreme. One of my cousins is due in Washington the middle of the month, but the others will probably remain with us to the end.

August 23, the day you were enjoying again the sights in Franconia Notch, we all went to Weetamoo for the day. There was a big wagon full, with only ourselves (cousins included), as all four children went, and the mammy was the only member of the family left at home, with the exception of my father who is too absorbed in his work to wish to go anywhere. It was very warm climbing, but we took our time, so that even Albert, the five-year-old, did not complain.

After dinner, my uncle, aunt, and I left the others to return to Mr. Blair and the wagon at the Roby Farm, and struck down through the woods on the southern side toward the upper clearings of the Beebe Valley. In crossing a belt of woods among the high pastures, we came upon a hedgehog who slowly climbed a tree bristling his back at us.

Thursday of the same week, all but one of the same party walked to Mt. Prospect. Last week we accomplished nothing in the way of excursions. During the warm weather we have enjoyed the bathing very much. I have also made two examinations of the bogs in the neighboring woods, and think I have added another variety to our list of ferns. Today it has grown clear and cooler, and we are making plans to go to Pollard's on Tuesday if the weather holds. We hope to start early enough to be able to go up Loon Pond Mountain the same day. The next day, my cousins proposed to devote to the Notch, while my mother, uncle, and I may find something of interest in the East Branch Valley. Thursday will probably bring us home again. Two of the party, who are novices in the mountains, have been anxious to camp out, and, as this desire has not been gratified so far, we are going on Sunset Hill this afternoon, taking our supper with us, to give them the pleasure of at least seeing the sunset from a height. You have often done the same on Sugar Hill I believe.

Our little evening picnic is over and I return to you. The late light on the mountains was lovely and the candidates for camping had the pleasure of sitting by a fire until the twilight deepened. I wonder if you did not notice at sunset those long brown smoke bands in the north.

It seems to me a difficult matter to impose a name on mountain or waterfall. Adam in Paradise knew how to call all creatures appropriately, but I am afraid that is one of the many gifts that have been lost for me. Personally, where a poetical name does not grow naturally, I should incline toward a matter-of-fact one that would best describe the place, but this is merely individual feeling. "Flume Knob" or "Spur", which would seem the most obvious name, has the great disadvantage of having been already used for the great pyramid of Flume Mountain on this side of the mountains. The town might impose the name "Easton Knob" or "Spur", but persons could then say it was rather a western spur!

The new route to be opened to Moosilauke will go in from the neighborhood of West Thornton, and pass between Mounts Kineo and Cushman. This is very direct from the Camptons, and I believe is the lowest notch between the two valleys, so that the bridle path could be turned into a road some day. I have a vague remembrance of having heard that a bridle path was contemplated, perhaps completed, from North Woodstock by way of Moosilauke Brook and the Blue Ridge to the summit of Moosilauke.

Beside the Pollard trip, we have also in view Tripyramid (the three peaks this time), Black Mountain and Kineo. If they come off I will write you about them, for I know on such themes your patience to read is as inexhaustible as my willingness to write.

My father heard I was writing you and wishes me to send his kindest remembrances. My mother also joins me in sending kindest regards to you and to your father and mother when you write to them. We would be glad to have you drop down upon us here by the stage. Your letters are always a pleasure to us.

                              Yours very sincerely,
                              Marian Pychowska

Marian Pychowska writes to Isabella Stone.

Blair's House
Campton, N.H.
September 24, 1880

Dear Miss Stone,

I suppose I must think of you now at home in Framingham, perhaps looking at the sky and the hills and imagining how clear the mountains must be. You seem to have met a great many pleasant people this summer, and this must have been some compensation for the inactivity to which you had to resign yourself.

In the letter my mother had from him some days ago, Professor Fay spoke as though much pleased with Sugar Hill and his visit there. There is a prospect of going to work immediately on the new route to Moosilauke, and the plan includes a branch trail to the summit of Kineo and the clearing of said summit. I am afraid that if we get there, as is hoped next week, it will still be necessary to climb a tree to get the view.

Two of the expeditions planned can now be crossed off the list— three in fact. As you may suppose, the heavy smoke that came down the second week in September, put off our trip to Pollard's. One morning that we had made all our arrangements to start, including an early breakfast, my mother determined to go somewhere where the smoke would not make such a difference to us, so we drove to Newfound Lake. Mr. Blair himself had never been there as it is in an out of the way place among the hills beyond Plymouth, about fifteen miles from here. We had a very pleasant but rather tantalizing day, for as we sat by the shore the strong northwest wind that freshened the lake into whitecaps, also poured down volumes of smoke. The outlines of the hills on the other shore were barely discernable, and if one only looked at the water line, one could imagine the waves rolling in were from a shoreless sea. The lake is seven miles long and quite broad, and the views must be very lovely in clear weather. Mr. Blair put up his horses at a little boardinghouse newly built in a fine situation and called, I think, the "Lake View House". We drove home another way across the hills.

After the smoke, followed much needed rain, and for a week my mother was not well so Pollards was still postponed. Monday, the 13th, my uncle, two ladies of our party and I went to Black Mountain. As we needed a long day, we had to make an early start, at seven, when the heavy fog was still about us as we drove up the valley. When this lifted, the western sky was dark with threatening clouds. Our ascent was by the old path which follows the ravine and reaches the crest by a slide of broken rock. The new path, by which we came down, keeps along the high ridge by Jenning's and Noon Peaks, and reaches the road only two miles from Greeley's. The forests on our upward route were grand, but when we came out on the open side above them, the clouds had crept over the sky and had enveloped Moosilauke and the higher mountains. At one we stood on top, and had a few moments to enjoy the view that was allowed us by mingled smoke and cloud, then the mist swept over and shut us in. When we had eaten our provisions and inscribed the names of the party in the Appalachian bottle[20], we were glad to crouch by the fire my uncle built and get warmed through before starting down. Though the clouds darkened as we descended, we scarcely anticipated the rain that began to patter through the trees as we left Noon Peak. The highway reached, we found a dry spot under a bridge in which to wait for Mr. Blair. Our fourteen mile drive home was a rather wet one, as the wagon had no cover and we had not even an umbrella to shelter us from the persistent showers. I think our amiable landlord was well pleased with his party for neither loosing its temper nor taking cold.

Tuesday, the 21st we woke to be surprised by a splendidly clear day after Monday's storm. At last everything and everybody was ready for Pollard's. My mother, uncle, aunt, and two of the cousin party, with myself, set out after dinner to take that beautiful drive toward the Notch that is still in store for you. So clear and cold, such a brilliant sunshine and splendid masses of cloud and autumn color, all made it delightful. I should have said that my uncle started on foot at eleven o'clock. As the rest of us drove up to Pollard's door, we saw him sitting in the parlor window with his face beaming with fun. When we got in, we discovered the cause to be a volume of "John Phoenix" nonsense, that he had found on the table. His absurd take off of the reports on the government surveying parties kept us amused all evening. We had the house to ourselves, and the Pollards did all they could to make us comfortable. Those of the party who had not been there before were agreeably disappointed. In fact the only thing lacking at the table was good bread.

My mother made inquiries about climbing the mountain the next day and was told that there were two trails to Loon Pond, one from Pollard's which we could take if the East Branch was low enough to cross, and one from Sharon, three miles down the valley. Of course we preferred the first, and were pleased to hear next morning, that the old man had been down to the stream and thought we could get over it. Heavy clouds driven by a northwest wind still swept the top of Moosilauke, but

---

[20] The Appalachian bottle, refers to registers (stored in metallic bottles) that had been placed on mountain summits by the Appalachian Mountain Club to collect excursion data. Some of these old registers have been saved and are located at the AMC library in Boston. The signatures of Miss Stone, the Pychowskas, Cooks, and their climbing companions are recorded in the registers from many different summits during this time period.

they promised to lift later, and at least the atmosphere was as clear as could be.

Mr. Dura Pollard, the older son, was our guide, as we did not wish to lose time finding the way. We walked down to the bank and while Mr. Pollard cut us some sticks and made a sapling bridge over the first stretch of the water, we looked at the wide stream running over its bed of boulders and pebbles, and wondered if we were going to get over dry shod. This we soon found was not expected of us, for Mr. Pollard said that if we were afraid of taking cold, it would be well to wet our heads before going into the water! Having crossed the little bridge to the first rock, there was nothing to do but jump from stone to stone, choosing if possible one above water, or at least not more than two or three inches under it. The lucky ones were not wet above the ankle, but two slipped in, skirts and all. My mother went through bravely, helped by Mr. Pollard who walked into the water to help us. It was great fun for those who did not have wet skirts to carry up the mountain, for the feet soon dried.

The blazed trail to the lake is about two miles, and passes easily up through fine woods to the ledges. The large pond, which must be near two thousand feet above the sea, is a lovely sheet of water and a resort for fishermen. One has fine views of the mountains from the ledges about it, but we were attracted by the bare heights that lie beyond. Mr. Pollard had never been on them, hunting and fishing having been his business when on the mountain before. A scramble over the bleached trunks of the old forest swept off by fire and through the young thickets that have grown up about them, brought us to the top. It was splendid to look so nearly at those wonderful peaks of Liberty and Flume with Lafayette between them, and a part of your Hooket looking over from behind. One has a fine view of the Twin Range, the Hancock and Carrigain group, and if the clouds had not been so low we should have seen the Presidentials in line over the Willey Range. Kinsman and Moosilauke are fine, and one can see several of the Green Mountains beyond. If we had time, it would have been a pleasure to study the details of the valley toward the south, with all the familiar heights about Campton, but we were due at Pollard's at half past two.

On the way down to the lake, Mr. Pollard pointed out a bear track and several hoof marks of the deer. Again we forded the East Branch, and had time to get into dry clothes before we were called to an excellent dinner. Pollard's is taking on a new air, for they are building a good porch on two sides of the house, which will give it a much more attractive appearance.

After dinner my uncle started on foot, and the rest of us with Mr. Blair drove home. It took us three hours, and my uncle five, to accomplish the eighteen or nineteen miles. After all our waiting, the excursion so long looked forward to was put through. It was well that we took the first available day for toward the end of the week, one of Mr. Blair's children was taken so ill, that we thought it better to leave a few days earlier than we had intended. We turned our backs on Kineo still unclimbed and reached New Jersey by the boat on Sunday morning. Next Monday my mother and I expect to spend a few days with friends who have a house on the Jersey Shore near Long Branch, and so finish the summer with a breath of the sea. After this flitting, the butterflies must settle down into bees once more. My mother, having returned to her big geologies and fern books, is having all the pleasure of classifying the few trophies of this season.

Please remember me to Dr. and Mrs. Stone and believe me always,

Your friend,
Marian Pychowska
Hoboken, N.J.
September 30, 1880

1881

"Best of all was the greeting from the grand old mountains, 'my multitudinous mountains sitting in the magic circle', each peak an everlasting friend aglow in sunset radiance."

Isabella Stone writes to Charles Philbrook.

Framingham, Mass.
June 8, 1881

Mr. Charles E. Philbrook[1]
Dear Sir,
On my way from Portland to Jefferson, I wish to see what are the attractions of Shelburne as I am in search of a desirable summer home for our family party on that side of the mountains; we have spent many seasons on the western side. Dr. James Shepard of Boston recommended your place to me. To save you time and trouble I will leave after each question a blank space in which I will request you to write the answer and return this sheet to me with your circular or card.

Can I have a single room at your house for a day or two about the third day of July?
No.
Or sometime during the first week in July?
No.
What is your price per day?
One dollar.
I desire especially to have a good bed. Do you have spring beds?
Yes.

---

[1] Charles E. Philbrook of Philbrook's Boardinghouse in Shelburne, NH. This house was located three miles west of the Philbrook Farm Inn which was run by his brother, Augustus E. Philbrook.

Charles Philbrook's Boardinghouse

What kind of mattresses?
Hair and wool excelsior.
Can you furnish a guide trustworthy and suitable to escort ladies?
Yes.
And what would be the time and expense required for each of these
excursions:
Ascent of Mt. Baldcap? *One day.*
Ascent of Mt. Hayes? *One day.*
Visit to Glen Ellis Falls? *One day.*
Visit to Giant Falls or Cascade of the Clouds? *One day.*
Is your house nearer Gorham than the other Philbrooks[2]?
Yes.
What do you charge for a horse and buggy and driver per half day?
Three dollars.
Or for the ride to Gilead?
One dollar and fifty cents.
Have you a covered carriage, comfortable and easy to carry one or
two persons? What do you charge apiece?

---

[2] The Philbrook Farm Inn in Shelburne, NH. Augustus E. Philbrook was the
proprietor. The inn was opened in 1861 by Augustus' father Harvey and has been
operated continuously ever since by his descendants. Today's hosts are now the fifth
consecutive generation of the Philbrook family to manage the establishment.

Philbrook Farm Inn

According to distance.
What would you charge to drive one passenger, with a small trunk, to the Waumbek House[3], Jefferson?
Five dollars.
How much a piece for a party of three or five or more, with but one trunk?
Three dollars each.
Is there a regular stage from Gorham to Jefferson over Randolph Hill?
No.
Please answer immediately and you will confer a favor.
                              Yours truly,
                              M. I. Stone, Box 112
Note: We shall not have room for any one after July 2.
                              Yours truly,
                              Charles Philbrook, Shelburne, N.H.
                              June 11, 1881

---

[3] A boardinghouse in Jefferson, NH. In 1860, Benjamin Hunking Plaisted built the first unit of the Waumbek. Many additions followed and the Waumbek was eventually considered to be a fine hotel. Patriot and preacher Thomas Starr King is credited with choosing both the location for the house and the Abenaki Indian name "Waumbek," which has been interpreted to mean "mountains with snowy foreheads."

James Hovey writes to Isabella Stone.

Chelsea, Mass.
June 10, 1881

Dear Miss Stone,
We were disappointed on Wednesday that you could not visit. We hope you will consider the invitation on some more favorable occasion.

I have made a little diagram of the route from Gilead, Maine on the Grand Trunk Railroad. I will suppose you are going alone or with a companion and afoot. Take the Eastern Railroad for Portland and Gilead, Maine in the morning (through ticket), arrive at the Gilead Station at 4:00 P.M., cross the wire bridge and on the road leading up that side of the river, go to Philbrook's three miles to stay overnight or longer. The views at Gates' Cottage on the way up to Lead Mine Bridge and at the bridge are admirable, and should be seen in the early morning (6:00 or 7:00 A.M.), better at 6:00 or 7:00 P.M. Cross Lead Mine Bridge and up the other side to Philbrook's Boarding House. Hire this Mr. Philbrook to drive you to within one or two miles of the summit of Randolph Hill, so that you may be there at 5:30 P.M. Then enjoy a delightful walk over to the Ravine House[4] where you stay overnight. The next day walk to the Mount Adams House[5] six miles, and on to Jefferson Hill six miles more.

From Jefferson Hill you may take rail to Whitefield several times during the day, but for views walk over Bray Hill to Mr. Aldrich. There take rail to Littleton to meet Goodnow's team, or better, walk to Bethlehem, eight miles on one day, next day eight miles to Goodnow's.

You have done mountain walking enough to know that you must travel light—no baggage. You will find fair mountain beds and living at the places I have mentioned. At the Ravine House tell them that Mr. Hovey sent you. There you will get good bread and butter and consider the location. If we could have made arrangements so that I could take you along from Gilead, I think I could have pointed out many objects of interest which may escape your observation.

I think you will enjoy this trip on foot.

Very truly your friend,
James Hovey

---

[4] A boardinghouse in Randolph, NH. Built by Abel N. Watson and his son Laban M. Watson, the house was opened with accommodations for twenty guests in 1876 under the name of the Mount Madison House. In 1877, the name was changed to the Ravine House. For years it served as headquarters for explorations and hiking excursions in the area and it was the "permanent" summer home to many who were involved in the activities of the AMC. The business changed hands many times and remained in operation until 1963 when it was demolished.

[5] A boardinghouse in Jefferson Highlands, NH.

Marian Pychowska writes to Isabella Stone.

Hoboken, N.J.
June 18, 1881

Dear Miss Stone,

Your long and full letters always give us a great deal of pleasure, and I assure you it flatters me that you should take the trouble to write to me now that you have another and better matched correspondent here. Under these circumstances, it would not be fair to count letters with you, and as during the summer my pen and my tongue are somewhat loosened, I intend to write you whenever I feel inclined.

The 28th is the day set for the decampment of the first division to the Black Mountain House[6]. My uncle and aunt will follow about the middle of July. We are looking forward with pleasure to having new walks and new ferning grounds, though with much doubt whether we shall find the same comforts and benevolent spirit in the house management which makes Blair's so pleasant.

The Black Mountain House is an old rendez-vous of Professor Fay and some other Appalachians. It would be very agreeable to meet them again especially as all our small efforts have been so well received. Evidently there are not many members who trouble themselves even to do as much, for in the last *Appalachia* we figure again under the head of exploration and ferns.

Mr. Hinkley and Mr. Sargent have made plans to spend part of the summer at Campton. They seem to amuse themselves very well in such a quiet place, Mr. Hinkley in bugging, ferning, and talking, and Mr. Sargent in the excursions and in teasing his friend. Mr. Sargent returned from the west several months ago and has been with his family in Newport. In one of his letters to my aunt, he describes himself as trying to persuade his family to go with him to Campton, but strange to say, they were not to be enticed away from their accustomed life in the wilds of the Pemigewasset.

That was indeed a sad event that you tell me of and one to darken the spirits of those who were near witnesses. If those poor souls who are tempted to go out of this troublesome world by force would only take to themselves so much true philosophy as Hamlet did, they could not have the cowardly courage to plunge into the undiscovered country. Indeed I hope many who commit suicide are not in a responsible condition of mind.

My aunt commissions me to thank you for your letter to her and proposes to answer it soon. With regards to your father and mother and best wishes for a happy summer to you all, I remain,

Sincerely your friend,
Marian Pychowska

_____

[6] The Black Mountain House was a boardinghouse in Campton, NH, where the Pychowskas and Cooks spent the summer of 1881. The house was managed by the Willis family.

Edith Cook writes to Isabella Stone.

Hoboken, N.J.
July 4, 1881

My dear Miss Stone,

I have been reserving a number of letters to answer when my sister's departure for the mountains would reduce our household to my brother, myself and the servants and when too the companionship by letter with one's absent friends might be even more pleasant than at ordinary times.

So I take up your letter this morning of our national holiday when my brother is outside in the garden diverting himself with his juvenile friends, supplying them with fire crackers and toy cannons and other accompaniments of the "Glorious Fourth" which we so gratefully celebrate today in that the life of President Garfield is still spared and that we may even hope for his recovery. While, as Americans, we deplore the dastardly deed with indignation and sorrow, we cannot but rejoice in the one common feeling of protest and sympathy that rises from an outraged people. And we trust that out of this evil may be wrought some good for the whole country, that the political conscience, if there be such a thing, will be awakened to the fact that the President of the United States holds his office for the good of the whole country, not as the dispenser of spoils or the means of the personal aggrandizement of the "wire pullers" that elected him. The whole people should not leave their whole country to the mercy of the unscrupulous few. In the midst of the suspense of today, it is still comforting to see all the flags run up to the peak, not melancholy half-mast telling of the nation's loss.

I have told you of my brother's method of celebrating the day, you, as a housekeeper, will smile when I tell you that the other portion of the household, our two servants, has chosen rather to enjoy itself over the washtub and clothesline than take the holiday offered for outside relaxation. Our cook has been very merry over our washing and the conjunction of the comet with the shooting of the president.

I believe Marian wrote you just before leaving for the mountains. Saturday I had my first letter from her from our summer quarters which are found extremely comfortable and surpassing, even in the outside surroundings, the memory that remained of them from our frequent drivings by when at Blair's. The house seems to be more like Goodnow's than Blair's, with high ceilings, wide halls, one parlor, two sitting rooms and two pianos!! But if the summer proves only as pleasant as was the one at Sugar Hill and gives us as good friends, we will not mind the hundred guests nor the two pianos nor even the telephone which our hosts have set up in their house for the better communication with the metropolitan center of Plymouth. We know how much the neighborhood offers and then we have the pleasant friendly human intercourse of the summer to look forward to, that knitting of friendly ties for which the mountains have so subtle a power.

We expect both our old Sugar Hill friends to spend part of their summer with us, Mr. Hinkley and Mr. Sargent. Mr. Hinkley may possibly bring some other friends with him, while Mr. Sargent will be our faithful escort to any distant peak we may choose to climb or to any hidden waterfall we may seek to discover.

I do indeed remember our climb of Cannon Mountain and our walk home through those thrush-haunted woods in the hollow of the Ham Branch. It was a day to remember with the weird mists sailing up the notch and lightly enriching the crests of Cannon and then that ruby light on Lafayette as we gained the top of the steep hill above the mill, that trial to impatient feet at the close of the day's labor. I wish you might join us some day in such another expedition.

Thank you very much for writing me. Your letters are always pleasant visitors. Remember me most kindly to your mother and father and believe me,

Sincerely your friend,
Edith W. Cook

* * * * * * * * * * * *

Marian Pychowska writes to Isabella Stone.

Black Mountain House
Campton, N.H.
July 17, 1881

Dear Miss Stone,

We learned from Mr. Willis that you had enjoyed your drive, duly admired the Pemigewasset Valley, and put up for the night at Dearborn's[7]. Upon Mr. Willis' description, we recalled the pretty little cottage and the maple tree with its surrounding platform across the road, but we had supposed this place to be a part of the Russell[8] establishment just below. I do not remember what view these houses have.

The evening you left us, we sat out in the meadow across the road until about half past eight enjoying the warm balmy breeze without a thought of dampness. What a delicious change that was which prepared that beautiful Thursday for you! You must have enjoyed it exceedingly where you were, but I wished that you could have seen these mountains relieved of their smoke veil. Thursday afternoon my mother and I went

---

[7] Dearborn's Boardinghouse in North Woodstock, NH. David Dearborn was the proprietor.
[8] Russell's Boardinghouse in North Woodstock, NH. George F. Russell was the proprietor. Isabella spent the summers of 1882, 1883, and 1885 at the Russell House.

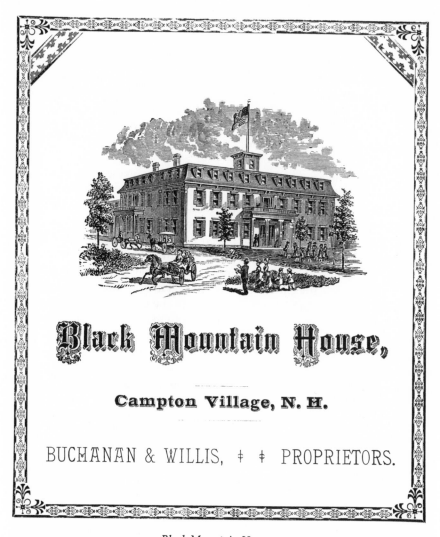

Black Mountain House

on Hodgeman's Hill, intending, at first, only to explore the road that climbs its side, but finally beguiled toward the bare top. The view is not very different from others we have seen from neighboring hills, but you know a day like that throws a new charm over old things. On the way home, we tried to find a way of crossing the Mad River without going around by the bridge, but after some time spent in scrambling through the tangled thickets along the bank, we finally came to a place where the stream divides to form an island. We crossed to the island by means of some logs, but the other branch of the river had no such convenient bridge, and we were obliged to wade over. This ignominious transit was made in sight of the village bridge that we had taken such pains to avoid. I do not think we shall try that "shortcut" again.

On Friday we induced my father to go with us to the top of Wallace Hill. He was very much pleased with everything, except the brush fences that we were obliged to climb. Yesterday, Saturday, you must have seen magnificent sights from Goodnow's. The shower we had here was glorious, with an episode of big hail stones and was followed by an equally glorious sunset.

July 24

I put off finishing my letter, waiting for a new inspiration, but I must not let it get too old. The last *Echo* informed me of your arrival at Goodnow's. I see also in the list the names of other friends, Mrs. Short and Miss Mary Short, from New York. Perhaps you have already made their acquaintance, in which case I need not tell you they are very agreeable people. Professor Short, who has gone abroad for his vacation, is the professor of Greek, I think, in Columbia College. Miss Short is an Appalachian, having made the Club's acquaintance at the Mt. Adams House. She is not able to walk much, but is interested in the Club's work. I suppose you have seen the account of the field meeting in the *Echo*. I am afraid the weather was not very favorable for the excursions that were to follow it.

Of course you were interested by the proposition to rename the Franconia "Haystack", under impulse of the sympathy excited by our President's condition[9]. I was pleased that the President and members of the AMC could so well hide any personal inclination for or against the change, under the Club's wise regulation of noninterference in such matters. My conservatism could scarcely defend "the ignominious name of Haystack", but it intrenches itself in the name I learned from you, "Hooket", which seems to suit the weird peak perfectly. If Bethlehem only had a different name, I could rail at its citified airs more at my ease.

My aunt and uncle arrived last Thursday at the same time with Mr. Hinkley and his sister. There is a prospect that this house will soon be filled.

Hoping to hear from you soon, I remain always,
Your friend,
M. M. Pychowska

---

[9] Mount Garfield, which connects the Franconia and Twin Mountain ranges, was originally called Mount Haystack or Mount Hooket. The name was changed to honor the memory of President James Abram Garfield who was shot July 2, 1881, and died from related complications on September 6, 1881. The name change was first adopted by the selectmen of Franconia in August, 1881, and approved by the AMC on the date of President Garfield's death.

Isabella Stone writes to Marian Pychowska (draft copy).

Goodnow House
Sugar Hill, N.H.
July 20, 1881

My dear Miss Pychowska,

Much as I should have liked to remain longer with you all at the Black Mountain House, the weather during the few days after leaving was so perfect that I could but rejoice in taking the trip just then; especially as we have had gloom and clouds almost ever since, with frequent heavy showers.

Probably, Mr. Willis told you of our ride to North Woodstock and his leaving me at Mrs. Dearborn's little cottage. The good woman had her house full of boarders, but as I came on Mr. Gerry's[10] recommendation, she made up a cot in the parlor, and did everything in her power to make me comfortable and to enable me to see all the beauty in the vicinity. Indeed everybody was very kind to me during the entire journey, as usual when I start out alone.

In going to the Post Office at the Russell House (which is but a few steps south of Dearborn's) I was surprised by the most unexpected sight of an old Framingham friend, now a teacher in Wellesley College, Mass. She was very desirous to have me come over there and spend a few days. Mrs. Russell's best chamber happened to be vacant, and was given to me Thursday night.

Thursday P.M. a little party of four of us rode to Agassiz Basins; then down the west side of the Pemigewasset to Woodstock and back on the east side, crossing the old bridge at Sawyer's, where you had your "superb near view of the Notch and of Moosilauke", I presume. Then we drove up to Pollard's, saw the old man and his son, the guide. The new piazza is scarcely finished. Their next neighbor is building a new house for boarders. And the view from "Pollard's Bridge" is even finer than from Sawyer's and how beautiful the river is everywhere around Woodstock! We drove ourselves and were quite independent. The "Basins" were well worth visiting and resemble both the Pool and the Basin in Franconia Notch. I clambered about on the rocks and obtained one good view directly down upon the waterfall, which from the banks of the brook is hidden by an immense rock held in firm grip between the high towering walls of granite between which, low down, the stream rushes and winds. I could spend an afternoon there delightfully.

Did you go up on the grassy bluff back of the Russell House called "the Ridge"? From here the view is far better than from the highway. You

---

[10] Samuel Lancaster Gerry was an artist who painted many White Mountain landscapes during his distinguished career.

are surrounded by mountains and the prospect is particularly picturesque on account of the varying outlines of near and distant peaks, and there is an unobstructed sight of the beautiful "Gateway of the Notch".

At two o'clock, I left North Woodstock in a comfortable carriage with Mr. George Russell for driver; he is a quiet, slow, plain, honest-hearted farmer, with a hidden appreciation of mountain beauties which my enthusiasm seemed to draw out. His boys and girls are bright and helpful at home, the oldest fourteen. He talked about his family, his experience when the war broke out, a severe illness of three years which broke down a strong constitution at a peculiarly trying time. He insisted upon my alighting to see all the "nice places", though I would not have asked him to stop, knowing he would not reach home again till between nine and ten o'clock. He took me a short distance through the woods to a miniature Flume and series of cascades on the Pemigewasset River which he thought "was real kind of purty". So they were.

Mr. Russell had been spoken of by some of the boarders at North Woodstock rather contemptuously, but I am inclined rather to despise the speakers for it instead of the man! He told me of a family who engaged rooms of him, but on arrival left at once, dissatisfied and prevented their friends from coming, who had also engaged, leaving him disappointed. Friends here have told me the same story and the names and it appears to me quite unfair, but I revealed nothing. I was quite pleased with the place and table, and the low price is a great attraction; and Mrs. Russell is a good cook, pleasant and kind.

At teatime we arrived at Goodnow House where I received a cordial welcome from the family and found a few old acquaintances among the boarders. Best of all was the greeting from the grand old mountains, "my multitudinous mountains sitting in the magic circle", each peak an everlasting friend aglow in sunset radiance. You who are familiar with that ride up the valley do not need to be told how brimful of happiness for me was every hour. The views fully equalled my anticipations and among the most pleasant memories of the trip will be the little surprise visit to you. My friendly regards, please, to your family party, all reunited now.

There have been many improvements here, as usual from year to year; and especially in the table this season, which is really excellent. A party recently returned from an excursion of several days to Crawford Notch and up Mt. Washington and expressed satisfaction with Goodnow House in every respect, saying that while the table at Crawford House[11]

---

[11] This was the second Crawford House. Crawford's was one of the five grand hotels located in the town of Carroll and was able to seat one hundred people in its dining room when it opened on July 4, 1859. The hotel was operated until 1967, and then failed to open for business the following year. The building fell into disrepair and was eventually burned in 1977.

afforded more variety, nothing was so nicely prepared as at Goodnow's. In the party were Kate Sanborn, Professor of Literature at Smith College, North Hampton, a D.D. from New York, Miss Carson, the noted lecturer on cooking, Doctress Brayton, etc.

There is a Mrs. Short of New York here and her daughter Mary. In talking together we discovered that we both knew you. Are they old and particular friends of yours?

Letters from home tell me father continues to improve, though not yet as strong as usual. Business to be attended to in Boston and elsewhere, deferred on account of his illness, may delay father's and mother's coming here. Of course our friends from Framingham are with me much, but they do not care to walk more than a mile and ride occasionally.

What should you think of a lady of thirty, perhaps, married to an admirable man, who is so fond of gaiety that she exclaims, "O dear! it is so quiet, so silent in the woods and fields and Flume, etc, it tires me. And the mountains make me nervous staying so still always in the same places. I wish they'd move about, I'd like to change them around!"? Isn't that funny? Stillness tires one! Well, tastes differ.

There has been time to exchange calls with several acquaintances boarding in the vicinity, among them artist Gerry and daughter; and to renew my friendships with some of the farmer's families, seeing a child's laugh or a sick woman's brightening face over some little token brought them from the city.

O, my dear Miss Pychowska, have you heard the dreary news that a railroad up Mt. Lafayette has been determined upon and surveys will be commenced this summer? Alas! Can we hope it is a false rumor? Can nothing be done to prevent? I can see your father's face of disgust!

I enclose one of our circulars. Some of the distances are foreshortened considerably. Loon Pond Mountain has an alluring look from Dearborn's and I understand how it was a fond dream of your mother's and yours to climb it. With love to her and Miss Cook,

Yours truly,
Isabella Stone

* * * * * * * * * * * *

Marian Pychowska writes to Isabella Stone.

Black Mountain House
Campton, N.H.
August 15, 1881

Dear Miss Stone,

Your long full letter made me wish I had waited for its inspiration before writing to you. I am so glad you stayed over at North Woodstock, and so got the views from different points. We have never been on the hill

Old Man of the Mountains

you speak of back of Russell's, but I can imagine, judging by similar experiences, how much finer the view is than from the high road. You have added a valuable item to our knowledge of the valley by staying at Russell's and giving such a favorable account of it. I would like to follow in your steps and stop there a while and take in that view which a bird of passage can not appreciate.

Since you wrote me, I suppose you have seen that the Lafayette railroad is not the only enormity being planned. Shortly after you were here, our house harbored for several days the surveyors of the new road from Plymouth to the Profile[12]. After their departure, returning to my secluded bathing place in the Pemigewasset River, I found trees and bushes thinned out, and a stake, marking position and distance, driven into the bank. The road keeps on the east side of the river, at least in the lower part of the valley, and I can already imagine how its embankment will scar the green meadows and wooded shores of our quiet stream. Are you not now dou-

---

[12] The "Old Man of the Mountains" in Franconia Notch is a rock outcrop that has a shape which resembles the profile of a man.

Glen House

bly delighted at having seen this valley before the all-pervading rapid transit takes possession?

Mr. Hinkley and his sister, Mrs. West, were with us till about ten days ago. They then returned to Boston to meet their mother with whom they have since gone to the Glen House[13] for two or three weeks. Mr. Hinkley expects to return here later, and has left some boxes of moths, collected here, as a hostage for his reappearance. While we had these guests with us we did not do much walking. The first all day trip was August 2, when my mother and I escorted a party of five boys to Mt. Weetamoo. I suggested we looked like a school out for a holiday. We drove to the base and walked by the upper road over Hodgeman's Hill.

During the hot weather our walks were confined to the forest toward the Pemigewasset River. I imagine you have scarcely seen the top of Mt. Washington more than once or twice through this last week, but at least if we have clouds now, the old yellow smoke is driven out.

Last Monday (the 8th), after dinner, we walked down to Blair's to visit our friends there. All gave us a hearty welcome, and sitting on the porch there with the beautiful familiar view before us, there seemed no reason for going away. Mr. and Mrs. Blair were particularly cordial and would have had us stay all night, but after tea we were ferried over the

---

[13] The Glen House was located north of Pinkham Notch at the base of the Mount Washington Carriage Road. The first public house at this site was opened in 1852 and after much expansion it accommodated five hundred guests. This grand hotel was destroyed by fire on October 1, 1884, the day it was being closed for the season. Three more Glen House hotels were subsequently built at various dates on the same site and were all destroyed by fire as well.

river and started for our present home. Towser, our old companion of many walks evidently remembered us, and when he saw us start out, he thought old times had come back. The dear old foolish dog swam the river after us, and disobediently refused to go home. We thought to leave him at the first farm house and steal away, but he soon broke loose from the man in whose charge we had left him, and came galloping after us. At the next house, being unable to persuade the man to take any trouble in the matter, we took it into our own hands, invited Towser into the kitchen, shut the door on him and hurried off as fast as we could go. This morning he came over with a party from Blair's, as foolish and affectionate as ever.

Tuesday was overcast, but we risked the weather and went to Welch Mountain. This was my second visit, but my aunt had not been there before and so I had her new pleasure to give a spice to the trip. It is a wonderful little climb up the steep roof-like sheets of granite, and through two "lemon-squeezers", as they are known to us, in other words narrow clefts in the ledge. On Welch my aunt had the pleasure of finding the "Northern Scrub Pine" which is not set down in *Gray*[14] as growing this far south. From Dickey, the higher of the twin peaks, the view was as beautiful as it could be on the clearest of blue days for this time, under the cloudy sky, the mountains were all shades of soft gray, except where the sun, striking through a rift, brought out a patch of vivid green. For a long time it lighted the peak of Lafayette showing, even at that distance, the bright pink of its granite.

I will pass over other pleasant walks of this week to speak of our discovery of yesterday afternoon. We had been told of a short cut to Goose Hollow, which is a small hamlet on the Mad River, where the roads to Sandwich and to Weetamoo cross the stream. The high road swings way round and climbs several unnecessary hills, but the wood road, a true short cut for once, strikes up the intervale, giving one a lovely variety of meadow, forest and sugar-bush, with glimpses of the rushing stream and mountains rising over. It is just a walk you would thoroughly enjoy. There is such a satisfaction in cheating the high road, especially when you really save distance.

The rambles of this week have also resulted in finding two new ferns, new that is to us. Our list for this locality is now thirty distinct species and six additional varieties. All these I believe have been found in the immediate vicinity of Campton Village, except one at Plymouth and one at the base of Tripyramid.

If you were to come in upon us now and see the dining room with five tables full of people, you would hardly recognize the quiet place you took your meals in. The house has been quite full for about a week, but

---

[14] A botanical guide by Asa Gray.

will soon thin out again. In our sky parlour we cannot complain of noise, although there are, I believe, sixteen or more children in the establishment.

I hoped to keep this letter a day or so and finish it with some account of a trip to Black Mountain, which we had planned for tomorrow, but at sunset the clouds were thicker than ever over Moosilauke, so it will not come off just yet I fear.

Please remember me to Dr. and Mrs. Stone, who we learn from the *Echo* have arrived at Sugar Hill, and greet our Hoboken friends, the Gibsons, if you have found them in the haystack that I imagine Goodnow's to be at present.

Yours very truly,
M. M. Pychowska

* * * * * * * * * * * *

Marian Pychowska writes to Isabella Stone.

Black Mountain House
Campton, N.H.
September 8, 1881

Dear Miss Stone,

How funny that "la vareuse" should turn up again. If we keep our curiosities long enough they are pretty sure to be satisfied. The summer must have benefitted you a great deal, if I may judge by the valiant way you speak of walking. I congratulate you on your renewed reason for extolling the climate of Sugar Hill. I hope it has equally benefitted your parent's health. I wish you could accomplish the trip to Moosilauke. From my memories, I am sure the ascent would repay you, perhaps more than that of any other mountain. My only knowledge of the "Tunnel Brook" path is from the map and a few words in *Osgood's Guide* (1880 edition). Our Moosilauke excursion has not yet taken place, and I fear will not this year, unless some new impulse is given to the party.

The day after my last writing to you, my mother, my aunt and I went by our winter road to Goose Hollow, then crossing the river, continued up the right bank and reconnoitred some high pastures and lovely streams at the base of Black Mountain. It threatened rain all day, and our homeward march was rather hurried.

The next day was that superb Wednesday, August 17, and we availed ourselves of it to go on Black Mountain. We had a nice little family party, so there was no room for delay or dissatisfaction.

This was my mother's first big mountain since Osceola two years ago, but she went up slowly and steadily, making only three rests of any length in the three miles and a quarter. We had two full hours on top, thus having time to go over the splendid view of mountains and lakes, first geographically and then for the beauty. Mt. Washington was at first clear and then lightly wreathed with cloud. We thought Mr. Hinkley and Mrs. West might have gone up from the Glen that day, and so that evening we got a dispatch, by telegraph and telephone, from them "among the clouds"[15].

I had been ailing for several days and trying to keep myself up by a careful diet, but on Thursday, after Black Mountain had been bagged, I was taken sick and was confined to bed for a few days. (Not to be attributed to drainage!) Since then we have walked very little, and indeed, if other things had not prevented, the weather has not been suitable for much exercise.

Toward the end of August Mr. Hinkley returned here. He had a very unsatisfactory time at the Glen, though his mother's health had much improved there. A severe cold taken on Mt. Washington developed such serious symptoms after he had been there two or three days, that our good doctor advised him to go home where he could have proper care. So on Sunday he was driven to Plymouth, and on Monday my aunt went down with him to Boston and put him into the hands of his brother. That night he was threatened with pneumonia, but care has brought him through, and he now writes encouragingly of his convalescence. Last year Mr. Hinkley was ill at Blair's for some time and so this year had reason to dread the forlornness of being away from his family at such a time. The anxiety about these invalids, told on my mother's health, but now she is gaining once more.

September 9

The Goodnow House, I suppose, has still a fair show of boarders. This house was very full through August, but two weeks ago the people began to drop off. Last Tuesday and Wednesday departed Mrs. Underhill and her mother and a family of Parkers from Detroit, leaving the house entirely to ourselves with the exception of a young bicyclist who expects to go to Boston on his machine in a few days. These two western families are as pleasant as any we have met here this season and we had some very enjoyable evenings with them. I think Mrs. Underhill enjoyed her week at Sugar Hill more than any part of her mountain stay, for while she was here the weather was not pleasant and she waited in vain for a suitable day to drive to Waterville.

---

[15] This refers to the summit of Mount Washington which is often obscured by clouds. *Among the Clouds* was also the name of a newspaper that was printed daily on the summit of Mount Washington during the summer season beginning on July 20, 1877. It was the only newspaper ever published regularly on a mountain top. In 1908, a fire destroyed the printing office and after a lapse of two summers, publication was resumed at the Base Station of the Cog Railway. When World War I temporarily suspended operation of the railway in 1917, the paper was discontinued permanently.

While you were having so much rain near the Notch, we were merely having cloudy weather giving us beautiful cloud effects on Black Mountain and Tripyramid. During my sickness, we moved into a front room so we now have the best of the view from our window. The afternoon we moved, Tripyramid was covered with a veil of rainbow light. Those days were beautiful with their clear atmosphere and vivid green, but since then the smoke has discolored everything, being sometimes so thick as to obliterate Wallace and Hodgeman's Hills. The sulphurous dark day was very remarkable here, but by the newspaper accounts must have been much more so further south. I suppose you saw the comparisons made with other similar days and especially with the "dark day" of 1780. It seems that even that long ago Professor Williams of Harvard suggested distant forest fires as a cause of this phenomenon. The great humidity of the air was one of the strangest things here last Tuesday, and the next day was a striking contrast by its burning dryness. At least this time the AMC has had the smoke pest brought painfully to its notice, and I hope the members were duly impressed by it. At the same time, they had yesterday to see how nice it is without the smoke. If they went to the Percy Peaks yesterday I hope you were of the party. We enjoyed the coolness and cleanness at home as we expected Mr. Sargent and his friend Mr. Eddy to arrive, but instead came a letter saying they could not get off for a day or so. Another pleasant addition to our party is in prospect, for Mr. Willis brought us word from Professor Fay, whom he saw in Plymouth, that he hoped to get here before the season was over. I wish you could be here to listen to the comparing of notes between the Campton lovers.

The Club, I see, has accepted the renaming of Hooket, but I think I know several members who will still use the old name. How glad I shall be to have some account of the meeting from you.

This morning I was reading to my mother from a small U.S. History that I have taken up, while our tall Vermont maiden, Helen, was arranging the room. Trying to recall the date of the settlement of St. Augustine, I was stumbling over 158_, when Helen said quietly, "1565, was it not?" This opened a pleasant conversation in which she told us of her home near Montpelier and how having taught school for seventeen terms, she thought she would like to come to the mountains and do housework for a change.

It is time for me to put an end to my chronicle for the present, and leave it to your kindness. As we are not likely to leave here till the end of the month, I hope to have a more entertaining budget next time I write.

My mother joins me in kind regards to Dr. and Mrs. Stone and in love to you.

Always your friend,
M. M. Pychowska

P.S. Upon second thoughts, it seems hard hearted to complain of the smoke here when the fire is doing such dreadful damage in Michigan.

Marian Pychowska writes to Isabella Stone.

Black Mountain House
Campton, N.H.
September 20, 1881

Dear Miss Stone,

Where are you in this beautiful weather that is paying us for weeks of smoke? Shall I think of you as still in sight of Washington and Lafayette, or at home in Framingham?

Everywhere today, throughout the country the flags are at half mast for our dead President, and Mrs. Garfield and many another widow are in the fresh grief of their loss, while I sit down to write to you, full of the lovely season and the excursions we have been making.

I am sure our little enjoyments would seem very, very small if our minds were able to realize the sorrow of the world, but if we might rise higher and see things as they are, the world's sorrow too would disappear in the presence of Eternity. Fortunately, however, we are not required to realize, but only to do the best we can with what is sent us, saying "Sufficient for the day is the evil there of".

Since my last letter, Professor Fay has been here, but only for an hour on his way home. Perhaps you know the party did not get on Percy Peaks that beautiful Thursday. There was some lack of connection of trains, so they did not reach the mountain till Friday when nothing was visible. Ten days ago came Mr. Sargent and his friend. They were gone four or five days on their walking trip, which included the Franconia Notch, ascent of Mt. Washington by Crawford bridle path and descent the same day to the Glen by Tuckerman's Ravine, then home by road through Bartlett and Livermore Path to Waterville. It was a very severe walk and smoky nearly all the time. While they were off, we had a pleasant day exploring Cone Mountain and Pond.

Last Saturday the long talked of excursion to Peaked Hill came off. Mr. Willis drove us to where the road forks below West Thornton and from there we climbed the lonely farm road to the pond. There are signs of an old dam at the outlet, which may account for the generous proportions of the pond as given on the map. Now it is a small affair and not so picturesque as is Cone Pond. An old logging road led us high on the hillside, whence we reached the top through some fallen timber and hobble-bush. The great thing was to discover if any part of the Presidential Range can be seen from Peaked Hill, but with all our eyes, we could not see through Scar Ridge. The view of Franconias, Twins, Hancock, Carrigain and the Waterville mountains did very well in the absence of Mt. Washington. On the other side and just at our feet lay Ellsworth Pond all blue and wind ruffled. My mother was with us that day, and also on Cone Mountain.

Perhaps you remember that Mt. Kineo has long been an attractive point to us. Last Sunday my uncle organized his party, and we duly studied Mr. Scott's account of the Thornton-Warren Path in *Appalachia*. Monday morning the equinoctial storm seemed to be brewing, and there was an angry gathering of clouds pointing northeast and southwest, but we hoped the weather would give us time to accomplish our plan and started.

The wagon was left at the Tannery fork at ten minutes to ten. My mother had driven over with us, intending to go with us at least part way on the path, but a threatening of headache decided her to go home in the wagon. The path makers have availed themselves of a logging road that follows Hubbard Brook for several miles. This road is evidently in present use by the Tannery people, for it has just been fixed for the winter's work by filling the inequalities with saplings loosely thrown down.

About two and one-half miles in, the road ends and the path starts on its own account through the high valley until it meets a wood road from Warren. This part of the way is like a high plateau, where the stream descends very quietly and one can walk rapidly through the beautiful forest. It is somewhat more than four miles from the Tannery to the Club camp[16], which divides the path midway. From this point we sharpened our eyes to see some indication of the blazed line to Kineo, promised by Mr. Scott. In another mile we were confronted by the Kineo shingle and recrossed the brook to follow the blazes. It was already past one o'clock and now the travelling began to be slow and laborious, up hill in earnest over fallen logs and through luxuriant hobble-bush. The distance to the top is probably less than a mile and a half, but it took us an hour and a half to make it. The clearing of the top has not been done as thoroughly as I hope it will be one day (not by fire), but still the view obtained by dodging the trees is very fine. There was no mistake about seeing the Presidentials from here. We overlooked Cushman lying on the other side of the long valley we had come up. The grand object was Moosilauke rising near and way above us. The Warren farms and Moosilauke turnpike were to be seen just below us, and we could realize that we belonged much more to the Baker's River Valley than to the Pemigewasset. An hour passed quickly in seeing, eating our late dinner and registering ourselves in the little patronized AMC bottle, which we found fastened to a tree.

At half past three my uncle said the magic word, "Time", and we began the descent. To avoid the time lost in looking for trailblazes, we took an independent course down the mountain side and struck the path

---

[16] There is mention of the need of establishing an AMC camp at this location in *Appalachia* Vol.I, No.1, 1876. It was eventually constructed during the summer of 1880 by William M. Sargent of Thornton, NH. The camp was built of logs, with a roof of split shingles, open in front, and large enough to shelter eight or ten persons.

near where we had left it. After a short rest by the brook, we marched on steadily till a quarter to seven, when we reached our wagon, which had been waiting more than an hour. During the last half hour of walking, the deepening twilight made the woods very solemn. This morning we were in the smoke again, but now smoke and clouds have vanished before a cold northwest wind.

September 22

At last the storm has begun, giving me leisure to continue the chronicle of our doings. A day of rest after Mt. Kineo prepared us all to take advantage of yesterday. The atmosphere was piercingly clear and the temperature correspondingly keen and bracing as we drove out to Greeley's. There the party divided, my uncle and the two young men taking the path for Livermore where they planned to spend the night and then ascend Mt. Carrigain the next day. My mother, aunt and I were to ascend Mt. Tecumseh, and, as my father objected to our going alone, we engaged Mr. Brown, a one-armed man who is the regular guide at Waterville. It was an unaccustomed luxury to have our wraps carried for us, and to be served with a can of delicious water at our dinner on top.

Like all the paths at Waterville, the Tecumseh trail traverses the most beautiful luxuriant forest. Two hours and ten minutes carried us easily up the three miles to the bare summit. The mountain view is, in my opinion, finer than from Black Mountain, and a stay of two hours did not suffice to master it even geographically. How you would have enjoyed seeing the internal construction of the wilderness behind Lafayette with old Hooket, the Twin Range, Hancock, and Carrigain. Mt. Mansfield looked very near, and farther south we could see a range of mountains behind the nearer Green Mountains. Of course the wilds of Kineo and Cushman were studied with due care, and we had the satisfaction of seeing how distinct Mt. Fay is from Kineo proper. Ellsworth and Peaked Hill Ponds and a little corner of Newfound Lake glistened in the sun. We got home just in time for tea, and found that Mrs. Willis had been true to her word and had kept some ice cream for us. This is the time for all sorts of little luxuries that are impossible in the height of the season.

A few transients come and go still, and we have, for some days, a Canadian family and a solitary young man from Cambridge. I do not know what the Carrigain party will do this cloudy day, whether they will wait over or make the climb in the clouds. Mr. Sargent and Mr. Eddy will leave the end of this week, I believe, and in another week we shall also be on our way home. Hoping to have an account of the end of your summer, I remain,

Yours very sincerely,
M. M. Pychowska

Edith Cook writes to Isabella Stone.

Hoboken, N.J.
October 9, 1881

My dear Miss Stone,

Lest you should think I have quite forgotten or failed to appreciate your long letter received at the Black Mountain House in August, I will no longer delay my answer, though writing today at the risk, I fear, of proving extremely uninteresting. During the later days of our stay among the mountains I knew you were kept well posted by my niece in all our little and great expeditions, knowing too how satisfactorily our adventures would be set forth for you by your fellow Appalachians. So there remain only a few threads of the summer web for me to spin for you, the hurried lines the spider makes at the end of his house building just before he sits himself in the center to devote his energies to the serious business of filling his larder.

Marian wrote you, I think, after the stormy ascent of Mt. Lowell made by my brother and Mr. Sargent and so gave you an account also of the more successful ascent of Mt. Tecumseh made by herself, her mother and myself assisted by the most praiseworthy of guides who, finding us such adepts on a trail, confined his attentions to carrying up our wraps with water for our lunch, building us a fire on top to temper the chilliness of the air, and giving us bits of mountain information. We in return, identified certain distant points for him, with which he was not familiar. He also gave me a huge roll of birch bark for artistic purposes, having seen my sketches on top of the mountain and having had experience through the summer visitors at Greeley's of the decorative value of the bark.

I suppose Marian also wrote you of our failure to find on our Kineo exploration a certain wonderful Gorge mentioned in the guidebook as lying one-quarter of a mile off the Warren path. My brother was resolved not to be baffled in the finding of this, so our last exploration was the search for this gorge, made in only a half a day's excursion by taking the high road in a wagon. Ignoring the Moosilauke path we took to the bed of the stream, knowing that in this way, we could not fail to find that of which we were in search, walking, by turns on the boulders and rocks, through the bushes or along some friendly wood road following for a while the course of the stream. My brother and his companion, a chess acquaintance and citizen of Campton, outstepped the ladies of the party, my sister, niece and myself, who, following at our own pace, soon became our own pilots, with all the zest of individual discovery until, at the head of the glen, rejoining the male members of the party among the hugest of the boulders. We were glad of a strong hand to pull us up a long step or two to reach the rather lofty throws of success to which we had attained. We had found "the Gorge" indeed, and found it wild and rough and interesting, and we had seen much more of it than would the ordinary visitor to it by the blazed path, but we could not recommend our route to the ordinary mountain walker, since missteps into the water and bruises are most probable concomitants of that route.

Of course we were glad to have made the expedition so, but for our return we took to the woods in a line to strike the Appalachian path from Thornton to Warren and, on reaching the top of the steep hillside, we came upon the blazed trail leading down to the Gorge. We followed it down to see where it struck the stream and then we followed it a very long quarter of a mile to the junction of the two, the junction being so much farther back from the stream and from Thornton than we had supposed while, to our great satisfaction, we found how we had managed to miss seeing the path the day we went on Kineo. Part of the path to Warren is, as you know, a used logging road and the loggers have been widening part of it during the past summer. Consequently felled trees lay across the entrance of the Gorge path blocking it up and making all edge of the road alike while the post with the sign board had been removed to within the shadow of the wood some feet back from the edge of the road and set at such an angle that it could bear no witness of itself to the passerby on the main path. We were gratified to find that it had been circumstance, not our stupidity, that had prevented our noticing the path the first time. We moved the sign post back to the edge of the road where the next seeker for the Gorge path could not fail to find it, so fulfilling our duty as Appalachians and charitable minded mountaineers.

Our two last days at Campton were devoted in part, by Marian and myself, to collecting roots for taking home. We had marked some weeks before, a certain piece of arbutus that grew admirably for transplanting, it being an isolated root and in a place exposed to the sun so fitting it better for our city garden than a more trailing piece from under the shadow of the pines. Then I wanted to collect some fern roots for my window garden for this winter and so we had two beautiful wood walks for our last rambles of the summer, one through the pine woods that stretch from the Black Mountain House down to the Pemigewasset River, the other over Wallace Hill, that mine of fern treasures. I was so fortunate to find on one of these walks a single arbutus blossom, one that could not wait for the spring or, as one might think, hurried its blooming time, that it might give a intense and unwonted pleasure to an ardent lover. You can imagine with what enthusiasm the vision of the little white star and its exquisite perfume were received by the gratified eyes and heart. The next day we found blue and white violets and a ripe strawberry.

The mountains, for some reasons, were for me, harder to leave than usual. The warm September seemed to have deprived us of certain ideal weather that makes our autumn right in the hills while the extremely late changing of the leaves was also for us a loss of beauty on the wood paths that we are not accustomed to do without.

Now, we are fairly settled down at home once more, the house in its proper running order and the winter seeming already begun. Perhaps Marian has told you how very little I used my brushes during the summer, a most imperfect artist at best, I was even more imperfect than usual this summer and many circumstances prevented even my usual scant allowance of work. But the summer is richer for me in other ways.

With kind remembrance to your mother and father,
Sincerely yours,
Edith W. Cook

* * * * * * * * * * * *

Marian Pychowska writes to Isabella Stone.

Hoboken, N.J.
November 29, 1881

Dear Miss Stone,

I congratulate you that "Bridal Veil Falls" are no longer a veiled mystery and that through your instrumentality they are accessible to others. It will make a beautiful walk independently of the fall itself, the forest and stream are lovely, especially when one's attention will no longer be absorbed by hobble bush and moss pitfalls. We did not see the *Echo* regularly last summer, but I remember seeing that this path was proposed to the Club. It was too bad to have your proposition so misunderstood when you were yourself doing all the disagreeable work. All the red tape of rights of way, etc. that was necessary, is very repugnant to the true Crusoe who feels monarch of all that he walks over. However, landowners have rights, even to the extent of making brush fires. From the little we have seen of Mr. Scott, I should think he would be a very cordial promoter of any good scheme belonging to his department.

My mother's letter to Professor Fay contained nothing, I believe, that I had not written you about. The south side of the mountains in general is so well explored by "Apes" and others, that this, among other reasons, makes my mother and myself turn our eyes secretly to the north side once more, secretly because the others are so satisfied with the Pemigewasset Valley. We dare do no more than whisper to one another of a change. Besides, summer is a long way off, and Providence usually saves us the trouble of deciding things.

As you are kind enough to ask about my mother's health, you will be glad to hear that she is unusually well and free from her headaches. My father has just come through with a seven or eight weeks siege with a sore eye. The trouble began with two sties and continued with inflammation and swelling for some weeks, until my father submitted himself to our doctor. He soon put an end to it with a simple injection. Of course the long days of enforced idleness were very tedious, especially as my father has given up smoking lately.

My aunt has found time, in the midst of domestic matters, to illustrate a poem of my mother's called "In the Valley of the Pemigewasset", with sepia pictures of the most interesting views of the Campton neighborhood. Another of her Christmas labors has been to make an artistically arranged collection of the Campton ferns. This is intended for Miss Maria Tilden.

Last Sunday my mother and I had the shadow of a mountain walk. We went to an afternoon service at the monastery church on the hill, about two and a half miles from here. It is a shame to have so glorious a view so near and yet only see it once or twice a year. From the eastern edge of the hill, the river and the big city are spread out before you, very rich in purple color in the evening light. From the western height you look across the wide Jersey meadows to the distant hills, with the Hackensack River winding between. These meadows raise their fair share of smoke for the composition of the Indian summer atmosphere, for the rank grass is always catching fire in the autumn.

We are all curious to know who Elizabeth Thompson may be, who has given her name in full to a Franconia mountain. Please instruct our ignorance. In speaking of this mania for naming, my uncle wondered why the township should have the privilege of putting up names on other person's property. What a difference the point of view makes! When people offend our taste in the matter of calling names, we take our stand on the rights of property, but it is another matter when the proprietors put up toll gates.

We did not see either Booth or Rossi during their engagements in New York, but my mother indulges me in an occasional symphony rehearsal. I plod along with my finger drill, my father always hoping for the end, and I, generally, desponding. With Dante at least, I am getting nearer to Paradise.

My mother sends love and thanks for your card. With kind regards to Dr. and Mrs. Stone, I remain,

Sincerely your friend,
M. M. Pychowska

1882

"Miss Barstow has convinced me that the woods are never so wonderful as in the rain."

Edith Cook writes to Isabella Stone.

Hoboken, N.J.
January 7, 1882

My dear Miss Stone,

Thank you so much for your letter. Each unexpected greeting at this season adds its very perceptible portion to the little pile of affection we claim, as of right, at this time. I dislike much to remove the pretty row of kind thoughts when the time comes that one must realize that Christmas is really over, to hide them in a dark box or even among the leaves of some favorite books; it seems like laying aside one's holiday garments to go back to the work of every day when our faces are apt to drop too much earthward.

I am beginning the new year with a mind somewhat too dull to realize the full values of good resolutions for these same work-days, having been since last Tuesday a prisoner in my room from a sore throat that put me in a quarantine and in exile from all visitors except my sister, my ever-watchful guardian. Yesterday the doctor lifted the embargo, but my sister is still unwilling to have me leave the warm room for the possible draughts of the rest of the house as I am still a subject of chlorate of potash. You will see I have not been seriously ill when I tell you most of my time has been spent in lessening the pile of unanswered Christmas letters or in hours of dull meditation sitting up by a little wood-stove trying to keep warm in these coldest days of the winter, so far. I think you know how rare an occurrence with me is any physical disability. I feel, indeed, as if it were rather a blow to my pride and reputation to have to succumb now. I do not know whether my friends will theoretically, be more consoled at finding me mortal, like the rest of the world, or disturbed by having their pet example of womanly health defaced in its fair proportions.

I have had a fine opportunity, during my exile, of making studies in human and cat nature especially the latter since I have been banished from my own room which is without fire to our guest room which gives upon, what a cook of a friend of ours called "the backs of things". Backyards and shutters and sheds, the chief arena of the cat life of the neighborhood.

And now I will answer some of the questions in your letter. My ferns, I am sorry to say, not being under glass, show that patient endurance of the tortures of civilized life that these creatures of the wilderness are apt to develop except under the most skillful hands. Some of them have turned brown either wholly or along the edges, but I believe all still live, waiting only the late spring days to unfold their green fronds once more and give the world assurance of a fern. My house plants, in general, have not done as well this winter as usual, not having yet given one any blossoms: I think they like winter to be more himself without.

I wish I might answer your question if none of us ever come to Boston, with a "yes". Certainly I know such a visit on my part would be full of pleasure. I have not been in Boston to stay since '76, we have but passed through since, hurrying to catch a train, or stopping over just a few hours to see a friend. With our summer in New England, each year seems to make an additional reason why it would be pleasant to stay awhile in Boston. Someday I shall hope to have the pleasure, and then I shall surely let you know where I am to be and shall most gladly, if possible, spend a day with you in Framingham, that "leaf-anchored Hebe" as Dr. Oliver Wendell Holmes calls your town, of the Bay Queen. Lillie[1] and Marian, I am afraid, are even less likely to be in Boston than myself, not withstanding the tempting Appalachian excursions from there that they receive notices of from time to time.

Miss Tilden sent me the other day a slip from the Boston papers with regard to the railway up Mt. Lafayette. Said railway is to connect near the Profile House[2] with the Pemigewasset Valley road and this, after we were assured last summer that the Pemigewasset road was to stop short of the Notch, its object not being summer travel, but the opening up of the vast lumber country of the East Branch and Moosilauke. Alas! for the stage route up the valley and the bridle path up the mountain. I suppose, though, there will still be beauty for those who come after us, even though it has less of the flavor of the wilderness and those who follow will not know the hills otherwise. But one must regret this too close circling of the hills

---

[1] Lillie was a nickname for Lucia that was often used by Edith.

[2] The Profile House was a grand hotel located in Franconia Notch near the base of the profile of the "Old Man of the Mountains." The hotel was originally opened in 1853 with 110 guestrooms. Further additions greatly increased its capacity. It was torn down in the autumn of 1905. On July 1, 1906, the New Profile House was opened to the public.

and Lafayette's shoulders do not seem broad enough to bear this burden. Watching the climbing trains will become one of the amusements of the Goodnow House, though I suppose the road will climb the mountain on the side near Mt. Lincoln.

Please remember me most kindly to your father and mother and believe me, with hearty thanks for your New Year thought,

Sincerely your friend,
Edith W. Cook

* * * * * * * * * * * *

Marian Pychowska writes to Isabella Stone.

Hoboken, N.J.
January 20, 1882

Dear Miss Stone,

Your kind letter and gift have been waiting a long time for an acknowledgement. My aunt being nearly restored, last Saturday I took my turn at being sick, so that my poor mother might not get out of practice in the nursing art. It proved to be an attack like last summer's. Today I am sitting up in my room, appetite and strength returning.

The book-marker you sent me could not have been more fitly chosen for me. I am a member of a society of young girls whose special object is to honor and to imitate Mary Immaculate, who is the woman par excellence, Eve unfallen, the valiant woman, "who put out her hand to strong things and yet disdained not to take hold of the spindle", and who was all this, that she might be worthy to bring into the world the Incarnate Word of God. In one of the discourses of Major Beebe, describing some Peruvian traditions, he told of a mysterious cleft rock that could only be penetrated by one being—a white dove. This might symbolize many things, but as my mother listened to the Major, his words brought to her mind the grace of the Immaculate Conception as a fulfillment of the type. When the Lord God cursed the serpent He said: "I will put enmities between thee and the woman, and thy seed and her seed: she shall crush thy head and thou shalt lie in wait for her heel." Catholic expositors apply these words to the Blessed Virgin, who, being exempted from original sin by the foreseen merits of her Son and Redeemer, thus triumphed over the power of the evil one. She, then, might be the one white dove that alone could pass through the cleft of the rock. The poetry of the myths cannot out do the beauty of the truth, "for by the greatness of the beauty and of the creature, the Creator of them may be seen so as to be known thereby".

If I had not great faith in the interest you take in how your friends think, I should not take the liberty of dilating on my favorite theme.

To turn to another favorite topic, how do you like the new Appalachian "Member's Ticket" with its alpine picture containing a party of happy

Appalachians, including, if I make out, two ladies? I suppose this will secure hotel keepers, etc. against persons wrongly claiming the privileges of the Club. We are evidently growing.

My mother and I continue to hold secret meetings in regard to the advantages of the north side of the mountains and especially of the "Ravine House" where we had a friend last summer. The place is about 1,300 feet up, just opposite to King's Ravine[3], one of the grandest things in the region. It would be moderately near our old haunts in the Androscoggin Valley[4], for it is but six miles from Gorham where there is a nice little Catholic church. The other way, it is only ten miles from Jefferson. My compass sets that way, but we breath not the name of the Ravine House, as yet, to my uncle and aunt. Next month we shall see what they will say.

My father has given up smoking altogether. He complained at first of feeling very sleepy and dull for the lack of it, but now says he does not miss it. His reason for leaving off was that he found smoking was beginning to affect his health unfavorably.

I have not forgotten that last Spring I promised to send you to read F. Theband's *Gentilism*, but, knowing you were very busy, I refrained. If you have leisure and would be interested to see the book, tell me in your next, and I will send it.

With sincere regards to your father and mother, I remain always,

Your friend,

Marian Pychowska

＊ ＊ ＊ ＊ ＊ ＊ ＊ ＊ ＊ ＊ ＊ ＊

Isabella Stone writes in her diary about a trip from the Russell House in North Woodstock to Georgiana Falls.

July 14, 1882

Mr. Russell drives me on buckboard about two and one-half miles north to Steven Russell's where we leave our team all day. We leave the house about nine o'clock and enter the fields opposite Mr. Steven Russell's about fifteen minutes to ten. We walk northwest to a wooden promontory, cross a brook and enter the woods and travel nearly west, cross a swamp and listen for the rushing sound of Harvard Brook soon striking it. We came into the path on the right side of Harvard Brook built by Mr. Pope of Boston in 1877. From the stage road to Georgiana Falls is three miles; by our course we save nearly a mile on the path. With frequent rests, a moderate pace and several climbs down into the brook, and min-

---

[3] Named in honor of patriot, preacher and author, Thomas Starr King.
[4] The Pychowskas and Cooks stayed at the Philbrook Farm Inn in Shelburne, NH, during the summers of 1872 and 1873, which familiarized them with the Androscoggin River Valley.

⚜ RUSSELL ⬧ HOUSE, ⚜

North Woodstock, N. H.

GEO. F. RUSSELL, ⚜ **Proprietor.**

THIS house is reached by the Boston, Concord and Lowell railroad, being but a few rods from the terminal station of the P. V. division. From its grounds extensive views of Mts. Moosilauke, Lafayette, Haystack, Garfield, and many other noted mountains, can be obtained. The location of the house renders all points of interest in the Franconia Notch, or Pemigewassett Valley easily accessable, making it a desirable place for the tourist, the invalid or the sportsman.

Russell House Advertisement

utes spent gazing at the cascades and at two fine waterfalls, we reach the highest falls, the real Georgiana Falls of eighty feet where the path ends, at 12:15.

The rocky projection opposite the Falls, about east, was formerly the best view point, but is now made hideous and well nigh impassable by fallen trees burnt from a neglected campfire. Through these we fought our way and lunched at the top of the highest falls on a big rock close to the plunging flood. We have a fine outlook down the Valley and across on to Loon Pond Mountain to the southeast. We drink the brook water but it is not refreshing. At 1:30 we start up the brook through the pathless forest to see what we can find, Mr. Russell never having been any farther.

Two or three times we take to the boulders of the bed of the brook and hand in hand go springing up. We find two large and noble waterfalls each fifteen or twenty feet in height, the latter consists of seven different large cascades pouring into the stream around a huge rock resting sideways in the center of the brook. The whole makes a picturesque cataract. We continue on the right bank of the brook until it becomes a small placid noiseless stream and forks into two rivulets. I suspect that we have diverged from the main stream, but Mr. Russell says "no." At last we reach a swampy lagoon, probably the outskirts of Bog Pond, where further passage is impossible without a boat! Mr. Russell climbs a tree to get our bearings. Time 3:00 P.M.

We retrace our steps to where we had lunch, then make a detour around the burnt wood, cross the dry bed of a branch stream and at 4:35

P.M. stand once more at the beginning of "Pope's Path." We climb down the precipice on to a huge rock in the center of the stream at the foot of the highest fall to get the spray and see its splendor. A heavy shower would have drenched us, but we crept under some big rocks into a grotto where we could sit upright and be completely sheltered. Here we chat about the trip to Moosilauke and the underground tunnel.

PRICE LIST OF DRIVES —PER SEAT FROM THE— *Russell House.*	
Profile House and Echo Lake,	$1.50
Flume and Pool,	1.00
Basin and Doghead,	1.25
Walker's Cascades,	1.25
Mt. Lafayette,	1.50
Bald Mountain,	1.75
Georgeanna Falls,	.50
Agassiz Basin,	.50
Pond Brook,	.25
Pollards,	.50
Russell Pond,	.50
Elbow Pond,	1.00
Bryant's Ledge,	.50
Pilot Hill Basin,	.75
Sunset Gorge,	1.00
Mill Brook Cascade,	2.00
Tecumseh,	2.00
Woodstock Drive,	.50
Thornton Drive.	1.00

From the Russell House

We start home at five o'clock and remember there is a delicious spring of water a few rods from the path just east of the spot where we entered it in the morning, where Mr. Russell broke a sapling across the path. We emerge at Steven Russell's at 7:15 P.M. and arrive home at eight o'clock.

* * * * * * * * * * * *

Marian Pychowska writes to Isabella Stone.

Ravine House
Randolph, N.H.
July 25, 1882

Dear Miss Stone,

Your long wished for and most satisfactory letter came in last evening's mail. I have been so full of things to tell you, I believe you would have heard from me before now if I had known where to address. While reading your descriptions last night, I felt as if transported into the old Pemigewasset haunts. How pleasant it would be indeed if we could explore together once more, either in Woodstock or in Randolph, but in default of that, I shall enter as fully as possible into your plans, and try to interest you in ours. Your letter makes me believe you are stronger than is usual when you first come into the hills, and I hope you may have strength to do all the pleasant things you have in your mind.

The mention of you in *Appalachia* is first in the treasurer's report, and then in Mr. Scott's report, where he says, speaking of Bridal Veil Falls path, "Miss M. I. Stone, of Framingham, took hold of the work with great energy, raised the required amount, and obtained rights of way or permission to pass over lands of various owners". As you did not respond to the invitation to present a paper on Bridal Veil Falls, I hope you will prepare one on some of your this year's explorations. There are so few in the Club who seem willing or able to write, it is an encouragement to us all who have the material and the will to put it in shape. The fact of our having been near enough to attend three of the Field Meetings has only been a pleasant accident. My aunt, in looking through some White Mountain letters in the *Boston Traveller*, came across this amusing passage: "We are disgusted with the arrogant claims of educated tramps and 'culchowed' pedestrians who have set up a sole-leather aristocracy, insisting that nobody can 'do' the mountains except under the aegis of the Appalachian Club, or on foot, alone with scribe and staff, wallet, hammer and impaling needles".

I wish I could do more to help you in identifying the mountains east and west of you, but those same (to us) nameless foothills also mystified us on our trips through your region. We never went up the Thornton Gore road, and Hatch Hill, Wonosha, etc. are only names to me. You may remember seeing in driving up the valley through Campton, between the Tecumseh group and Loon Pond Mountain, a high rounded mountain with a long slide running obliquely down its side, and to the right stretching out a serrated ridge toward Tecumseh and Osceola. The mountain with the slide is Scar Ridge (well described in an early *Appalachia*), and the most conspicuous tooth of the ridge Professor Fay says he has heard called "Bread-trough Mountain" by an old lady living in that district. It is hard to reconcile one's observation of these mountains with what the map gives. My remembrance is that from the inn at West Thornton you see Osceola rising over a depression in the nearer ridge. You see the edge of the abrupt white face that it shows to Greeley's, Waterville, its round head and the long ridge with curious sharp peaks it sends out northwest. How its ridge is related to the continuation of Scar Ridge, I cannot tell, but I think the latter is south of the former and would perhaps hide it from the near view point of Wyatt Hill. I hope I have not made "confusion worse confounded".

Let me do all I can to persuade you to go to Loon Pond Mountain. There are two paths, one from Pollards' and the other from the settlement on the east side of the Pemigewasset. The latter obviates the necessity of fording the East Branch, but I know not what sort of a way it is. I cannot remember whether or not there were blazes on Pollard's path. There was a faint trail as far as the pond, and I think the distance is about two miles. So far it is very easy, and the pond and view repay one for the climb, but by all means go on to the summit. There are several successive rocky heads east of the pond. The old burnt district is pretty scrubby, but the distance is not great, and the view superb from the final top. I would like to advise in matter of guide, more than to give my opinion that you would be surer of a successful and easy trip if you took one of the Pollards who has been up before. Fortunately I have the note I made of part of the view, beginning with Mounts Lafayette, Liberty and the Coolidges, Flume, (part

Ravine House

of Hooket?), the big unnamed mountain between Franconia Branch and Red Rock Brook (which I think I have since heard called "Owl's Head" by a Waterville guide), Potash Mountain, a steep whitish thing rising from the East Branch, the Twin Range, the Willey Range with the Presidentials over it, and Black Mountain this side (on whose top we look down), then Hitchcock, and beyond it to the right Hancock, to the right of the extreme top of Hancock is Carrigain. Now our view of the Waterville peaks is shut off by the broad end of Scar Ridge which connects with Loon Pond Mountain, but rises high above it. To the right of this big black mass I think you see the top of Tecumseh with its subalterns, and over the farms of Thornton Gore the southern Pemigewasset Valley, a scrap of Newfound Lake and beyond the southern Kearsarge and the bold scallops of Cardigan. I believe it is a good place to study Kineo, Cushman, and Waternomee. The clouds were down on the higher peaks when we were on Loon Pond Mountain, so I would be obliged for any corrections and additions your trip may develop.

We have never been on Mt. Pemigewasset, but noticed its attractive little top from Loon Pond Mountain.

You will not be astonished that my uncle cannot give a very detailed account of Georgiana Falls, if you remember that was the day he and Mr. Sargent took a buggy and did up Georgiana Falls, Walker's Falls and Lonesome Lake! He does remember the cave you describe.

I expect you to find many more places of interest in your vicinity, and I want to hear about them all, if you will be so good as to write me. The place on the East Branch that Mrs. Pollard took you to, is probably above where we crossed. At our crossing the stream is wider and shallower and the stones smaller. It would be a charming walk to continue as far as one liked on the wood path that follows the stream for several miles into the wilderness.

Now you shall hear about our experiment in Randolph. In the first place our sea voyage was a great success all except the sea!! Even when we went out of sight of land beyond Cape Cod, the Atlantic was as level as a quiet lake so there was no chance for us to test our sailing qualifications. We arrived here on the first of July in an easterly storm—cataracts of cloud pouring over the big mountains as we drove over the famous Randolph Hill.

How pleasant it is to like one's hosts! We have that pleasure as well as you, for the Watsons are excellent people, good to one another and liberal to their guests. The younger Mr. Watson, Laban[5] as he is known in general, is a tall handsome man of about thirty, a thorough woodsman and extraordinarily energetic in making paths and opening up the beauties of his neighborhood. The house only has fourteen rooms to let, all but two being on the second floor. My mother and I occupy a large front room facing the mountains. Some persons might complain of a lack of fresh vegetables here, but the table is so excellent in the way of bread, butter, milk, eggs, and the general cooking, that it suits us entirely. No ice is used in the establishment for our water, brought in through logs from a most copious spring, has almost the temperature of ice water when set on the table. The meat is gotten day by day.

We were the first to come. The next comers were Mr. Peek[6] from Chicago and his daughter (a deaf and dumb girl with a good talent for painting). I mention this gentleman's name because he has been here several summers, exploring and painting. He is a perfect enthusiast for the place, and has been an aid and a pleasant companion in our explorations. Then followed an agreeable family from Portsmouth; they have been joined

---

[5] Laban Morrill Watson was born in Randolph, NH, on May 14, 1850. He was an active member of the AMC and a lifelong resident of Randolph. Laban, along with his father Abel, was the founder of the Ravine House. He was the maker of the Watson Path, the Mount Madison Path (Valley Way), and many other trails in Randolph. Watson was also the principal builder of the first AMC hut (Madison Hut) in 1888. During many years of volunteer service, he served as both Selectman and State Representative. He died on October 1, 1936.

[6] William H. Peek was born in London, England in 1820 and came to the United States in 1838. He was a bookseller, a publisher, and later the owner of a furniture manufacturing company. Peek was the perennial partner of Eugene Cook with whom he helped build more miles of trails than anyone else in the White Mountains during the 1800s. He spent twenty-five summers in Randolph (1880-1904). Peek died in Chicago. IL, in 1905.

by some young ladies who make the quiet house pleasantly lively.

I want to give you as exact an idea as possible of our location, but the difficulty is the Walling map[7] is all out in the placing of King's Ravine and adjacent brooks. The Moose River does not rise in the ravine but on Nowell's Ridge[8] to the west of it. Cold Brook, a fine large stream justly named, drains King's Ravine which heads directly into Mt. Adams. The next stream to the east is Snyder Brook[9], which rises in the col between Adams and Madison and runs into the Moose River, a short way east of our house. Next comes Bumpus Brook which is fairly given on the map rising on the north slope of Madison, and then Triple Falls Brook between Bumpus Brook and Miss Barnes Brook. Each of these streams has one or more beautiful waterfalls, varying in distance from here, between three-quarters of a mile and two and one-half miles. You can mark our house on the map beside the western most of the two little parallel brooks that run out of Randolph Mountain.

Charles Lowe[10], the famous guide, lives two miles west of us, where the Mt. Adams (Lowe's) Path starts. Just across the road from the Ravine House runs the Moose River whose soft music is our nightly lullaby, beyond there is a strip of meadow land and then the bare summits of Madison and Adams, the first crowns the steep forest clothed ravine of Snyder Brook, and the other the barer wall of King's Ravine. Pine Mountain and the Moriah-Carter Range finish our view most beautifully to the east, and to the west lies distant Cherry Mountain, giving us a fine position for sunset effects. Perhaps you know the view from Randolph Hill. The best view point is a little over a mile back of us, by a pleasant wood path. The elevation of the Ravine House is between twelve and thirteen hundred feet.

------

[7] A topographical map of the White Mountains that was produced from surveys directed by H.F. Walling.

[8] Named in honor of Dr. William Grey Nowell of Malden, MA. Nowell was a founding member of the AMC, serving as Councillor of Improvements from 1876 to 1878. He was both an ordained minister and a physician. He first came to Randolph in 1873 and spent many summers thereafter. Along with Charles Lowe, he built Lowe's Path, the Nineteen-Mile Brook Trail and the Carter-Moriah Trail. He is also credited with building the Log Cabin on Mount Adams in 1890. William Nowell died in 1929.

[9] Snyder Brook was named by William G. Nowell on September 2, 1875, in honor of Charles E. Lowe's little dog, which bore the same name as Rip Van Winkle's dog.

[10] Charles E. Lowe was born in 1838. His parents, Clovis and Alpha, were prosperous farmers. His brother was Thaddeus S.C. Lowe, the renowned inventor, physicist and balloonist. He was, among many things, an innkeeper, a trained surveyor, and a famous guide. With William G. Nowell, he built Lowe's Path (1875-76), the Nineteen-Mile Brook Trail (1877), and the Carter-Moriah Trail (1883). As a guide, he was said to be the best for the Northern Peaks, being cautious, intelligent and companionable. On February 17, 1887, he made the first recorded winter ascent of Mount Adams. Charles Lowe died in 1907.

Mounts Madison, Adams and King Ravine from Randolph

Having told you some of the advantages of the place, I must not omit mentioning that black flies and midges, almost unknown in Campton, have been very plenty here until very lately. They not only infest the woods, but troubled us on the porch, so that a smudge was made in the evenings to drive them off. We have always found these little blood suckers in the woods and fields on this side of the mountains, but they have seldom come so about the house, the reason of their so doing here being the proximity of the woods.

A short time before we came, one of Mr. Watson's calves was badly clawed by a bear in a near pasture. I believe the poor thing was saved from death by the rest of the herd, who are supposed to have run at the bear and scared him off.

The morning of the Appalachian meeting my mother and I drove over to Jefferson and were welcomed at the Waumbek House by Professor Fay. Professor Edward Pickering opened proceedings by a short explanatory address intended for the outsiders who were present in numbers. Then the intended excursions were explained. Professor Fay announced an international meeting of Alpine Clubs in Saltzburg in August and Mr. William H. Pickering[11] was appointed our delegate. Mr. Scott's paper was merely an account from memory, assisted by a few notes, of an exploration of the Pemigewasset forest begun at Pollard's and ended at the Crawford House.

---

[11] William H. Pickering was the younger brother of Edward Pickering. He too was a founding member of the AMC. He served as President (1910,1911), Councillor of Exploration, and Councillor of Art. In 1882 he published a contour map of the White Mountains as well as the *Walking Guide to the Mount Washington Range*.

His description was very graphic and interesting. The party was several times puzzled, following the wrong stream where forks occurred, found five falls yet unnoted, and on the last day found themselves on a crest wrapped in cloud and not knowing where they were. A rift in the mist revealed Mt. Webster opposite them, and they quickly made their way to the Crawford House, and thence to Jackson in time for the AMC meeting. Miss M. F. Whitman[12] was one of this hardy party. When Mr. Scott had finished, Professor Langley[13], the astronomer, gave a most interesting description of his scientific journey to the top of Mt. Whitney in the Sierra Nevada. Among other small things was read a note from my mother announcing the opening of a new path[14] from the Ravine House to top of Mt. Madison. A resolution was passed thanking Mr. Watson for his public spirit in putting through this work.

After dinner a party was formed to climb Starr King Mountain. My mother put me under the care of Mr. Scott, and on this pleasant little trip I continued the acquaintance made at dinner with Miss Whitman and Miss Knowles[15]. The former is the sturdiest lady walker I have ever seen and withal unassuming. The view from Starr King is not very remarkable as compared with the view from Jefferson Hill itself, but of course it interested me to make out the southern mountains as well as the smoky atmosphere would allow. When I got down at teatime, I found my aunt arrived from Hoboken as expected. She spent the night at Jefferson with us, my uncle having gone on to the Ravine House.

Next day the plans were for different parties to go into King's Ravine or on Mt. Adams, some intending to pass a night at the camp on the latter. At the time appointed for starting, eight o'clock, it was raining, but toward midday it cleared and plans were relaid. The camping party started after dinner to spend the night on the mountain, and next day make the climb. Mr. Scott and Professor Fay were the leaders of this division. We drove home with them, intending to join Professor Pickering's party into the ravine the next morning.

Thursday also opened very dubiously, but my mother and I, with

---

[12] Martha Fairfield Whitman was an avid hiker and known as one of the sturdiest women explorers of her day. Her identity as a member of the Scott-Ricker adventure (further described in the letters of August 2, August 27, and September 4, 1882) was hitherto unknown prior to the discovery of these letters. She, along with Marian, Lucia, Edith and Isabella, was one of the few women publishing accounts of her explorations in early volumes of *Appalachia*. She had completed her medical studies and was a resident physician when she died on December 12, 1884.

[13] Samuel Pierpoint Langley (1834-1906) was an astronomer, physicist and pioneer in aeronautics.

[14] This trail is known today as the Watson Path.

[15] Miss Martha A. Knowles of Boston, MA.

Waumbek House

Professor Langley and Mr. Kennard[16] (Treasurer of AMC) who had come to the Ravine House to see the place, were driven to Lowe's. After a heavy shower, the weather promised better things, and we started on the path about eleven o'clock. Mr. Kennard, Miss Bartlett from our house and we two made an independent little party, having pleasant encounters with the others by the way, but not bound by their movements.

When we reached the view point on the floor of the ravine I left the others, and went forward among the famous boulders to the ice caves, where I met a party of four who had come down the headwall.

Mr. Lowe had refused to guide the ladies of the camping party down the difficult wall, asserting the greater danger of the descent over the ascent, so the leaders had decided to bring the party across the side of Madison and down the new Watson path. You would have opened your eyes at the array of stout and elderly ladies who managed to get into King's

---

[16] Mr. Charles W. Kennard of Boston, MA.

Ravine under the auspices of the Club. We got home in time to dress ourselves comfortably for tea, and then sat on the porch watching for the mountain party to emerge from the woods opposite. They all straggled in before dark in various states of well and ill being, and after a taste of our milk, drove back to Jefferson. Mr. Kennard left on Friday, much pleased with our place and hoping to return later with his family.

Saturday (July 22) was a magnificent day and we decided at breakfast to test the new Madison path. For several years there has been a good way up Snyder Brook to the Upper Salmacis Fall, about two and one-half miles. Leaving the brook, the path then climbs out of the ravine on to the mountain and comes out on the rock about a mile from the top. The whole distance is about four to four and one-half miles. Our family four with Mr. Peek duly registered ourselves in the AMC bottle, and then gave our attention to lunch and the view. The northern view is very fine; the air was so clear we could see Rangeley Lakes and mountains beyond. Mt. Washington, the Great Gulf and Carter Notch were very grand. This climb was made easy by the exhilarating day and my mother felt it so little that she could not rest till she had been on Adams too.

Monday we explored for a shortcut up Cold Brook to intersect the ravine path and visited two falls on our route. Wednesday my mother succeeded in making a party for Mt. Adams with my uncle, Mr. Peek and I consenting to go, but my aunt declining on account of the heat and the smoke. We got started about 8:30 A.M., walked to Lowe's and toiled slowly up the four miles of path reaching the top about 1:20 P.M. When we got out on the rocks I was stimulated by the sight of a party in front of us. Coming up with them we found two of the ladies were speaking acquaintances made on the AMC excursion. Mr. Lowe and another guide were laden with their traps. They intended camping on the col between Adams and Madison, and the next day going over the peaks to Washington. They winded their way round the head of the ravine, while we followed the cairns on to the summit. At least we were cool enough on top, for the wind was strong.

Madison is an exceedingly sharp peak as seen from Adams, and very picturesque with Star Lake nestling on the col. The huge bulk of Washington with the winding road up its side is very imposing. Smoke was so thick we could only faintly distinguish Lafayette. Among other interesting things in the natural history line, we found a full sized potato bug on the very top pile of rocks! These rocks are the same gray broken things as on top of Mt. Washington, tedious to walk over. One gets quite enough of them walking down Nowell's Ridge to the tree line. About three-quarters of mile before coming out to Lowe's we tried another short cut home. A very direct wood road led us to the old mill on Cold Brook not far from home. It was pretty badly overgrown in some places, but we all agreed it was far preferable to the sunny highroad. You understand that view of the matter.

Since Adams, the warm thick weather has allowed us to rest and given me opportunity to finish on Friday this document begun on Tuesday. Such a missive from its size and weight deserves the name of a missile. If the length of yours frightened you, this is my revenge. I hope my details will not exhaust your patience.

My aunt sends the scraps about Mr. Booth. She and my mother wish me to send their very kindest regards to Dr. and Mrs. Stone and to you. In all their good wishes I join, remaining,

Your sincere friend,
M. M. Pychowska

P.S. Have you seen Mr. W. H. Pickering's view map of the Great Range? It is very accurate in regard to the peaks, but our streams are woefully out. Gorham is not necessary in our address, for we are the Randolph Post Office.

* * * * * * * * * * * *

Isabella Stone writes to Marian Pychowska (draft copy).

Russell House
North Woodstock, N.H.
July 27, 1882

My dear Miss Pychowska,

The heat, haze, and dust make walking and riding both intolerable, and thus a little leisure is gained for letter writing.

I presume my long letter of July 19 reached you in safety. You will hardly care to hear of our long day spent in Franconia Notch, at Profile Lake and Echo Lake, and on Bald Mountain, whence I saw the "Goodnow House" once more and all the dear familiar region around Sugar Hill, for which I must confess to have had a little homesick yearning during the first week of my sojourn here. But the fresh views and many attractive excursions in this vicinity made me contented very soon, more easily because a visit to Goodnow's is to end the summer's pleasuring, and I can anticipate the sight of my beloved peaks and the retracing of a few favorite rambles there. Here the Pemigewasset River and many small brooks supply the one element of beauty lacking at Goodnow's. The sunsets are very fine seen from the plateau behind the house yet the mountains take on no such wondrous all enveloping tints as there, but a peculiar radiant mist pours into the gorges between their giant forms, similar to that seen at Shelburne that your aunt spoke of at one time. The view reminds me of "Aurora Leigh's" sight of Italy: "The old miraculous mountains heaved in sight. One straining past another along the shore. The way of grand dull Odyssean ghosts...Peak pushing peak they stood."

Can you believe that I have actually made the ascent of Lafayette?

And in a charming manner, too, not with a large chattering party. Mr. Russell's son Fred (about fifteen years old) drove Miss E. (of whom I wrote you) and myself in the beach-wagon up to the Profile House one beautiful cool morning last week. We hired two horses and the head guide, mounted at the entrance of the bridle path in scientific manner by springing into our saddles from the ground with one foot in the guide's hand, and started on our steep and winding way, with lunch and wraps. The guide held on to the tail of Miss E's horse, while mine followed with Fred clinging to its tail! A comical sight we must have been to an outsider, but there were no spectators, for we had the mountain quite to ourselves all day. We had a fine view, far better than the average the guide said, though somewhat hazy in the extreme distance. We had occasional glimpses of the view as we wound along, but just before coming to Eagle Lake, we emerged from the woods and the superb ravines and mighty brother peaks close to Lafayette burst upon our vision in all their indescribable grandeur, while high above us, a mile distant, rose the rocky wind-swept crest, the goal of my aspirations for so many summers of the past. At one place only were we obliged to dismount on account of the roughness of the way for a few yards. We rode bravely up to the beacon on top, and then walked down to the spring and lunched, sheltered from the fierce wind and in full view of the Mt. Washington Range which it was a special joy once more to behold. We spent a full hour and a half in gazing at the magnificent prospect, and in picking out old friends and making new acquaintances.

For the first half or three-quarters of a mile we walked down slowly, reluctant to leave that glorious view point, and feeling safer on our own feet where the path was so fearfully steep and rocky. Afterwards we rode nearly all the way, not without inward tremors and many audible exclamations. My companion was accustomed to riding, but this was the first time I had ever mounted a horse. You can perhaps imagine that my sensations were not always delightful, especially when on the ascent my horse more deliberately than once turned round and started rapidly down the mountain, or on the descent lurched into a sort of trot around the sharp corners in haste to keep up with Miss E's horse. The latter animal on the ascent exhibited some ugliness of disposition which alarmed the lady so that she insisted upon having the guide almost constantly at her bridle. In spite of jokes and dolorous predictions, I mounted every time successfully and never once lost my seat. It was a fascinating experience and has hung many beautiful new pictures in memory's gallery. Moreover it was a satisfaction to prove Lafayette a perfectly feasible undertaking for me, because now I shall do it again next year! It would be pleasant to ride up only and then dismiss guide and horses and walk down at our own convenience. To walk up would be too fatiguing for me I feel sure. The ten-mile ride home (after a rest at Echo Lake) was delightful.

Again tonight two *Echos* have come for yours truly, and the kind sender of one is unknown to me.

Some of our pedestrians have departed, and I feel it will be impossible to arrange a party to walk through the Thornton-Warren (AMC) Path and spend a night on Moosilauke, but I do so long to accomplish the trip under guidance of a man recommended to me as eminently trustworthy and efficient by Mr. Scott. Perhaps we can muster enough who would like to visit "the Gorge" on said path, which your aunt wrote me about your party exploring. Will you kindly write me as exactly as possible the best and shortest way to reach it? On which side of the AMC path do you turn off? The guide above mentioned is at work in the forest most of the time, and when at home lives miles away.

Our last excursion was an exploration of the old disused road running westward along Beaver Brook to the base of Waternomee. It affords fine views of Moosilauke, Franconia Notch and even Mt. Washington, and is interesting for its wild pastures and woody dells, and deserted houses fallen to ruins not yet picturesque though hinting at the pathos of a vain struggle for a livelihood and a home; sometimes a rose bush still hangs over a bit of front yard fence, its blossom laden boughs, or a few gnarled old apple trees still keep guard behind a stone wall.

My friend on her wedding journey has arrived to spend a week and her artist husband is delighted with the beautiful "subjects" for sketches that we have found in two or three days of search together.

What do you have for indoor work this summer? And do you like Randolph as well as Campton, or better?

Goodbye, with love to your dear mother,

I am ever yours sincerely,

Isabella Stone

P.S. My Walling Map was lost on one excursion and a letter to the Secretary of AMC enclosing money for a new one has as yet elicited no reply. It is a necessity at the mountains and I am disconsolate without it.

* * * * * * * * * * * *

Marian Pychowska writes to Isabella Stone

Ravine House
Randolph, N.H.
August 2, 1882

Dear Miss Stone,

I am so very glad you have at last made the ascent of Lafayette, and in such a satisfactory way. Your description of the behavior of the horses brought vividly to mind our ascent by the old path in '77. My aunt especially recalls the fierce trot her beast indulged in when coming down, and his insisting on going to the very edge of the precipice which was a favorite view point on the old path.

Your Beaver Brook exploration attracts me much. Those old roads high up among the hills are usually very fine places for views, as well as lovely in their immediate surroundings. The number of such roads in the neighborhood of our two Campton sojourns was one of their great attractions for us, and made up in great part for the grander mountain climbing that we have here.

You ask me if I really prefer Randolph to Campton. Perhaps you took my last letter for an answer, but I will indulge myself in talking a little more about it. Our climate here I certainly find more exhilarating, the water of the streams and springs colder, the comforts of indoors as great, and the biggest mountains in reach of our two feet. But I think Campton just as beautiful and attractive to the mountaineer, though in a gentler way. If I may judge by such a variable thing as my mother's health and mine, this is the better place for those who need stimulating.

Losing your map was a serious thing. The last time we wrote for a new one, the only copies left were those bound with *Appalachia* (Vol. I, No. 1). They had a number of these for sale. I hope your appeal to the Secretary will have been answered ere this.

It is a pity your trip to Moosilauke is balked. I would like to know how you had planned to do it. "The Gorge" is easily found if the lumber men have not again removed the AMC sign board and stuck it out of sight in the bushes, as was the case when we were there. You know the path starts where the West Thornton Tannery road branches off from the main road. You cross fence and stream. The way across the pasture was marked by tall poles stuck in the ground at intervals and there is another sign board at the entrance of the woods. You soon come out again on a pasture above the Tannery pond, follow poles up hill and enter woods again. From here I believe there will be no trouble in keeping the main path. The Gorge branch turns off to the right after you have climbed the hill and come to an almost level plateau, where the road cutting is very wide with young trees laid across it to facilitate the running of the sledges of bark. Perhaps the name we gave to this piece of road will give you a better idea than my description. We called it the "boulevard". The opening of the Gorge path may be obscured by brush, but there is a good sign in black and white paint, if the workmen have allowed it to stay. Perhaps when you arrive at the Gorge you will be inclined to say 'Is this all?' for you have much more wonderful places nearer Russell's.

The only all day expedition we have taken since my finishing my last letter, has been to the Ravine of the Cascades. This is the next ravine west of King's and in it is one of the sources of Israel's river. We climbed Lowe's Path once more as far as the AMC camp[17] on Mt. Adams, and then took a branch, about a mile in length, down into the new river valley. On the way we had a fine view of the Castellated Ridge of Mt. Jefferson just opposite us. At the first cascade the rocks seemed to have combined for the purpose of making the water fall over them in as many different ways as possible, sliding down inclines and shooting over edges, pouring through gullies and trickling from threads of moss. We climbed on, sometimes in the stream bed and then on the treacherously moss clad bank, my aunt suggesting it was quite as arduous as the way to Coppermine Brook Falls! In the distance of about half a mile there are four fine cascades. The views out toward Jefferson Hill are lovely, but the best thing was looking up toward the headwall, seemingly so very high above us, with its forest mantle growing gradually thinner and paler up to the tree line. We could see the beginnings of our stream coming down this green wall, in little steps at first and then lower in broad sheets of flashing white. I hope some day to go farther up this beautiful ravine and see these upper falls nearer.

When we got back to the camp we found a fire started up, a big coffee pot filling at the spring and Mr. Lowe's companion guide, Hubbard Hunt[18], making new bough beds, for a party who had gone that day into King's Ravine and were going next morning on the mountain.

At sunset that evening we had an unusual sight. The tops of Adams and Madison were quite clear, but the Moriah-Carter Range was imbedded in thick cloud pouring over from east or south. The crimson and golden lights on mountains here make me think of Sugar Hill. Of course you have been enjoying the moon this week as much as we have.

You would have liked the little walk my aunt and I took yesterday. Randolph Mountain has its shows as well as its big opposite neighbors. We followed one wood path to this "Mossy Glen", then sat by the stream and refreshed our eyes looking at the pretty cascades falling over luxuriant green moss into clear brown pools. On our way home by another path we stopped long to watch the growing shadows in the big ravines, and the peaks framed in by spruces and birch trees.

---

[17] Known as "Lowe's Camp," this crude three-sided shelter was located near the same site as today's Log Cabin on Mount Adams. This structure, completed July 21, 1876, was the first established AMC camp.

[18] Born in 1834, Hubbard Hunt moved to Randolph from Whitefield, NH, and bought a parcel of land near the Bowman homestead where he built a fine farm of his own. A trusted guide, he, along with Laban Watson and Charles Lowe, was one of the most active trail workers of Randolph's year-round population. He built the Castle Trail on Mount Jefferson under the direction of Eugene Cook and William Peek (1883-84) and helped cut the Carter-Moriah Trail. During the summer of 1892, he maintained all the trails on the Northern Presidential Range for a fee of twenty dollars. Hunt died in February of 1903.

An amusing thing happened at the Jefferson meeting which I believe I did not write you. Last September on the Kineo Trail, my aunt found a tin cup of an ordinary shape but with a peculiar arrangement in the handle. She scratched "Kineo" and the date on it and gave it to me to carry this summer. Knowing Mr. Scott had opened the Kineo trail, we showed him the cup and asked if he had lost it. Miss Whitman, who was standing by, spoke up and said it was her cup and had made its first trip with her into Tuckerman's Ravine. She had lent it to Mr. Scott for that occasion and he had dropped it by the Kineo brook early in July. I offered to return it, but was allowed to keep my historic dipper, ennobled by the use of two members of AMC before it fell into possession of another.

You ask often my indoor occupations. The excitement of exploring a new region prevents much being done indoors. However, the off days I reread a canto of *Divine Comedy*, take a small dose of German and read some French. We have just finished a novel, *LaSoupe Noire*, illustrative of the persecution of the United Greek Ruthenians by the Russians about twelve years ago. A heartrending piece of history. Now, to do justice to Russian civilization, I have commenced a life of Mozart, an excellent work by a very enthusiastic Russian. One of our extra distractions this summer is tennis, which my aunt and I are trying to learn.

My long ramble must stop sometime. Hoping to hear often I remain always,

Your friend,

M. M. Pychowska

P.S. I forgot to say the distance to Gorge is less than two miles. Is the name of your guide recommended by Mr. Scott, William Sargent[19]?

On coming in to tea my mother finds a letter from Mr. Addey[20] of the *Echo* in which he says Mr. Scott, Miss Whitman, and party are about to make an exploration of the Twin Mountain Range, descend into the wilderness and come out either over Mt. Garfield or Mt. Willey[21]. What a splendid walk it will be.

---

[19] William M. Sargent of Thornton, NH. Sargent was a woodsman, guide and trail builder who, under the direction of Isabella, built trails on Mount Moosilauke and its surrounding peaks as well as to Bridal Veil and Georgiana Falls.

[20] Mr. Markinfield Addey was the founder and editor for twenty years of the *White Mountain Echo*.

[21] This exploration was known as the Scott-Ricker adventure, a remarkable seven day bushwhacking expedition over the then trailless Twin Mountain Range. Miss Charlotte E. Ricker, who was a journalist, accompanied this party and was all but overwhelmed by the arduous journey. Two scouts (Allan Thompson and a youth named Odin), two woodsmen (possibly William Sargent and William Pollard) and an unidentified woman (possibly Martha A. Knowles) also braved the wilderness with A. E. Scott, Miss Whitman, and Miss Ricker in search of a future trail route over these mountains.

Marian Pychowska writes to Isabella Stone.

Ravine House
Randolph, N.H.
August 4, 1882

Dear Miss Stone,

Here am I writing to you again, but fortunately you will not know it for sometime yet. Our yesterday's excursion and my aunt's appropriate sketch impel me to try your patience by a detailed description of King's Ravine. You can see a part of its bold headwall on the right of the drawing, with the sharp peak of Adams above it. The lesser double head to the left of Adams is the so called "John Quincy". Between this and Madison is Madison Spring, in which rises Snyder Brook whose ravine you can trace by the winding shadow in the picture. On the extreme left you can see the beginning of the ravine of Bumpus Brook. This is a part of what we see from the slope of Randolph Hill. The view from the house is the same, but foreshortened.

Yesterday morning after breakfast, two parties started out from the Ravine House, one, composed of three young men, for Mt. Madison via the Watson path, the other bound for the same summit by way of King's Ravine. The second party, consisting of my uncle, aunt, Mr. Peek and myself, instead of going up to Lowe's and following his path from the beginning, went up Cold Brook by one of our private cuts[22], striking the path well up toward the ravine. The well, worn track was a pleasant change from our scraggly wood road. At the crossing of the West Branch stream, Mr. Peek produced his thermometer, which being put in the water, went down to forty degrees. We soon came to the main Cold Brook, the very air of which chills one, and in this water the instrument marked thirty-four degrees and a small fraction. Now we came into the boulder region. The enormous masses of angular rock are clothed with short spruces and birches, and deep, green moss, but the way is still excellent. About three and a half miles from home we came out on the "floor" of the great amphitheatre, where there is a splendid view in both directions. Looking out, the Randolph and Pliny mountain wilderness and the scrap of cultivated valley far below, are framed in by the steep, symmetrical curves of the pine clad side walls. Looking in, you see a great basin of broken rock whose angles are only here and there shrouded by the stunted growth. The high wall, which shuts you in from everything but the sky, is scored by slides and sounding waterfalls and crowned by a battlement of crags whence came these "bowlders" at your feet.

Now begins the climbing. Fortunately the way is marked, where

---

[22] This trail is known today as the Amphibrach.

possible by cairns, blazes, and marks of passing feet so there is a clue to guide one through this labyrinth. There is plenty of variety in crossing the chaotic mass of rock, walking slant roofs, hauling yourself up by convenient roots, squeezing through underground passages, where one is glad to be thin and have a small pack. Caves open on every side, out of which blows a cold blast betraying the ice stowed away beneath. At one place where the ice was accessible, we got down and broke off big pieces, most refreshing to our dry lips. My uncle carried a bit along in his cup, with which to cool himself in climbing the long slide[23]. We came out into one open spot surrounded by cave openings, where the air was so chilled as to take the mercury down to fifty degrees, while that same afternoon it stood at seventy-two degrees on the top of Madison. The whole boulder region is, I suppose, less than half a mile through, and emerging from it, we began the ascent of the long slide, perhaps six or seven hundred feet in height, that marks the northeast wall. This was toilsome and needed care not to dislodge the nicely balanced stones, but not difficult. Many were the little stops to look across at Nowell's Ridge and down at the boulders lessening behind us and up at the pinnacles that we were nearing.

The Gateway itself is a most beautiful place. The rough slide ends, and there is a gentle slope of grass full of alpine plants, which leads, like a road, through the battlements of the ravine wall. On the right is an immense even sweep of rock highly inclined, and on the left the broken and ragged crag out of the crumblings of which the slide was made. As my aunt and I neared the opening, the picture was completed by my uncle's figure standing between the cliffs with nothing behind it but the deep blue sky. Rising a little higher, we saw the sharp, symmetrical cone of Madison taking my uncle's place in the gap. Here we rested awhile, watching the other party from our house clambering down to Madison Spring. As it was now half past one, we soon joined them there and ate our dinner. One of our plans is to camp by this spring under Mr. Lowe's superintendence, and next day walk over the peaks to Washington. Some stretched themselves on the bough bed of a deserted camp, glad, even five thousand feet above sea, to get in the shade of the stunted spruces. The young men made some inquiries about the ravine, and determined to return the way we had come. We took care not to excite their scorn by picturing the difficulties before them, simply giving directions for finding the path.

At three o'clock we stood on Madison, spent half an hour enjoying the afternoon lights and contributing to the AMC bottle, then hurried down our own lovely path, stopping for a momentary glimpse at Salmacis Falls. We got home at a quarter to six, the other party coming in about an hour, enchanted with the ravine, which had exceeded their expectations in gran-

---

[23] The site of the upper section of today's King Ravine Trail.

deur and difficulty.

I am finishing this dry account in the grove this Sunday afternoon. Though we ate ice last Thursday, and saw one patch of snow still resting at the head of the Great Gulf, this warm weather makes us fear for the survival of the usual late season snow arch that forms in Tuckerman's Ravine. When we went through there on August 9, five years ago there was not a speck of snow left. Two pedestrians, who are spending Sunday here, report the arch as still extant but rapidly melting. Our plans are laid to drive round the Glen tomorrow and go up into the ravine, so I hope to end this letter with some account of the other great amphitheatre.

August 15

The weather on Monday was warm and promised showers, but this was only another reason to visit the snow. The Pinkham Woods Road was new to me, not having been over it since I was old enough to take in what I saw, so the views of the Carter Mountains and the beautiful high Notch outlined against the sky, were of special interest. We drove three miles beyond the Glen, to where the path[24] to the Ravine and to Crystal Cascade enters the woods. Just before reaching this point, we saw one of the grandest of our mountain views under exceptional circumstances. The great mass of Washington was before us, with the two portals of Tuckerman's Ravine and Huntington's opening into it, the former partly enclosed by the bold flanks of the Lion Head and Boott's Spur. A strong west wind was driving black clouds up behind this picture, and, in strong contrast to their dark shadow, the sun shone in patches on the brilliant green of the alpine growth high among the stern rocks. Our snow was plainly seen under the head wall. About eleven o'clock we left our wagon, my mother, aunt, uncle and I starting at once on the path; Mr. Peek and Mr. McGinley soon following.

When we came through the Ravine in '77 we were led off by the superior plainness of the path that leads out to the Mt. Washington road near the second mile post. Since then the AMC has much improved the other path, so that the snow arch is reached by two and three-quarter miles of easy traveling. The forest is very beautiful, and the grand views begin as one nears Hermit Lakes. The two tiny tarns do not amount to much in themselves, but they make fine openings and foreground for the ravine picture.

Do you remember the view, purporting to be of King's Ravine in Thomas Starr King's *White Hills*? It is much more like Tuckerman's, though not a striking likeness of either. King's Ravine looks to me as if a giant had stood on the top of Adams and taken a single deep shovelful out of the mountain. It is so open, so exposed in every part, as one looks at it from the heights opposite, the headwall surmounted by the peak of Adams,

---

[24] The Tuckerman Ravine Trail.

very fine, but the sides fading down abruptly to the valley, not a work of constructing, but a digging out. Tuckerman's Ravine is seemingly more withdrawn into the mountain, better protected by the side fortresses built up about it, no less curious than King's, but more beautiful.

There is a steep short climb from the lower floor, where the lakes lie, to the upper amphitheater. At our first visit the stream was a most convenient passage way through the obstinate dwarf spruce and alder, but now there is an excellent path. It was easy to see why the way was so well worn, for we met several parties of what my aunt called "descendants of Washington" among whom were some acquaintances of my uncle's. Now we felt the full force of the wind that swept over the headwall, making us forget it was a hot day in the valleys. This wind explains many things in this ravine; the dwarf trees with their arms stretched out toward the east, the garden of alpine plants whose seeds have blown down from the grassy flats of Boott's Spur above, and the late lying snow which must pile up here to an immense depth in winter. The arch was still extant, spanning the stream that is formed by the convergence of a thousand trickles down the wall[25]. No such water as this flows from the ice caves in our own ravine. It is warmed on its course over the cliffs, and we were glad to cool it with lumps of snow. The drift was still nearly a hundred feet long, resting on pillars of compacted snow, but generally with a space of from one to eight or nine feet between the snow and the rock. You know, from the pictures, how the roof is made of umbrella shaped cavities. The water pours in streams from all the points where these cavities join together, so I went through the arch with my sun shade up. If this curious thing were made of pure white snow it might be very beautiful, but the effect is marred by the lines of black dirt that accentuate the drawing. We got two rare alpine plants among the many lovely ones in the upper basin.

You will see how easy the trip was, when I tell you we were only two hours in walking from the road to the arch. Before four o'clock we had regained our wagon and about six we were at home.

The next thing on the programme was to explore the Ravine of Bumpus Brook. My uncle, aunt, and Mr. Peek, who formed the party this time, reported fine views of Madison, waterfalls, and a tough scramble of the first class. My uncle went to the top of Madison, the other two remaining a little below, and they all came down the Watson path, while that heavy shower of last Thursday wet them through.

Saturday my uncle took the same party with the addition of my mother and myself, on the highest point of Randolph Mountain. It has an unpromising look like Cushman and Waternomee, but for that very reason we were the more determined it should yield us something. By the

---

[25] The Falls of a Thousand Streams.

Snow Arch, Tuckerman's Ravine

shortcut we gained the upper road on Randolph Hill. (Oh, how I wish you could see that view and watch with us the evening's lights on the big mountains and ravines in front, dear Moriah-Carter, the distant blue hills down the Androscoggin, and then the clear cut northern mountains. What was the use of immersing ourselves in overgrown wood roads and all sorts of debris for a possible glimpse of what we already had without trouble?) The roads, such as they were, helped us to gain the main ridge, and from there a short piece of fairly open woods was easily passed to reach the top. What should greet our view on the unfrequented summit (as was the case before on the "formidable peak" of Kinsman) but the old signals of the U.S. Coast Survey with the usual notice not to disturb them. They had evidently been put there a good while ago, for the keg, fastened to a tall pine, had nearly fallen to pieces. Before reaching this point, we had a glimpse, through the trees, of the Pond of Safety[26] lying in the wilderness behind Randolph Mountain, and from the southwest ledge we saw Lafayette and the Twins. Near the signal was a cutting which opened for us a superb view of Madison, Adams, and Jefferson—King's Ravine looking more than ever like a gigantic spade hole. By circling the whole crown of our summit we found openings in nearly every direction, and what we could not see from the ground, my uncle, aunt and I saw from

---

[26] During the Revolutionary War, this pond and its surroundings served as a refuge for four American soldiers who refused to take up arms a second time after being released as prisoners of war.

the upper boughs of convenient young spruces. What interested me most was the view across the Upper Ammonoosuc wilderness to the Pilot Range, Percy Peaks, etc. It was worthwhile after all. We got home early in the afternoon, having added a new mountain to our possessions, as Mr. Peek is fond of saying.

There are few people I should dare to surfeit with all these guidebook details, and even with you I am afraid of being a bore, because I know I am writing for my own pleasure in the first place. But for that same good reason I will risk boring you.

The Mt. Adams House is about six miles from here. My mother, my aunt and I were driven there yesterday morning, and climbed the half mile of easy path to the top of Boy Mountain. The whole Great Range is spread out in this view, but is not as beautiful to my eye, as from our own heights. Lafayette and Hooket, the Twin Range, Hale, etc. are also well seen, with a wide stretch of hilly country and distant mountains to the west. After dinner we sauntered down and along the road toward home, stopping at all the places recommended us by Mr. Peek as good for views. The mountains grew more and more lovely as the shadows lengthened. We lingered long at one place where my aunt drew. Beyond a narrow bit of cultivated land we could follow the winding of the forest clothed gorge of Israel's River, ending in the scarred Ravine of the Castles, the beautiful Castellated Ridge on one side, its fortress rocks casting long straight shadows down the slope, and the whole crowned by the strong dome-like form of Mt. Jefferson. To vary our treat, we took a small journey into the woods to see a pretty little cascade. Does this not fascinate you? We have plenty such gentle excursions and afternoon walks, but for brevity sake(!) I only tell you about the big things.

August 17

Yesterday, in spite of the unusual heat, the four "wild geese", my uncle, aunt, Mr. Peek and I attacked the "Ice Gulch", a most curious place in the ridge between Randolph and Crescent Mountains. Mr. Peek was there last year with Mr. Watson and his brother who is acquainted with the mysteries of this most complicated logging region. Taking the shortcut to Randolph Hill we there took a very good wood road that led us down a back way into the valley of Moose Brook. The mill here is the center of a vast system of roads cutting the Randolph-Crescent slopes in every direction as we found to our east. If there was nothing but the compass and stream to guide us, we should probably have had no trouble, but the deceitful appearances of a well travelled road carried us far to the eastward of our object. Abandoning this we crossed a tract where hemlock trees and heaps of bark were lying in wild confusion, struck a road which promised a better direction, and finally having travelled six miles or more from home, we found ourselves on the ridge about half way between the Gulch and the top of Crescent Mountain.

It was now one o'clock, so we ate dinner by a cold rivulet, and then started southwest along the ridge. Oh! what masses of prostrate trees and brush. It was one continuous logging road for nearly a mile. Now we could see we were coming to a gap in the crest, and going down into this, we soon struck the beginning of the Gulch. It was nearly 2:30 and we had just reached the entrance of the formidable place of whose difficulties we had heard so much! However, though the climbing needed care and time, there was nothing like the tedious labor of the brush district we had come through. The Gulch is about three-quarters of a mile long, very narrow, the cliffs on each side from one to two hundred feet in height and beautifully crowned by spruces and hemlocks. The bottom is entirely filled with angular rocks, fallen from above, of the same aspect as, but smaller than those in King's Ravine. As we got fairly into the Gulch, we were met by a blast of cold air, and presently saw a white vapor pouring out of the big black holes between the rocks. Through a great part of the length, the compact white ice, which fills the interstices to an unknown depth, is much exposed to light and air. Of course we walked on it and ate it. The rocks are clothed with moss of beautiful shades of green, yellow and red, but what gives the strangest aspect to the place is that the perpetual cold that reigns has stunted the evergreens and birches, and induced a growth of alpine plants such as one finds at the tree line on the big mountains. At the lower end, where the ice ceases and the brook flows free, there is a small basin of brilliant moss filled with genuine ice water, a fairy like spot. Our way home was much shorter but not more lovely than the mornings scramble, the wood roads not going our way and only serving to entangle us. At last, after much tacking, we came on the first rate way that we had followed down to the mill. We hailed our tracks with joy and at a quarter to seven, emerged on top of Randolph Hill in time to see the last glow on the peaks and their clinging clouds.

If I do not send off this chronicle now, it will grow beyond all reading.

Yours very sincerely,

M. M. Pychowska

P.S. Did you notice a little paragraph by my mother in the *Echo*?

Isabella Stone writes to Marian Pychowska (draft copy).

Goodnow House
Sugar Hill, N.H.
August 27, 1882

Dear Miss Pychowska,

This "cut" will give you some idea of the stylish establishment into which what was once the Goodnow Farmhouse has developed. Since August the table has been entirely satisfactory, the servants are attentive and everything moves on smoothly. You need not credit any rumors of poor living here. During the hot spell in July there was some trouble with sour bread, but at present no one but chronic grumblers could find fault with anything. The scenery and air are as enchanting and exhilarating as ever and I rejoice hourly over my return home to Sugar Hill! Various little internal improvements have been made, and the entire kitchen department has been reconstructed on a much larger scale with numerous modern hotel appliances, all of which Mr. and Mrs. Goodnow seemed to take pleasure in asking me out to examine, and the new cottage likewise. There is no one more interested than I am in their success, and their cordial reception of me each year is very pleasant.

I have read again your last extremely interesting letter, and marvel anew at the great things you accomplish. Tuckerman's Ravine is "an easy trip" because "you were only two hours walking to the snow arch from the wagon." To appreciate the full force of such a remark, a person should have made one or two walking excursions with your party. All the expeditions of which you write are very attractive, but Randolph Mountain and Boy Mountain with its saunter home in the exquisite afternoon lights and shadows, little cascade and all, do especially fascinate me. I echo your wish that I could watch with you that glorious view from "the upper road on Randolph Hill." It is pleasant to know that on your charming rambles you do occasionally think of me and wish that I were alongside. Do you mind telling me how Miss Cook and you manage to climb trees so readily without dropping your dress skirts? What a tough tumbling walk that must have been to and over the Ice Gulch! And a wonderful place, too! You know there is no need of fearing to bore me with your descriptions. Four sheets full are quite what I expect now. Ha! Ha!

Of various minor strolls at North Woodstock you may not care to hear, but will you not jump up and clap your hands when you read that I have actually stood upon the tiptop summit, the queer crumbling double headed rock, of Loon Pond Mountain? Week after week the rushing waters of the East Branch, the grand towering mountain wall wrapped in its mantle of somber pines, did call and beckon me upward, and I comprehended well how the alluring charm of the mountain made your mother feel, as you once wrote me, that it was the dream of her life, to go to

Pollard's and ascend Loon Pond Mountain. At last, the party of seven—
including five ladies—was organized and I engaged as guide, Dura Pollard, who advised us to carry dry boots and stocking over the river, and
plenty of wraps to the summit, and asked, "Do they know its a mighty
tough tramp? They may go to the pond, but I don't believe there's any of
'em 'll want to go way beyond to the very top."

In July, one of the ladies at our house had an extremely narrow escape from drowning, having fallen into one of the treacherous deep pools
in the Pemigewasset River, from which she was saved by her own coura-
geous presence of mind, and slight knowledge of swimming before the
arrival of help summoned by the screams of her frightened companions.
Father and mother were opposed to the Loon Pond trip, the former on
account of the hard climb, the latter because of the necessity of fording the
river. Father and I walked to Pollard's and Mr. Dura showed us the fording
place, where at present there was certainly no danger of drowning even if
one fell in. I purposely told him of the trip to Moran Lake and down the
Cascade Brook, which he said he knew by experience, was a hard tramp,
and laughed at my dreading to attempt Loon Pond Mountain after that.
This encouraged father (as I hoped), and your letter urging me to go helped,
and finally all obstacles succumbed to my enthusiasm, which truly was
tempered with strict justice, for I told all who proposed going whatever I
knew of the difficulties.

The day was cool and beautiful, preceded and followed by days of
preternatural clearness, but the view satisfied us though somewhat smoky
southward. The Pollard brothers kindly took pains to make sapling
bridges, frail and slippery, over the worst places, so that only three of the
party got wet feet. At 8:30 we began the steep ascent through the woods
by the blazed trees. The pauses were frequent to rest, to gather moss or
birch-bark, to examine ferns, etc. for "Why should we hurry with all day
before us?" some one said; while Mr. Pollard entertained me with praises
of your rapid climbing. "Never seed ladies go like them, they never
stopped to rest; and as for that Mr. Cook he do walk faster than a horse
can travel. He beat the team goin' home, and I reckon their party would
tucker out any o' the men folks here about." Was he not mistaken in saying that you were but two hours from the river to the true summit?

One young gentleman and I endeavored to introduce some discipline into our little band by decreeing three minute rests only at stated
intervals and all agreed to obey our calls. Thus we went easily up, obtaining a glimpse of the little pond, waving a signal from the midway ledges,
whence Russell House was visible, and inspiring views began to appear,
stimulating me to hasten on. We suffered for water, until reaching the
spring by the large pond whose northern shore we skirted for one-half or
three-quarters of a mile, passing on our left superb granite ledges which
in one place projected over our heads while we crept across the lapping

waters on long logs which our guide said were submerged at high water making impassable our present route. Here we discovered a resounding echo from the opposite shore. The lake seemed enchantingly beautiful, with its deep bright blue waters glittering in the sunlight and ruffles into waves by the cool breeze, and in its setting of wild dense forest and bare craggy peaks among which Mr. Pollard pointed out the true summit ascertained by your party in 1880, since which he had taken no one to the top.

We lunched by a delicious spring on the shore of the lake at 11:45. After a long rest, everyone desired to push on for the top, for which we started at 12:50, reaching it in one hour and five minutes after a rough scramble up hill and down dale, across a ravine and up the opposite side, finding on our way fresh bear tracks, the foot prints of deer and signs of his browsing on the mountain ash.

On the summit, a fierce cold gale was blowing which forced us to tie down our hats, bundle on our wraps, and cling to each other. It threatened instant destruction to my new map which had to be directly folded up. Many thanks for your memorandum of the view; with this and the compass I had to be satisfied. How beautiful and grand it is! The Presidentials were free from clouds and Mt. Washington looked specially fine. At his left were Clay and Jefferson and possibly Adams, to the right Monroe and Franklin. In front of these to the right of the Willey Range was a long ridge scarred with rocky cliffs which we thought might be Webster. Bond and Guyot also look fine. Do you remember on the left of Cannon how rise the big nameless scallops[27] between it and Kinsman? Then come the interminable crests of Kinsman sweeping around to Blue Ridge and Moosilauke in the west. Kinsman Notch is not apparent and the Blue Ridge rises to the same regal height as Kinsman and Moosilauke, and all are unutterably beautiful. The big Franconias also thrilled me with a different sensation from this new standpoint. It is Garfield, I think, far away beyond Flume Mountain. Long did I gaze, over Black Mountain, Hitchcock, Hancock, etc.

Mr. Pollard built a fire on what we called the gravel bank. What kind of rock is it? And how do you account for its curious disintegration? The weather in time will wear it quite down to the ordinary ledges on which it stands now like some weird monument. We spent an hour on top.

On returning to the pond we found Will Pollard out on a raft fishing which accounted for the sudden appearance of the dog who had surprised us toiling summit-ward. On our descent we were accidentally led somewhat away from the usual route and thereby found the cave and scaled a mighty ledge, from the top of which was a view of the Presidentials almost equal to that from the summit, and afterwards obtained a grand over-

---

[27] Known today as the Cannon Balls.

look into the wilderness of the "Coolidges" and slide riven flanks of "Little Haystack." Two friends from Russell's were in the wagon to meet us and hear about the trip. We drove home by the sunset light, all highly elated with success though not ashamed to confess that we were very tired. This expedition was called "a good send off for Miss Stone," my departure occurring two days after.

Sunday eve, ten o'clock

This evening four of us have been up Sugar Hill to tea, remaining for the last glow of the sunset and coming down by moonlight, a charming walk new to all my companions who were highly delighted.

Have you read the interesting account in the *Echo* by Charlotte Ricker of the tramp made by Mr. Scott's party? Poor Miss Ricker had a hard time left behind with the pack-boy and guide. She ran a great risk in undertaking such a severe walk.

Will you be so very kind as to write me how the ascent of Kinsman compares in difficulty and length with that of Loon Pond Mountain? Does the view repay one as well? Can the directions in the *Osgood*, 1881 edition, be depended upon? And can you add any "items" of information which would be useful to an "ascendent?" Did you ascend by Slide Brook? And is the foot path and brook mentioned by Professor Gaetano Lanza[28] easy to find from the road? None such appear on the map. Has your uncle, or has anyone, measured or estimated the height of Loon Pond Mountain? What is considered the length of the bridle path to Moran Lake? O, dear! I did not mean to write such a catechism!

Your industry is astonishing; French, German, Italian, music, <u>such excursions</u>, and long letters, those to me alone must occupy considerable time, and doubtless other friends are equally favored. Lawn tennis, too! The drought here is becoming serious, and even the woods are losing their beauty. Father and Mother are still at North Woodstock, or they would send a message of friendly remembrance to your mother and aunt and yourself. With love, ever yours,

Isabella Stone

P.S. What time have you planned to leave Randolph? Not before October?

---

[28] Gaetano Lanza of Boston, MA, was a founding member of the AMC. He served as Vice-President in 1882.

Marian Pychowska writes to Isabella stone.

Ravine House
Randolph, N.H.
September 3, 1882

Dear Miss Stone,

Please do not imagine to yourself that the variety of my occupations argues great industry on my part. A very small amount of each one suffices. As to the few persons, besides yourself, to whom I write, they do not inspire me to indulge in very numerous or extended letters, and can hardly be called correspondents at all, since I am thankful to hear even once from each during the summer. Do not wonder then that it delights me to pour out my little store for you, when I am so royally "treated" in return.

Since the Gulch, August 16, my aunt and myself have not gone on the all day excursions. My mother and uncle have been on Pine Mountain and reported an interesting view and fine cliffs. My uncle has visited the Pond of Safety. He and Mr. Peek have measured Crescent Mountain proving it by both their barometers to be about equal in height to Randolph, that is, somewhat over 3,100 feet. Their most enviable trip has been that through the Ravine of the Castles. For this they had an early start, climbed Lowe's path to the shoulder of Adams, kept along the col toward Jefferson until they reached the headwall of their ravine, descended into it by a steep slide and followed the long stream valley out to the road. This ravine is of the same general character as King's, but scarcely as fine, in fact I could not but take a mean satisfaction in my uncle's avowal that they had seen nothing more beautiful than the view of Mt. Jefferson crowning the ravine, as seen from the Bowman Place, where they came out. This was the spot that so charmed us on our Boy Mountain day. They say that the Castles, so very striking from points this side, lose their character when seen from below.

My mother, aunt and I have employed three afternoons on the Mt. Madison path in measuring it. Mr. Watson supplied us with a surveyor's chain, which we have duly carried over the route to a point midway between the upper Salmacis Fall and the treeline. This point is two and three-quarter miles from the house, and we hope that a mile and a half more will put us on top of the mountain. Mr. Peek has painted signs to mark miles and half miles, and toward the top, the quarters too. It will require a whole day to finish the work, and I wish you could be here then to be proud with us of our own special way on to the Great Range done, even to the punctuation. Mr. Watson has already placed a large sign "Watson's Path" just above the treeline in order to draw attention to where it enters the woods, and made a line of cairns from there to the summit, so that a stranger coming over the Peaks could easily find the descent.

Not long ago a party of ladies and gentlemen from Philadelphia and elsewhere, under Mr. Lowe's guidance, went up his path and over to Washington one day, and the next day came down the Crawford bridle path. Later they completed the range by going up through King's Ravine and down our path. On this trip poor Mr. Lowe, by a misstep so slight that he can hardly account for the result, broke something in his leg, whether a small bone or a tendon he could not tell. This occurred near the top of Madison and the poor man had to limp all the way down here. Of course there is no more guiding for him this year, but unwilling to keep still as he ought, he goes about on crutches and sometimes drives down here to the Post Office and enjoys a good talk with my uncle and Mr. Peek. He has had much to do with surveying of town lots in Randolph, and lent my uncle his own private map to facilitate the finding of the Pond of Safety. The wood lots are fenced by lines of blazes which are a great aid in traversing the big wilderness back of us. I copied this map for my uncle and ought to feel learned in the properties of Randolph.

It is ten days since we did our last work on the path. Sunday we were in Gorham at church, having walked down Saturday. We anticipated returning also on foot, but my mother was so unwell we were obliged to take a team. She went through a little siege of disturbed digestion such as she and I are subject to especially at this season, in spite of all care. She sent for our old acquaintance Dr. Wight[29] of Gorham and soon rallied. The same trouble hangs obstinately about me in spite of medicine and dieting. I am not confined to my room nor supposed to be unfit for any amount of walking, but do not know if I dare hope to be one of the excursionists this week. At least I should be thankful for the store of pleasures I had earlier. Please do not think that this place is responsible for these troubles.

Having sufficiently displayed the dyspeptic egotist, let me atone by describing a lovely spot twenty or thirty rods from our house. It is the place our water comes from and is the most wonderful spring I ever saw. A beautiful shady yellow birch wood surrounds it and there, at the foot of a slope of broken rocks, gushes out the full fledged stream, the openings scarcely large enough to let out the impatient water. The long drought that has brought down the pride of larger brooks, seems not to have affected this in the least. It hurries down its beautiful mossy bed, hiding wherever it can among the rocks, till it crosses the road. Here it supplies, of its abundance, a splendid trough of ice cold water for man and beast. I once followed up the shallow, rock strewn hollow above the spring to see if I could find traces of surface water that fed it. Only a slight wash of long vanished rain water could I find, but peeping under the rocks, the

---

[29] Dr. Edward M. Wight came to Gorham, NH, from Casco, ME, in 1865 and continued his practice for forty-five years until his death in 1910. He was only the second physician to take up permanent residence in Gorham.

cool air that met me strengthened my fancy that our unfailing spring is fed by melting ice.

This evening's rain is hailed as a boon by all, and I cherish a hope that we sickly people may begin to sprout again. The late invasion of smoke makes us realize what a perfect atmosphere we have had this summer. We expect Mr. Sargent this week, to increase the number of transfers.

September 4

Now let me answer in detail your three long and interesting letters for which I have not yet had the grace to thank you.

A person occupying a single room in the Ravine House pays seven dollars a week. I believe Mr. Watson proposes putting a new wing out toward the east, and in this the rooms will be particularly desirable as being away from the morning noises of kitchen and stable. Front rooms are pleasant as having the view, but back rooms looking into the grove are cool. Milk is excellent and very abundant, butter and bread unusually good, meat unusually good, except the breakfast beef steak which is often tough. Living arrangements are all one could desire, and the charges very reasonable. Since the middle of August the black flies have retired higher up the mountains, and one can now sit in the grove without molestation.

"Sanborn's" in Campton seems to be a favorite place with artists, and the meadows are very beautiful and the house itself attractive, but it has always appeared to us to be situated too much under the hill to have much breeze or view. However, when I remember the utterly unfounded prejudice we had against the situation of the Black Mountain House before we went there, I am ready to think I may be prejudiced against Sanborn's too.

Seeing Miss Whitman dispelled a very wrong impression I had received from reading some things in *Appalachia*. She is a person of about thirty-five, evidently very independent, but ladylike and unassuming. I think she is the most thoroughly good lady mountaineer I have ever seen, short and stout and therefore somewhat scant of breath, but energetic and untiring. She seems to go through exposure, fatigue and campfood with unimpaired digestion, which certainly is not the case with poor Miss Ricker. Under the circumstances I think this novice showed a good deal of pluck, for the Twin Mountain excursion was really very trying. Their only hardship I can not quite appreciate is the constant thirst. A slice of lemon or a peppermint lozenge I have found a sufficient alleviation, but then I have never had such a continuous trial.

Miss Whitman's dress, when I saw her, was a dark blue flannel down to her boot tops and a rather long half fitting sack belted in, relieved with a little white trimming. I should think that for underbrush Miss Whitman must use something stronger than flannel. My aunt and I have found some nice fine woolen jean in Gorham for which she looked in vain in New York.

Do not depreciate your explorations. You being obliged to do them slowly gives you the advantage of thoroughly seeing and taking in what you go through, which is often not the case with us. You are thus better fitted to describe and I am sure this is abundant material for an interesting paper on the by-roads and little known views about North Woodstock. The Elbow Pond trip was no exploit to be sneezed at and the information regarding proper names of brooks is valuable to those who will bring out our new AMC map. I like your idea of keeping the old name of Lonesome Lake in Tamarack Brook, and think you ought to place that suggestion also before the map makers.

Most of my excursions have been over beaten ground and so would not be of special interest to the club. I have sketched out an account of the Gulch, and my mother one of Randolph Mountain. A more ambitious work I am going to attempt, is a map sketch of the northern slopes of Madison with the true streams and ridges. All the maps are so deplorably wrong.

You wonder how my aunt and I climb trees. Consider first that the middle sized spruces were conveniently branched down to the ground. The getting up is very easy as the skirts come naturally after. A graceful descent is more difficult, as the same skirts are apt to remain above, but my uncle and Mr. Peek considerately left us, so that grace did not have to be considered.

I do not remember how long we were climbing to Lonesome Lake. You know Mr. Hinkley was with us, and Major Beebe with several chickens and a gridiron. It rejoices me even more to think you have seen the view from Loon Pond Mountain than that you have stood on Lafayette, the first more recherche. Your description brings our expedition over the same ground so clearly before me—the ledge under which we passed in coming back round the pond, the cave, and the bear tracks. When we were on top it was also blowing a gale and was very cold. That crumbling rock is of the same character as the debris of the great Tripyramid slide, and the disintegration is owing to the rotting of the feldspar leaving a "gravel bank" of quartz and mica.

The Pollard's imaginative remembrance has treated us kindly. Miss Whitman reported that from their descriptions one would imagine all our party to be seven foot giants. We have no record here of what time we took in the ascent, but I think likely it was a little over two hours from the further side of the ford. We were nearly an hour getting all the party over the river, got started up the mountain about nine o'clock, were on the top a little after eleven and back at Pollard's for a two o'clock dinner. We estimated the height at something between 2,700 and 3,000 feet, Scar Ridge being 3,800 feet.

Kinsman is certainly a much more difficult climb, but I should think it quite possible for you with a sensible and experienced guide. Mr. Lanza's account gives you all (and more than) the information that my memory supplies with regard to the way. We did ascend by Slide Brook and found

its beautiful ledges quite worthy a visit for their own sake. To the foot of
the slide you would find no trouble, and even its ascent I hardly think
would overcome your powers. It is from this point to the top that good
guiding is required. My uncle took us through very little bad scrub, but I
have no doubt one could find a plenty. Moss bridged holes are certainly
abundant. The whole distance is about three miles.

To the description of the view, I only think of adding the number of
beautiful high mountain tarns you see. Lonesome Lake lies way down in
the forest (by the way, is that not a superb view of Kinsman from Mr.
Prime's[30] cottage?) and Gordon Ponds seem larger, or at least nearer than
the map warrants. Most cunning of all is little Kinsman Pond nestling just
under the topmost cliffs of the mountain's lower head, the chief one as
seen from the valley. I do not think the view nearly as rich in variety as
that from Loon Pond Mountain, but if you have never been over to Bolles'[31],
the mountain itself is very grand from there with its two heads and the
ravine of Slide Brook, and it would be easy to visit the latter. Having done
this, you could better judge of the advisability of scaling the summit.

My aunt wishes me to thank you for your letter to her, and will answer when my present fever abates for want of material to write about,
and gives her a chance to put in a word. Believe me always,

Yours very sincerely,

M. M. Pychowska

P.S. How long do you expect to be at Goodnow's?

* * * * * * * * * * * *

Marian Pychowska writes to Isabella Stone.

Bartlett House

Upper Bartlett, N.H.

September 14, 1882

Dear Miss Stone,

This vignette[32] at the top of my paper is more properly the Bartlett
Haystack, alias Mt. Silver Spring, and the puff of vapor above represents
the easterly storm that has housed us here at Mr. Frank George's[33]. My
industrious mother has visited the village store for sewing materials, and
has brought me the implements for writing you a continuation of my

---

[30] Dr. William C. Prime was a famous editor, traveller, and angler. He was the
author of *I Go A-Fishing*, *Along New England Roads* and *Among the Northern Hills*. He
spent many summers at his cottage near the Profile House in Franconia Notch.
    [31] Reverend Simon Bolles of Bethlehem, NH. He was the author of *The Early
History of Bethlehem*.
    [32] This embossed vignette depicts Italy's Mount Etna displaying its active
volcano.
    [33] The proprietor of the Bartlett House.

chronicle. Let us be methodical and go back to the beginning.

Mr. Sargent joined us last Wednesday as expected. On Friday we started early with the best intentions for finishing the measurement of the Mt. Madison Path. More than half the household, including a number of ladies, made our work the occasion of making the ascent of the mountain, workers and pleasure seekers being independent of each other. The weather promised rain and the clouds poured down the valley from the west, but when we got up about 4,000 feet we left them below us. The miles and half miles were duly marked by Mr. Peek's signs, and the chaining continued one-eighth mile above the treeline. Some time had been devoured by a number of small mishaps such as losing our hammer, so that midday was past, and the white sea of cloud was rising toward us, threatening to overwhelm the island peaks. Further measuring was postponed to a more favorable day, and three of us made a push for the top, before the mist should make the way over the rocks difficult to keep. We hardly dared to linger, for ghostlike shreds of vapor were stretching up their arms from King's Ravine and a sunlit flood poured over Adams. The sensible party enjoyed the same sights from the lower knobs, and all returned in good condition to the house. Most of these ladies were utterly unused to climbing, yet they could have reached the top with but little additional labor, if the weather had been suitable. Please remember this if ever you go to the Ravine House.

The day on Madison seemed to be the thing my mother and I needed to complete our cure and make us feel equal to Carter Dome. Sunday was too unnaturally black and clear to promise well for Monday. However, arrangements having been made for an early breakfast, and the morning giving a chance of clearing, Mr. Watson drove us off at 7:30 and got us to the Glen a little after nine. In a few minutes we climbed the pasture, where we might have spent a day studying the grand mountain wall whose peaks were still so clear against the gray sky. Entering the woods, we followed the aqueduct all the way to Nineteen-Mile Brook, where we found a shingle pointing to "Carter Pond". It is one of the loveliest paths I ever walked over, through an old unmarred forest, full of beautiful ferns. The ascent is long and gradual, between the ever nearing walls of Carter and Wildcat, of which one gets occasional glimpses. The crest of the Notch is very narrow, affording lovely views north and south. From here one goes down steeply about two hundred feet to the basin where the tiny ponds hide. Both of the Notch walls are very fine, but the dark towering cliffs of Wildcat are especially grand, reminding me of Eagle Cliffs above Echo Lake. We reserved the enjoyment of these beauties till our return wishing, if possible, to get some view from the Dome before the clouds shut down.

The long mile to the summit is very steep in the lower part, and it was breathless work hurrying up the path, making as few pauses as possible. When we neared the supreme arch of the curve, there was a vision of mist clinging to the spruces above us. Finally we emerged into a small clearing surrounded by spruces six or seven feet high, through which several vistas have been cut. Vistas to what? The broad dome-top was our world, beyond which nothing could be seen but an unvarying gray chaos. No view being obtainable, the record bottle claimed our attention. The only lady whose name we noticed therein is Miss Whitman heading the Appalachian party of two or three years ago. I believe our party was only the fourth recorded this season.

My mother was so chilly on top, she returned almost immediately to the notch. You perhaps know how she dreads anyone's lighting a fire in the woods. A burning crest near the Glen House had given her an occasion that morning to ask that none might be made where she was. But it was so penetratingly cold that, after she left us, no one objected to Mr. Watson's making a small fire. We warmed and rested ourselves an hour and a half, no change taking place meanwhile in the surrounding grayness.

At two o'clock we left our desert island, and, as we got below the cloud blanket, could see once more toward the south, the valleys and mountain skirts. We indemnified ourselves for the disappointment on top, by lingering round the ponds. On the south of their basin there is a rampart of broken rocks, like those in King's Ravine, and from the edge of this we had a good look down the Wildcat Valley to Jackson, beyond which we could imagine Kearsarge, Doublehead, etc. Near the ponds there is a very complete cabin-camp[34], with two rooms, a stove, etc.

At a quarter to five we mounted our wagon again at the Glen, the weather having so far favored us as not to rain. It was really a most delightful excursion and made us all wish to repeat it. Owing to the coolness of the day, we were able to make the four and one-half miles to the summit in five minutes over three hours.

That storm brought no rain to Randolph, but we found its traces in Bartlett, where the parched fields evidently needed it much more. Tuesday afternoon it cleared beautifully and a party of seven was organized for a three day's trip. Mr. Watson was determined to do himself credit and we set forth in style with a good four-horse team. The familiar Pinkham woods and the Glen seemed more lovely than ever, that perfect Wednesday morning, and I wondered what good use you were making of such an exceptional day.

My aunt had never been through Pinkham Notch before nor had she seen Glen Ellis. We halted some time to take in the grand view of

---

[34] This, along with Lowe's Camp on Mount Adams, was one of the first AMC camps and was the first enclosed cabin, predating Carter Notch Hut by at least thirty-two years. The cabin accommodated six sleepers comfortably.

Tuckerman and Huntington's ravines, and then lower down as we neared Jackson. All of us, except the two enthusiastic painters, Mr. Peek and Miss Barstow[35], dined sumptuously at the Glen Ellis House[36]. Afterward we joined the enthusiasts who were sketching on a neighboring hill, whence Mounts Washington, Doublehead, the Moats, Attitash and many lesser heights were visible.

At three we were en route for Upper Bartlett. Beyond Glen Station the road was entirely new to me, and I wished for four pair of eyes to see all round at once. Turning into the Saco Valley was like coming into a new world. Carter Dome looming behind was the last reminder of our northern region. What a delight it was to see the steep slope of the north peak of Tripyramid through a gap between the nearer mountains. Of course my map was on my knee to help in identifying each point that came into sight. The dark, slender cone of Mt. Silver Spring struck me as particularly beautiful. But Carrigain, the object of our desires, to visit which our party had set out, how magnificently it commands the Bartlett Valley!

At five o'clock we drew up at George's, and, depositing our things, some of us set out at once to explore the neighborhood. Around the corner toward the north runs a lovely side road through a maple wood to the Saco. From the long, shaky bridge we looked down the broad, pebbly river bed with its band of water and picturesque shore, to Kearsarge. Up the intervale the sun was sinking over the Sawyer's River Valley. The lines of Carrigain and Hancock are very fine. With high hopes we went to bed last night, but rose at six this morning to find a dull gray sky. However we must make the best of it as long as it does not positively rain. The party is reduced to the desperate four, my aunt, my uncle, Mr. Sargent and myself, my mother having made her plan to visit Mt. Langdon. Alas, even the Carrigain desperadoes were obliged to return. Mr. Watson had hardly driven us a half mile on our way, when it began to sprinkle, and there was no hope of an amendment. The whole country is so rejoicing in this downpour, it would be shameful to repine, especially when we had pleasure enough yesterday to last a week. One of us at least has made a good use of this rainy day. Miss Barstow came along with us with the special desire of making sketches about the Frankenstein Cliff. She made a successful negotiation with the Portland and Ogdensburg Railroad offi-

---

[35] Miss S. M. Barstow was an artist who disguised her identity by signing only her initials to her work, conceding that it would not sell as readily if known to be by a woman. She exhibited her paintings nationally for more than thirty years. Miss Barstow resided in Brooklyn, NY.

[36] A boardinghouse in Jackson, NH, that was opened to the public in 1876. The establishment was later known as the Fairview and was part of the Wentworth Hall complex. The Glen Ellis House was located on the Jackson Village Road next to the Thompson House.

cials, who were very obliging, letting her off where she wished and taking her in on a return trip. She returned a very wet but very satisfied lady.

The accommodation here is very good, and you know how many attractions it offers to the explorer. The nearness of the railroad is the only apparent draw back. My uncle and Mr. Sargent were so balked in their effort to reach Carrigain last year, that they are determined to wait for the proper weather, and I hope we can persuade my aunt to do the same. The rest of us are to start early for home, by Crawford Notch and Cherry Moun÷ tain Road. I hope to find a letter from you waiting for me at Randolph, and there finish this long scribble to you.

Randolph
September 17

"Line Storm" # 1 is over and it looks to me as if # 2 were brewing. After the thunderstorm of Thursday evening the stars came out, and Friday morning the thin clouds seemed to be melting fast and the beautiful circle of mountains looked out at us inviting us to stay longer. About eight o'clock we drove away from Mr. George's, dropped the two Carrigainers at the Sawyer's River Road with many good wishes, and a little envy, and then gave all our eyes to the beauties of the notch. You know them, I believe, from the railroad, which everyone says gives the best opportunity for views. This is my first trip through Crawford Notch and it has only whetted my appetite. I should dearly like to walk over the road stopping a week or more at George's and several days at the Willey House[37]. As we neared the latter place a fierce wind drove down the valley sweeping along columns of rain. Still, it was not thick enough to hide the grand mountain slopes on either hand. The view points along the high road are rare, but the yellow and white birch forest was so exquisite we had no mind to wish it away. The rain brought out all the lovely colouring of the trunks and foliage, and the interlacing of boughs above the wet leaf strewn road made more beautiful forest pictures than I had ever seen before, even in the Franconia Notch. Silver and Flume Cascades, which we stopped some time to enjoy, were finely swollen. Driving through the "Gate of the Notch" we met the full force of the wind, and the chilled rain beat in our faces.

At midday we were glad to stop at the old White Mountain House[38], and dry ourselves in the comfortable hall. After dinner the storm had

---

[37] This hostelry was originally built by Nathaniel T. P. Davis in 1792. In 1826, there was a disastrous landslide in which the new owner Samuel Willey, his wife, five children and two hired men were all killed. The damaged building was repaired, enlarged and occupied in 1844 by Horace Fabyan who was the next proprietor of the establishment. The Willey House burned in 1898.

[38] Horace Fabyan's original White Mountain House burned in 1853. This, the second White Mountain House, was located across the road from the Fabyan House and next to the railroad station in the town of Carroll.

White Mountain House

lulled, and, though the mountains were still invisible, we all thoroughly
enjoyed the Cherry Mountain Road with its rich varied forest so different
from that in the Notch. Miss Barstow has convinced me that the woods
are never so wonderful as in the rain. Our lively team got us home about
five o'clock. We thought my uncle and Mr. Sargent would have given up
Carrigain on Friday when the storm increased so, and would have waited
another day at Livermore Mills[39] or at George's, so we were rather surprised when they arrived home yesterday by way of the Portland &
Ogdensburg road and Jefferson.

Being somewhat sheltered by the mountains, they had kept on in the
teeth of the storm. An obscurity in the path obliged my uncle to make his
own way to the top, but coming down they had no trouble in keeping the
track and required only two hours to reach the Mills. Their only view was
a little glimpse of the Saco Valley, Kearsarge and Chocorua. So, although
the 'formidable' mountain has been conquered, it would not display its

---

[39] Located on the Sawyer River, Livermore Mills was the lumber processing
point for the logging operations in the surroundings of Mount Carrigain.

treasures, and I hope the next attack may be made by a larger force.

The Ravine House is still well filled and one party, besides ours expects to remain till the end of the month. It is getting more beautiful every day, and there is still quite a list of things to be done. I am anxious to know how you are spending these days. Please remember me to Dr. and Mrs. Stone if they are with you, and also to Mr. and Mrs. Goodnow and believe me always,

Your friend,
Marian Pychowska

* * * * * * * * * * * *

Marian Pychowska writes to Isabella Stone.

Ravine House
Randolph, N.H.
September 22, 1882

Dear Miss Stone,

You are making an unusually late stay in the hills, and I hope you are going to have a string of perfect days as a "bon bouche" before you go. A weather wise native here announces that we are only in the middle of this long drawn out equinoctial storm. Has it not seemed as if the winds were dancing round the mountains from east to west? We have had such a glorious summer that most of us have no excuse for complaining of the enforced rest, but it is somewhat hard for Mr. Sargent whose short two weeks are melting away. He has not yet had a fair view from any mountain top.

Tuesday, the day you spent in the notch, we also risked a wetting. We surveyed a new route[40] to Mt. Adams, which will bring its summit almost as near us as that of Madison. About two and a half miles up on the "Watson Path", instead of climbing out of Salmacis Glen to the east to reach Madison, the new path (if ever it be made) will climb the narrow spur that divides the above mentioned glen from King's Ravine. The rocks and "gate-ways" along this narrow crest are very fine and it affords superb views of the Ravine, and the peaks of Madison, "John Quincy", and Adams. If the project be carried out, it will be an easy matter for a good walker to visit the two great peaks, ascending one and coming down the other, the whole distance not exceeding nine and one-half miles. We dined once more at Madison Spring, and came down Snyder Brook to the path. A more beautiful brook I never saw. My uncle and I are now waiting for a suitable day to finish the measurement on Madison, my aunt and Mr. Sargent hope to ascend the Ravine and Adams.

---

[40] This trail is known today as the Scar Trail.

I hope your plan may be carried out, even though we may not be here to welcome you at the Ravine House. The time of our starting for home is not yet decided, but will probably be either Friday, 29th or Monday the 2nd. Friday is, I believe, the last day of the through express from Jefferson to New York. If we leave on Monday I do not know what line we shall take. Four new arrivals are expected here, so there will be a household of six or seven after our departure. Mrs. Watson thinks she can give you such a room as you require. If the two large front rooms where there are chimney privileges, be occupied, she can give you a front room that is warmed by the kitchen chimney. I hope we shall be here, at least for a day when you come, but if not, I am sure Miss Barstow, our artist acquaintance, will interest herself to show you some of our sights. Do come if it be possible.

How have you managed to get my yet unmade map and small descriptive papers already printed in *Appalachia*? Certainly if it ever be you shall know.

Yours very sincerely,
M. M. Pychowska

* * * * * * * * * * * *

Edith Cook writes to Isabella Stone.

Hoboken, N.J.
October 8, 1882

My dear Miss Stone,

It seems hardly your letter that I answer this afternoon though it lies open on my writing table before me, it seems rather yourself that I talk with and answer as you stood on the porch of the Ravine House last Monday morning or bade me within the door so sympathetic a goodbye. The fairness of the near past always seems strange and so, this afternoon it is as usual, hard to realize that it was but just a week ago that we watched the sunset lights from Randolph Hill and dropped down into the cool and golden shadows of our grassy short cut home.

I see from my window now the city in the sunshine, a bit of the blue river and the warm sky between the boughs and browning leaves of the lindens and the greener ones of maple and willow and I feel that the active life of the town is perhaps more perfect in its way than our life of refreshment among the hills—since we must in some things take more heed than the sparrows—but yet how gladly would I sun myself this afternoon, as on last Sunday, on the grassy heights among our summer hills to which the past week must have given so intensified a glory. We enjoyed much our morning ride to Gorham, save for the melancholy of feeling that the "mountain summer" was at an end, as doubtless you enjoyed your drive later to Shelburne. And the bright morning gave us dear views of all our old haunts and mountain friends along the Androscoggin Valley. Success, in especial, looming up, a massive mountain worthy to be admired, its bare white top a sharp contrast to the memory of the light green Alpine pasture that our campfire so sadly devastated.

Just before reaching Portland we bade goodbye to Mr. Sargent for there our ways parted, he keeping on to Boston where he was due about five o'clock, while we took our way over the Portland and Rochester road to keep on and on until nearly midnight when we at last found supper and rest on the boat at New London. You know none of us had ever been before on this route between Portland and Nashua and so it was supposed to possess in an eminent degree the pleasure of novelty, but our way passed through very dreary level lands for all the hours between one and after five, though the country might perhaps have seemed to us more interesting had we just come from the city instead of from the mountains, and such mountains! Still, we did have one fine view of the Mt. Washington range, a clear blue pile against the sky of the low horizon so far away, this view being somewhere, I think, in the neighborhood of the Saco River whose lowland waters made one think of the great Notch and the swollen waters of our rain bound stay at Upper Bartlett with its disappointments and its compensating beauties. This far away vista of the mountains seemed at least a noble farewell, though fleeting as the wave of a handkerchief from a station platform.

Still farther along the road we had views of lesser mountains on the horizon, supposedly Chocorua, Whiteface and Passaconaway and then our beloved New Hampshire hills were laid away in the cedar and sweet spices of memory for another year. After we passed Nashua and the strong twilight began to fill the sky, we had the firm and dark blue lines of Wachusett and the Peterborough hills against the light and over the rich rolling uplands of Massachusetts. And then with the darkness increased the weariness of the long day's travel, a day that grew almost sultry as the hours wore on in the dusty and crowded train. In the early morning on the boat, I tried to see the comet, dressing and leaving our state room for that purpose, but, though I saw a fine dawn over the dark Sound with its far shining light-houses, clouds covered where the comet should have been seen and I was just too late, my brother having been more fortunate in being earlier than I before the clouds had gathered just where they were, by me, least desired.

We reached New York in good time and were refreshed by the cool bright morning and by the smiling visage of our cook who, when we reached home, gave us the most enthusiastic welcome. The house we found delightfully clean owing to the faithful labors of both our handmaidens and I, as housekeeper, am now further delighted with the excellent appetites with which the family does justice to my marketing. We have all been very busy, of course, during these first days of our coming home. My first day was devoted to fitting myself once more to the shell of my room, winding, as it were, the silk of my cocoon about me only that we human chrysalids lie not so quietly in our winter wrap awaiting our butterfly summer. I often think my folded hands of the summer would scarcely give anyone a true idea of the life of their owner though they might betray her natural indolence and how kindly she took to ease.

Since our return I have put down stair carpets and helped Marian take down, dust and rehang all the pictures in the front parlor. Marian and I have dusted, too, all the books in the back parlor, a continuous work of nearly five hours. Tomorrow the pictures in the back parlor will have their turn and then Tuesday I go out of town for the day to see a favorite cousin who has lately had malarial fever. Wednesday there will doubtless be some other household work and then I devote my energies to making grape jelly and then, will it be poetry or painting? I fear not, but rather the busy needle started to set things in order for the winter though I have a vision of a little picture of Mt. Adams and John Quincy as one of the first things to be tried when I once more take up my brushes. In the mean time our friends drop in one by one as they hear of, or find time after, our return. We plan concerts to be attended, and, in the evenings, or at meals, or on the street, call back the mountain echoes of the summer.

I have written today a long letter to Miss Maria Tilden whom you will remember from our summer together at the Goodnow House, giving her an account of our last week at Randolph when so much was crowded into a few days, enough almost to make the feet of an invalid ache at the very thought of such activity. Miss Tilden, you know, is an Appalachian and is unselfish enough to enjoy by proxy the exploits of her friends, taking pride in their strength even when a prisoner in her own room.

Mr. Sargent writes me of the unlikeness of Boston pavements to mountain paths, as of the east wind and foggy weather to the late fall breezes of Randolph. There was an active inspiration in that east wind that blew over Madison the day that the Ravine House had its scouting parties so scattered over the mountain that is possibly lacking in the same wind by the sea level when the feet seem to have been clipped of the wings that bore them over the mountains. In town they become Pegasus in harness once more, and Pegasus when well broken can do very excellent work.

I have not forgotten my promise to copy and send you the "Success" sonnets, this shall be done when I have a little more time. Please remember me kindly to your father and mother and believe me,

                              Your friend sincerely,
                              Edith W. Cook

Marian Pychowska writes to Isabella Stone.

Hoboken, N.J.
October 27, 1882

My dear Miss Stone,

Here is a quiet evening hour I may use in a little letter communication with you. First let me thank you for the birthday greeting that surprised me last Monday morning. I remember as we were climbing Randolph Hill the last time, we each told a number of dates of birthdays in our respective families, but how did you remember mine out of such confusion? You were the only friend to send me a good wish.

At the end of this busy month we are getting fairly settled into winter quarters. In the midst of all the house cleaning, preserving and other home duties that have occupied our time, our summer life has been woven in by means of the many letters we have received from our summer friends. Our "eastern mail" has become a standing joke in the family. Nearly every day comes something from "downeast", and often the postman has half a dozen packages of various kinds, and all from the Boston way. My uncle's and Mr. Sargent's walk over the peaks[41] was noticed in the *Transcript* (with a few errors, of course) and copies were sent us both from Boston and Portsmouth. Professor Fay writes to my mother that, before this exploit, he had spoken to his pedestrian friends of the possibility of starting up Madison and over the whole range to the Crawford Notch in a day, but he evidently had not contemplated the little flourish of twenty-three or twenty-four miles on the road, as a finale. Our Appalachian walkers are so apt to have some scientific work to accomplish by the way, and to be, moreover, weighed down by twenty or thirty pounds of camera or micrometer level, that such a fly away feat is not convenient for them. Professor Fay writes also that the excursion to Pack Monadnock was a great success, and that they had a view sweeping round from Agamenticus, via Washington, etc., to Wachusett. Oh, how many plans we make of things we would do if we only lived in Boston, and every year draws us more strongly that way, but then how many other things would remain undone, if we had all those delightful distractions.

My mother has sent in her botanical notes to the Club, and I have made a map sketch of those much misrepresented northern slopes of Madi-

---

[41] On September 27, 1882, Eugene Cook and George Sargent traversed all the peaks on the Presidential Range (approximately twenty-four miles and 8,800 feet of uphill climbing). Beginning in Randolph at 5:00 A.M., they arrived in Crawford Notch in time for supper at the White Mountain House. After supper, they walked back to Randolph along the Cherry Mountain Road through Jefferson Meadows (another twenty-three or twenty-four miles). They arrived back at the Ravine House at 1:24 A.M. This remains today a magnificent feat and one of the greatest day-long hikes in the history of tramping in the White Mountains.

son and Adams and sent it in with some notes regarding topography, paths, etc. My uncle had a card, the other day, from Mr. Peek, with a very good watercolor drawing of the Castellated Ridge from near Hubbard Hunt's.

We have also had a long letter, from Mr. Watson, giving a graphic account of the state of things in Randolph. Miss Barstow and the Lyfords intended to stay on until the first of November and he still expected another boarder. The leaves had fallen so much they could see Snyder Brook from the house, and all the waterfalls were finer than they had been since spring. He could not begin building this fall, on account of his having accepted a large lumber contract, to be filled this winter. Thinks he may build in the spring. The Osgood guide people had written to him for a circular to embody in the new edition. He wished we were there to help him make a circular, and thought Miss Barstow would have to help. I believe the AMC meeting at Jefferson has brought Mr. Watson thus into notice. Mr. Kennard's little stay at the Ravine House was not for nothing. Mr. Watson's letter speaks of lovely mild October weather so I suppose our siege of easterly cloudiness has not extended so far. We see by the papers that you have had it, and that "in steady old Massachusetts even the weathercocks are invariable in their indications—they know no south, no north, no west!"

My aunt sends love and thanks for the postal card received. With kind remembrances to Dr. & Mrs. Stone, believe me always,

Your friend,

M. M. Pychowska

* * * * * * * * * * * *

Isabella Stone writes to Marian Pychowska (draft copy).

Framingham, Mass.
October 29, 1882

Dear Miss Pychowska,

Nearly two hours after your departure from the Ravine House, having enjoyed a hasty review of Miss Barstow's sketches, I drove away with one of the old shoes thrown after visitors for good luck. What a delightful ride it was looking backward nearly all the way to Gorham in order to watch every changing feature of the great peaks so rapidly receding, so crystal clear in the cold western wind and radiant sunshine! Carter Notch and Wildcat were duly noticed and the growing impressiveness of Baldcap and Moriah. At "Lary's"[42] came a pleasant call with Miss Ruth, Miss Ann and

---

[42] The Lary House in Gorham, NH, was built by Andrew Gilman Lary in 1835. Lary operated the boardinghouse until his death in 1884.

Lary House and Mount Hayes

Mrs. Hitchcock, Dawn,[43] all of whom well remembered Dr. and Mrs. Stone and their little girl, who had of course grown beyond their recognition.

Here Mr. Laban Watson became the driver to Harvey Philbrook's[44], where one of the best front rooms with a fire was assigned to me by Miss Fanny Philbrook[45], who is now practically the head of the household. An excellent dinner was deftly served for the half dozen boarders, pleasant Cambridge people intending to remain until October 19.

Mention was made of a route to "Crow's Nest" opened this season, and a lady who had twice ascended offered to lead me (after her customary siesta) to the entrance of the path, which they said was difficult for a stranger to find in the hilly pine covered pasture back of the house, traversed by misleading cow paths. It proved "difficult," for she searched a long time in vain. As the summit is invisible from the house and the lady could not tell its direction, while the hour was getting late (four o'clock),

---

[43] Dawn Lary Hitchcock was the wife of Colonel John R. Hitchcock. John, who died in 1879, was the proprietor of the first Alpine House in Gorham and the Tip-Top House on the summit of Mount Washington. Ruth and Ann were Dawn's sisters.

[44] The Philbrook Farm Inn. Although known as Harvey Philbrook's, his son Augustus was the proprietor by this time.

[45] Fanny was Harvey's daughter and Augustus' sister. She was the sixth of eight children.

discretion was the better part of valor and we consulted Mr. Augustus Philbrook, who at once showed us the right course. After a few yards, the lady, fatigued by our previous exertions, returned to the house leaving me alone to the charming little adventure of finding the way to the top by the fresh blazes, which were, for most of the distance quite small and infrequent, while the so called "path" became either faint underfoot, or was obscured by forking and intersecting logging roads, and finally disappeared altogether on the edge of a large clearing. The view from the summit is indeed beautiful and one must regret its already evident obstruction from the rising tops of a forest of young growth. While pitying you, whirled along in the smoky rattle and roar of the railway journey, I thought you would be pleased could you know at that moment how "my heart was delighted" with the spot whither you had wished to be my guide. The second knoll was visited also for the northeastern prospect and the house reached again in season to dress before the tea bell rang at six o'clock.

Next day was glorious weather and if you had been there would we not have tried Baldcap together, at least as far as Dream Lake? Instead, I walked to Lead Mine Bridge where river and mountains are so picturesque, and on to Charles E. Philbrook's (four and one-half miles) where I took dinner, examined rooms and wandered through the devious wood walks near the house, visited special view points mentioned by friends, and in the afternoon walked back with the occasional divergences to the bluffs of the river and a call at Gates' Cottage not forgetting the knoll opposite. Mother and daughter were pleased to hear from your family. As "The Crag" was in plain sight from the road, seeming like the first step toward Baldcap, I yielded to the temptation to strike for the summit, having for companion the large dog, Prince, from Gates' who volunteered his services. It is (as you know) quite a steep little climb though short, but in twenty-five minutes doggy and I were panting on the top most cliff, he wagging his tail in delight with his head in my lap. In default of a tail to wag, I hugged him tight and then danced about the rocks in a manner which could have dispelled your illusion of my being too dignified to sit on a fence for "O, what a good time I'm having today!" and "Isn't this a lovely view?" It surpasses that from "Crow's Nest." Do you think so? And what a contrast to the awe inspiring grandeur of King's Ravine! The clear frosty air and the glow of a gorgeous sunset made full of keen delight the homeward walk, from the base, of two miles, which was easily accomplished in thirty-five minutes. Prince would have been my escort the entire distance, but after half a mile I decided to send him back, first letting him present each forepaw for a handshake while his brown eyes beamed with intelligence.

The four peaks of Baldcap named in your Appalachian paper were immediately recognized and Dream Lake located between the Bald Ledge and the dark dome of the true summit. From Randolph Hill is not Mt. Joe hidden by Mt. Hayes? And did you not reckon Middle Mountain as the first peak of Baldcap counting first, second, third in the direction from Robinson's Peak towards Goose Eye? Mr. Philbrook emphatically denied that a path had been made to Dream Lake and also said that the proper name for "Giant Falls" was "Cascade of the Clouds" and that it had no existence except within twenty-four hours after heavy rains. He does no guiding himself, but can furnish a competent man when parties desire one, which is seldom. For natives and boarders, Baldcap seems to have acquired a name that is a "terror to evildoers" and good ones too, forbidding all approach.

Wednesday morning came the novel experience of fording the broad Androscoggin to Shelburne depot to take the train for Portland.

After a brief visit in Salem, once more in our little home, dear father and mother welcomed me to their arms both interested to hear of the Jefferson trip, the pleasant meeting with your family, and the nice boarding places discovered.

Having just finished a second reading of the book, *Gentilism*, I shall return it to you by this mail with sincere thanks for the loan. It is an instructive and interesting work well worth the attention of scholars. You mentioned the chapters on "Brahmanism" and "Buddhism" as particularly interesting. After reading these, a person desirous of obtaining a complete and fair idea of the religion of the Hindus ought to read at least certain portions of the volume on India of Samuel Johnson's work on *Oriental Religions and their relation to Universal Religion*. Do not attribute this suggestion to the partiality of friendship. Strangers and critics of great repute have pronounced his book one of the best ever published on its subject. He certainly shows a rare spiritual appreciation of those far off religions of antiquity, many of whose best elements seem difficult of comprehension to our Western and modern mode of thought, and he puts a just interpretation upon their philosophy and its practical results, even as we should wish a learned pagan to do who was writing in a similar manner the history of Christianity. A little book by C. D. B. Mills is also good, entitled *Indian Saint; Buddha and Buddhism*.

Please give kind regards to your father and tell him the memory of sweet strains he improvised in that little parlor among the hills will be a lasting joy to me, whose opportunities of hearing good music are sadly few, especially in the quiet way in which it comes as a benediction. Would that I could hear him play on the piano which is, as he says, "his own instrument."

Probably you have long ago seen the item in the *Transcript* about the wonderful tramp taken by Mr. Cook and Mr. Sargent. Do you not fear such a flattering notice in the leading newspaper of the "Hub of the Universe" will make those famous pedestrians more than ever "puffed up" and stimulate them to some feat next year which will surely lay them low upon a bed of suffering and woe?.

If there are no mountain excursions to write about now, remember that your doings and your thoughts are always of interest.

Your friend,
Isabella

* * * * * * * * * * * *

Marian Pychowska writes to Isabella Stone.

Hoboken, N.J.
November 1, 1882

Dear Isabella,

You do not know how I enjoyed your letter. It brought back so vividly those dear old spots about Shelburne, which I love even down to the little dingy railway station, where we used to get the first snuff of cool evening air, on our arrival. I am so glad you had that lovely weather for your stay there. That day, going down the valley in the cars, I watched for all the well remembered views, Baldcap, "Success", that beautiful Ingalls River valley with Goose Eye at the end, the grand distant view of Old Speck, Saddle Back, Puzzle, etc. from just below Bethel, and keeping my weather eye on the sharp blue peaks of Madison and Adams whenever the curves brought them in sight. I believe my aunt wrote you how, that perfect day, the mountains could be seen and recognized from way down between Portland and Rochester.

What a famous walk you had all the way up to Charles Philbrook's, and to think of your having enough superfluous energy to climb "Crag" on your home journey! You have taken possession of that country in true Appalachian style, as one of the "sole-leather aristocracy". It was pleasant to be escorted by "Prince". From your account of him, I should say he had improved since the days of his foolish puppyhood, when I knew him. I am very glad you like Philbrook's. I remember it as a most homelike place, with a delightful sense of ease and abundance about the whole establishment. Miss Fanny, with her native dignity and refinement of manner, stands in my mind for a type of New England woman that I fear was more often to be met with when Whittier was a younger man.

Baldcap seems to have relapsed into his old mysteriousness, since Mr. Chase left Gates' Cottage. So much terror about a mountain whose highest top hardly exceeds 3,000 feet! Surely one who has seen the peak of Adams so near, and looked down the mighty walls of King's Ravine, ought to laugh at such stories. I dare say Augustus never went to Dream Lake by Mr. Chase's blazes, but I should think, from your account, that the new way to Crow's Nest was about as difficult to find as the Baldcap trail. Old Baldcap <u>has</u> a great many sides and angles, and it is long before one can identify them from different points of view.

In reading your letter, my mother and I admired how you remembered so exactly the position of the mountains in the view from Randolph Hill! I think that, from there, Joe and Middle are both hidden by Mt. Hayes. The 1st, 2nd and 3rd heads pointed out are, the high, bare front usually visited, a wooded swell, which is properly no head at all, and the true summit. All along the road from Charles Philbrook's to the Lead Mine Bridge, the dark dome of the latter is seen looming over the gorge of the Giant Falls. As one gets nearer it disappears, and cannot be seen from any point on the road down the valley. I do not think it is visible even from the hills near Philbrook's. This highest peak is on the Berlin side of the mountain, and in order to complete our exploration we ought to ascertain the width of the central mass by crossing from this peak to the long eastern wall. Some day I hope it may be done.

Our impression is that the name of "Giant Falls" was derived from some of the natives, and I certainly think it to be preferred to "Cascade of the Clouds" on the various grounds of brevity, simplicity and originality. After a rain these falls, flashing and foaming down their ravine, are very noticeable from the road between Gates' and Lead Mine Bridge, but Augustus is rather hard on them to say that they have no existence under ordinary circumstances.

I could not quite satisfy myself, from your letter, that you had been at the view point on Crow's Nest. Was the second knoll you mention, the extreme eastern end of the ridge, considerably lower than the main hill, and separated from it by a steep little gully? Did you stand on the edge of a bold cliff and look right down into the Ingalls valley and up this to Success and Goose Eye? The view of the big mountains and Androscoggin intervale is finer, as you say, from Crag than from Crow's Nest. Since we were last on the latter hill, I think it has been swept by a new fire, which has probably destroyed the beautiful foreground of picturesque pitch pines that used to adorn our cliff. My aunt says that you have a portrait of one of these trees in your album, which she put there in old Goodnow days. So do the different summers get shaken together!

My father was much pleased when I told him what great pleasure his playing had given you.

My uncle has received a long, amusing letter from Mr. Peek. He has been hunting up Indian authorities, and gives an appalling variety of derivations for "Coos"[46]. Do you remember how hard we worked, one evening at Randolph, to find an appropriate Indian name for the Gulch, a name that should express "winter's last retreat"? Hiawatha was our only refer-

---

[46] Coos is short for Coo-ash-auke, a Native American word that translates to "crooked place," "rough place" or "pine tree place." Coos County, which is the northernmost county in New Hampshire, was established in 1803 and incorporated in 1805.

ence book then. Mr. Peek now brings quite a list of words relating to cold.

Please consider this as merely an appendix to last Friday's letter. You see from my non-conventional greeting, that I have more courage on paper than when face to face. We both have such fine names that a third party, reading the headings of our correspondence, might imagine he had gone back to the days of the primitive English novel. How surprised he would be to find, reading further on, that "Isabella" and "Marian" were only two members of the A(merican) M(onkey) C(lub).

Yours always,
M. M. Pychowska

1883

"Your letters are to me what you say mine are to you, an integral part of my summer pleasure. Would that our friendship might have a foundation even more solid than the mountains, and older than the hills!"

Marian Pychowska writes to Isabella Stone.

Hoboken, N.J.
January 7, 1883

Dear Isabella,

This is the way I snap you up and put you back in my debt, but you deserve everything for your sorceries. I am only astonished you were willing to let the cat out of the basket, and that it proved to be a good natured little tiger instead of a black nightmare! Thanks to the benevolent witch. You ought to be learned enough in herbs and simples not to suffer from the ills of common mortals, but I am glad you are able to write of your illness as being past.

The photograph of my mother was taken at the same time as the one you have of me. I do not know if you will like it. You can see in the expression of aggressive resignation that it was taken against her will. My aunt has had such poor success with photographs that she has not had one taken for years. You would imagine her, if you judge by some of her portraits, to be a large person of a very combative disposition. I will enclose a separate slip containing the times and distances you ask for.

This morning my aunt brought out her treasure, a long forgotten newspaper scrap, sent her by Mr. Gannett[1] in '76, in the days when Appalachians were looked upon as suspicious intruders, that is, by us New Jersey folk! It is "A Mountain Letter in Hexameters, respectively dedicated to the AMC" giving an account of a walk up Tuckerman Ravine and over the Peaks. The description of Mt. Adams, "the King of Mountains",

---

[1] Henry Gannett of the United States Geological Survey.

"the jolly, unwearied guide, friend Lowe and his little dog Schneider", but especially the account of the blackflies at Lowe's Camp, making us envy poor Io, who was driven from land to land by the efforts of only one gadfly, while we had a million, all this brings back delightfully the experiences of the last summer. The scrap is going to Boston or Newport for Mr. Sargent's perusal, and when it returns I will try to send it to you. Mr. Nowell is evidently "the great Appalachian Sachem", but who the other worthies are I cannot make out. Perhaps the witch will be able.

My uncle continues to get an occasional funny and cordial letter from Mr. Peek. He seems to dream of the coming summer quite as much as we do. Before Christmas, there arrived from him, an express package containing five water color drawings, one for each of us, leaving us to decide about the distribution ourselves. My uncle chose one in which Mr. Peek has depicted himself sitting on a wharf and looking out over the waters of Lake Michigan, a vision of his dear mountains appearing in the stormy sky. My aunt has a sketch of one of the lesser waterfalls of Randolph. My mother, one of Moat Mountain from Jackson, a memory of our three days' tour. I have Kearsarge over the Saco from Upper Bartlett, and my father, a view of "Moriah-Carter" from Randolph Hill. My uncle arranged an appropriate Christmas card for Mr. Peek, backed by a deluge of puns, of course. This was duly appreciated, the puns being returned with interest. Another surprise came for my mother from Miss Barstow, a lovely group of wild roses and daisies, done in oil, and quaintly framed in birch bark.

Yesterday evening my mother had down her big geological map of N.H. and I was studying the outlet of the "Pond of Safety" and other things that are beyond the limits of our old standby, the Walling map. Among other discoveries was that of the true position of Chickwolnepy Mountain, and I hasten to correct the information I gave you regarding it, for I am sure you remember exactly where the mountain lay to which I gave that name. My Chickwolnepy is only part of Mt. Hayes, the true one being several miles farther north, between Milan and the Success Wilderness.

Friends of whom we see a good deal, a professor in the Stevens Institute of Technology and his wife, spent part of their holidays in Boston. He is a Harvard graduate and they have many friends in Boston. They have come home so enraptured with the "Hub" as fairly to make our Appalachian mouths water. One cannot spend three months of every year in New England without developing a liking for Yankeedom, even to the extent of wishing to spend the whole twelve there. I fear though, it would be too distracting—Jersey is a better place for work.

Of course, at this season, there is an influx of books to be read and discussed. While I am writing this Sunday evening, Edith is reading *The Professor at the Breakfast Table*, and occasionally coming out with some wise, pathetic or funny passage for our benefit. My mother has just remarked, "a propos" of Holmes' description of the poor tutor, that if the "Epic of an

Alp", the newest of the new school of poetry, which she has been reading, contained such a bit of pathos, "it would burst"!

The chief dissipation of holiday week, was our going en masse (except my father) to hear the *Messiah*. Even my uncle, who never goes to public places where he has to sit, was of the party, and enjoyed it so much he thinks of indulging periodically in a like musical spree. He really has more natural ability and taste for music than any of us. My father, of course, primes my mother and me well before these treats, that we may listen intelligently.

A great attraction now in New York is the Raphael *Madonna*. We hear from Philadelphia that the people there are coming on "in droves" to see it. I hope it may be kept here, as a continual protest against the powerful new school of materialistic art. These benighted young "impressionists" dare rail at and criticize a beauty that three centuries have not put out of fashion. They may be sure their productions will not last so long. As I looked at the face of the Madonna, it fairly seemed to change color and expression while I gazed, as though a living soul were there. The Child, I would like to believe with the older connoisseurs, was never painted by Raphael, but by a pupil. A saucy Italian baby is not in keeping with such a mother.

I was a little surprised to read of your architectural drawings, not knowing you ever did anything of that kind, but I am not going to waste any more wonder on the products of Framingham.

With kindest remembrances to Dr. and Mrs. Stone, believe me always,
> Your friend,
> Marian P.

* * * * * * * * * * * *

Edith Cook writes to Isabella Stone.

> Hoboken, N.J.
> January 16, 1883

My dear Miss Stone,

I believe Marian promised to send you certain Appalachian notes when they returned from Mr. Sargent. These having returned yesterday from Newport, I make the sending of them to you the occasion also of answering your latest letter.

I suppose Marian told you of the resuscitation of those same hexameters from an old writing case of mine, where they had long lain forgotten until the thought of their once existence suddenly flashed through my mind one day and they were searched out and reread with an appreciation of persons, things, places and circumstances that was wanting when they were first read by Mill Brook at Shelburne, when "Schneider" and the merry guide had no personality for us, and Mt. Madison was not yet our playground, our front door yard. The name of the author was unknown to me, but Mr. Sargent writes me that he thinks it is Mr. Nathan Dole, of Boston. Will you, when you have sufficiently read the verses return them to Marian or myself, as I want to preserve them now for Mr. Peek's reading, keeping them for our possible meeting at Randolph, where perhaps he might enjoy them more thoroughly than now in Chicago in exile from his beloved mountains.

I suppose you have seen in the Boston papers that my brother has been chosen the Appalachian Councillor of Exploration for this year. He had declined the honor on the ground of his distance from the other councillors and the consequent difficulty in attending satisfactorily to the duties of the office, but the nominating Appalachians seemed to think that the matter of distance could be arranged and that it was the desire of many that Eugene should fill the post and so he has been elected. We all appreciate the compliment expressed in the wish of these gentlemen, and, I suppose our eyes and feet will be more busy than ever, if that were possible, to help make my brother's term of office one worthy of the compliment. It is one thing to be a "free lance" in the field, another to be responsible for a certain amount of work done, and some of that work the direction of others.

You ask if I have found time to embody my little vision of "John Quincy". Yes, I took time for the attempt and painted a very little picture of the two chief members of the Adams family as seen from that little knoll just above the descent into Mossy Glen, with the late September coloring and the light cloud resting just below the summit of the greater Adams, and the golden-leaved birches for the foreground. The coloring among those birches of Mossy Glen that last Sunday afternoon at Randolph is one of the loveliest landscape memories I have of last summer, so fertile in lovely things to remember, along with the deep cool shadows of the glen and those late lights on the mountains from Randolph Hill. Though I have painted once my little vision, I hope to try it again and do it better.

I have painted lately a little picture of the Pond of Safety as we saw it on that showery Saturday that finished for us the explorations of the summer so triumphantly. This picture is to go to Mr. Peek, the artist's tribute to the many pleasant summer hours owed to that gentleman's interest and enthusiasm. I have had more time for painting since the beginning of the new year, having painted also a bit of our Jersey seacoast for a wedding present for a friend whose house is just a little below Sandy Hook, while today I have been at work on an Adirondack lake, something I want to give to a friend who has a summer camping place on the shore of the lake. As I have, for this, to work from a pencil drawing and very imperfect oil sketches made some years ago when my eyes were even less trained than they are now and so have to depend much on a far away memory. My Adirondack lake has given me more trouble than the Pond of Safety, of which the memory is still so near and dear if the pencil outline is dim and but little suggestive.

Still another vision I have that I want to put on canvas is Madison Spring. I only wish I could draw some of the figures and situations that I saw on the hills last September. I never knew so wandering and picture suggesting a household as that of the Ravine House, and we have heard so pleasantly from so many of its members since leaving there.

I do not think I have thanked you for your remembrance of my birthday, the card arriving so punctually and pleasantly on the very morning of the day. It is pleasant to keep one's birthday in the bright light of Christmas.

I am glad "Success" gave you so much pleasure.

Affectionately Yours,
Edith W. Cook

* * * * * * * * * * * *

Merrill Greeley writes to Isabella Stone.

Greeley's Boarding House
Waterville, N.H.
April 11, 1883

M. Isabella Stone
Dear Madam,
Our rooms are all engaged for the summer. Can not accommodate you.

Yours truly,
Merrill Greeley, Proprietor

* * * * * * * * * * * *

Merrill Greeley writes to Isabella Stone.

Greeley's Boarding House
Waterville, N.H.
April 18, 1883

Miss Isabella Stone
Madam,
When your letter was answered Mrs. Greeley was very sick and we thought that as the rooms were all engaged you would not be particular about answering the questions, but if you wish it, I will do it most willingly.

In regard to the guide, he is a young man with one arm, he now has the confidence of the guests by his honesty and ability. They make their own bargains with him when they need his service. I think on account of his loss, gentlemen are quite liberal with him. Ladies say he is the best guide they ever knew.

Greeley's Boardinghouse

Professors Fay and Chickering[2], Mr. Cook, Dr. Buckley, Mr. Scott and many others whose names I can't recall, and have not the hotel register here, have walked through to Upper Bartlett.

Two or three years ago, when the Club had the Field Meeting at Waterville, two ladies walked through from Upper Bartlett to our place, Miss Knowles of Boston, and another lady, whose name I cannot recall, and several gentlemen and guide. They reached our house about six o'clock in the evening.

There is a party of gentlemen and ladies intending to go through, I think the last of June. They are to come up to our house, stay all night, and go on in the morning with a guide. I do not know any of the party except Miss Mary Dix of Rumney, New Hampshire. I mention this thinking your party would like to arrange to go with them as it would save some expense and we could accommodate a party at our house at that time.

In regard to the party in August, it would be doubtful about the lodging, but could furnish the guide. Since writing you before, a family who had rooms engaged has given them up and hired a cottage where they will lodge, so can give you a room early in the season.

Any further inquires in regard to Waterville you would like to make, I will answer most cheerfully.

Truly Yours,
M. Greeley

---

[2] John W. Chickering of Washington, DC, was a renowned botanist.

Isabella Stone writes to Merrill Greeley.

Framingham, Mass.
April 18, 1883

Dear Mr. Greeley,

Please write answers to the following questions in the blank spaces left after each one, and return this sheet to me.

Do you meet passengers at Plymouth and what price to drive them to your house? Or at Campton Village? and at what price?

The cars will run to near the village, the price has been $1.50. This summer probably will be more as it is further to the depot.

Does your water come from a distant spring through logs?

It does. It is a very abundant spring, large quantities coming from it daily, it is one of the best springs among the mountains.

How is your drainage fixed? This is a point of special interest for the health; and summer boarders are always anxious about it.

The closets are earth closets, there is fresh soil put into them every morning and every other morning they are entirely cleaned out and renewed with fresh earth.

Have you now disengaged a chamber for one person during the last two weeks in June?

Yes.

The first week in July?

Yes

Has it a good closet?

It has a wardrobe with curtains.

A stove?

Yes

The morning sun?

Yes

Up two flights or one flight of stairs?

One.

Near the kitchen or front of the house?

Front of the house.

Could I have a spring bed with a hair mattress?

The house was furnished throughout with good hair mattresses and spring beds last year.

What is the price per week for one person in a room for June and September?

Ten dollars ($10.00) a season

For two in a room?

Eight dollars ($8.00) a season

How much for one in a room in July and August?

The same.

What reduction do you make for those staying a long time?
None.
Is your table supplied with oatmeal? Plenty of cream? And berries?
Yes.
How often with fresh meat, such as roast beef, roast lamb, and chicken?
Every day and brook trout and fresh eggs besides.
By what date in September does your house "thin out" so that a person could depend on finding accommodations without writing beforehand to engage a room?
First week.
Price per day?
$2.00, two dollars.
Can you furnish a competent guide, suitable and trustworthy to escort ladies? What are his terms per day, how much for instance to go up Tecumseh?
Price depends on distance and amount of luggage he has to carry.
Is the Bridle path from your place through the woods to Upper Bartlett now passable for good lady walkers of the AMC?
Yes.
Will you have the kindness to write me full particulars of the best way of making the trip? Must arrangements be made for the cars of Sawyer River Railroad to meet the traveller? Or should they strike the high road and walk on to Upper Bartlett?
You can take the cars if you get through in season.
Could they go on horseback through the woods?
No.
How many miles that a wagon could not go?
Can not go with a wagon at all.
How long does it take to walk through?
All day for ladies.
With a gentleman escort in the party would a guide be necessary?
Yes.
How far (after leaving the woods path) to the nearest station on the Portland and Ogdensburg Railroad?
It is eight miles from Greeley's to the railroad.
What is the name of that station?
Sawyer's River Railroad Station.

Augustus Scott writes to Isabella Stone.

95 Milk Street
Boston, Mass.
July 5, 1883

Miss M. Isabella Stone,

Your letter of the second, addressed to Miss Dix relative to the Livermore-Waterville Path has been sent to me with the request that I should answer it.

Miss Dix did not make the excursion she had planned and hence could not give you the required information.

From Greeley's to the station called Livermore, on the Portland and Ogdensburg Railroad, is quite thirteen miles. A lumber railroad runs in from this point to the mills at Sawyer's River, less than two miles when the path was built, but I have information that this road has been pushed several miles farther up Sawyer's River, whether near our path or not I am not informed. But even if it is accessible from our path it cannot be relied on for conveyance.

From the mills toward the Swift River, for several miles, extensive lumbering is carried on in the winter which sadly interferes with our path at that end and I suspect it is considerably overgrown east of the Swift River. From Greeley's to the Swift River I doubt not it is still in fair condition. The path will be cleared out the whole length during the season, but I doubt if the work will be done as soon as you may like to make your excursion.

Of course in a path of that length through the mountains there must be considerable up and down hill, but hardly anything which would be called climbing.

The path crosses a number of streams without bridges (for bridges are not feasible on a mountain path), but it is easy enough to make crossings on logs or boulders. Only good walkers should attempt to do it in a day and the start should be made early in order to reach the mills or the station late in the afternoon.

There are no farm houses much nearer than Bartlett, but there are a number of frame houses at the mills and there is little doubt that two ladies could find comfortable shelter for the night. Arrangements can be made by writing Mr. Frank George, Upper Bartlett, to have a wagon meet you at the mills and take you from there to the Bartlett House. In case this is done you should write him to be there at a firm time, say 6 P.M., and wait your arrival.

I should call the time from breakfast at Greeley's to 6 P.M. at the mills ample for a leisurely walk for ladies accustomed to it.

If you prefer you can refer to the timetable of the Portland & Ogdensburg Railroad and plan to reach Livermore Station for an up train to Crawford House or down to Bartlett. Although the way from Swift River east may be somewhat overgrown it will be hardly possible to lose one's way in as much as all logging roads leading down stream converge to the mills.

I presume a man may be obtained at Greeley's who will take you safely through, but I strongly recommend your employing the man who cut the path, William M. Sargent of Thornton (his P.O. address is Woodstock, N.H.). He is a good woodsman, has been with me in the forests a great deal, and ladies may rely on him. He is now working for me on the Twin Mountains and I am not certain that he can give you a day until the last week in July. He is a good man to employ in case you would like to make any excursion to the East Branch region. I came out of that forest last week and had I known you were at Russell's I would have made you a call.

Yours very truly,
A. E. Scott

* * * * * * * * * * * *

Marian Pychowska writes to Isabella Stone.

Ravine House
Randolph, N.H.
July 11, 1883

My dear Isabella,

Your most welcome letter reached me last Saturday, and I should not have left it unanswered until now if the intervening days had not been unusually occupied. As you trusted, your long silence did not surprise me, knowing as I do the cares and illness that the winter is apt to bring to you, but when the time came for us to be turned out to pasture, I began to expect a letter. I thank you for realizing my expectation so bountifully. Your letters are to me what you say mine are to you, an integral part of my summer pleasure. Would that our friendship might have a foundation even more solid than the mountains, and older than the hills!

Where did the fiery dragon set you down on your journey to North Woodstock? Is there any talk of finishing the road through the Notch? I am glad of the improvements at Mr. Russell's and especially do I congratulate you and your mother upon the convenient platform behind the house. I can see what a great thing it will be for Mrs. Stone, enabling her to combine fresh air and that enchanting view with the rest which is so necessary to her. Strange to say I had heard not a word about the great slides in your neighborhood until I read your letter. None of the papers that fell into our hands mentioned them, but other persons here are better informed than we are. Can you tell me the date of their occurrence? Any account you will give me of either will be of great interest to us. Your promised description of the East Branch Slide seems to foreshadow a delightful trip that you are meditating. May it take place, both for your sake and mine.

I hope you will bring to completion all the Woodstock "jobs" and that the first part of the summer there will be most pleasant and invigorating. You may be sure that we shall be glad to welcome you to our side of the hills. I have a notion that a change in the middle of the summer is an excellent thing for health, especially when the air of the new place is more invigorating. Where do you think of staying in Jefferson? We certainly ought to be able to meet and have a tramp or two together and remember that we can always make room for you to pass the night with us, when such an arrangement would facilitate your plans.

By the time you get this missive your blistered feet will have no need of prescriptions, and indeed, if this mishap should befall·you again, the only alleviation I can suggest is to cover the blistered part with thin pliable sticking plaster. If the foot were very sore, I should think some kind of ointment would be desirable, but you will know more about such things than I. You know that woolen stockings are less likely to occasion blisters than cotton. I have taken to canvas shoes as both economical and comfortable. They are light, giving free passage to air and water. One's feet get wet on very little provocation, but also dry very quickly and there is none of the discomfort of wet leather. One useful hint I have taken from Mr. Pickering's *Walking Guide* and that is to rub the soles and counters of my shoes with common soap whenever they threaten to rub my feet. Another economical "find" is a material for an untearable walking skirt. It is that very thick cotton stuff that workmen's overalls are made of.

My parents and I took up our quarters here the evening of June 27, so that our summer is two weeks old today. We are all well, my mother and I unusually so, so that we needed no long resting time before beginning our climbs. Our very first climb on June 30, was up to your perch on Durand Ridge, and thence to the Gateway, Madison Spring, up the cone of Madison and home by that path. We consumed the whole day from a quarter to nine in the morning until after six in the evening, so that we could take it very slowly, my mother requiring very little absolute rest. After experiencing once more the steepness and roughness of the Madison Branch, we congratulated ourselves that we had made the choice of Durand Ridge for your trip. You were better paid for less labor there.

Our excuse for launching out so boldly immediately on our arrival here, was my mother's cherished desire to find in bloom the early alpine flowers. We were just in time to catch them—white, pink and purple beauties bearing names as imposing as Rhododendron, Azalea, Laurel etc.

Our first expedition was so successful that we started out again July 3. Mr. Watson drove us up to Lowe's whence we climbed the Mt. Adams path and botanized at our leisure over Nowell's Ridge and round the head of King's Ravine, returning home by our new Durand Ridge Path[3]. Then there was still a bank of snow about twenty-five feet long in one of the upper gullies. I could not resist climbing down to handle this product of winter and look at the dripping cavern beneath. It was curious and beautiful to see what beautiful growth was springing up in the wake of the departing snow, especially a large purple heath and a very delicate white one.

Last Sunday we visited our little church in Gorham, and came home on foot Monday morning. For our nooning place on Sunday we climbed a bold rock about the foot of which the Androscoggin winds, and whence we had a fine view of our peaks, the extreme top of Washington and the Carter-Moriah Range. It was a renewal of old Shelburne days to me, to watch those turbulent, steely blue waters sweeping by, so different from the gentle limpid Pemigewasset. If ever you stay in the vicinity be sure to walk from Shelburne to Gorham on the north side of the river. A carriage road[4] (for which the bridge at Gorham is now finished) is projected by this route, but I fear it will be years before the enterprise is carried out. Perhaps you took advantage of the crystal atmosphere on Monday to make some excursion, though you, as well as we here, have plenty to see from the front door.

My mother and I took an early (8:30 A.M.) start on Tuesday, traversing the familiar Salmacis way and up once more on Durand Ridge. Slowly and steadily we toiled up past the Gateway and along the base of "John Quincy", and scaled the sharp peak whence we looked down on all but Washington, reaching it at 1:05 P.M. How I wish you could have watched with us the brilliant sunshine and deep cloud shadows in the Great Gulf and on the grand sides of Mounts Washington, Clay, and Jefferson. Owing to our wet season, all the patches of alpine growth shine with such vivid green among the gray rocks. I saw no signs of life on the Washington Carriage Road though its whole upper course seemed so near us, but the streams in the Gulf were all alive with the heavy rains, flashing in the sun and sending up to us a pleasant murmur. You know how grand is the view from that turn in the road above the Halfway House, and you can imagine what it must be to look across the other way. My mother had brought the appropriate pages of the guide book which she keeps for mutilation, and we tried to identify some of the distant northern peaks that shone through the clean air. The AMC bottle also claimed our attention. Apparently the season on Mt. Adams had just commenced. The first record was on July 9 of a party from the Glen by way of the new path from

---

[3] The upper section of this path, which runs along the crest of Durand Ridge, is part of the present Air Line Trail. From Durand Ridge, the path followed the Scar-Valley Way route of today.

[4] This route is known today as the Hogan Road.

there just finished by the guide Osgood[5]. July 10, a party from Jefferson, having spent a night at Lowe's Camp, had preceded us. While we were discussing the view and lunch and record, there appeared on the scene a figure with spectacles and a botanical case, a Dartmouth student camping on Mt. Washington and collecting specimens for his college. As we had just had some experience in that line we exchanged notes before parting.

While my mother descended soberly along Nowell's Ridge, following the line of the cairns, I amused myself by skirmishing over F.3.2. (vulgarly called Sam Adams)[6] and round the head of the Ravine of the Cascades. It was now after three o'clock and the Castles so near me were throwing their long sharp shadows down the side of Jefferson. After a short dance through some patches of scrub spruce, I joined mother on Lowe's Path. My mother was tired when she first got home, this having been our longest walk and the weather, even on the summits, warm, but she was rested by bedtime, and was none the worse the next day.

To give a spice of adventure to my history, I must tell you that we hear a credible rumor that the following morning a bear was seen opposite Mr. Lowe's house. The most noxious beasts we have yet met are blackflies, from which we take refuge in our blue tarlatan wigs, and one potato bug which apparently had climbed up through the Gateway of the Ravine.

We are looking for my aunt and uncle to join us next Saturday, and the same day are expected Mr. and Mrs. Nowell (AMC), Mr. Peek and daughter and two young ladies who were here last season, are established once again. The house will soon be filled and Mr. Watson is now fitting up the deserted house on the way to Cold Brook Falls for persons who cannot find sleeping room here. Our party has the same rooms as last year and the Watsons, having abundant help, are able to give us every comfort we desire.

A new boardinghouse[7] is being put up on Randolph Hill very near

---

[5] Benjamin F. Osgood was a famous guide working under the auspices of the Glen House in Pinkham Notch. On December 7, 1858, he led the first winter ascent of Mount Washington. In 1878 he began to cut the path mentioned above, the Osgood Trail, which scales Mount Madison, ascending the ridge which also bears his name. Osgood died on September 7, 1907, at seventy-eight years of age.

[6] The AMC had its own system of nomenclature that divided the whole White Mountain district into a number of sections, each of which was designated by a capital letter. The various mountains in each section were then numbered, and the separate summits of each mountain were denoted by a second number. Employing this system, the club was able to assign each individual summit its own unique symbol. Although used for a number of years in topographical research, the system failed to gain acceptance, being observed as "dry and unaesthetic to the last degree."

[7] The Mount Crescent House, built during this year, was opened in 1884. In the course of nearly a century of business, proprietorship changed hands from Ingalls Leighton to Charles Lowe in 1895, to Joseph George in 1907, and then finally, to John Boothman in 1923. The Boothman family managed the Mount Crescent House until its demise when it quietly ceased operating in 1971.

the spot where we enjoyed that memorable sunset together. Mr. Ingalls Leighton of Randolph is the enterprising man. I hear that he proposes to fit the house for next season and to accommodate seventy-five guests. It ought to be a great success if it is well conducted. The town, in view of the advantages it will derive from the new enterprise, has exempted it from taxes for ten years. Mr. Watson fully enters into this view of the matter, and he was one of a small army of neighbors who helped to raise the building the other day.

We are planning to go to the AMC meeting at the Twin Mountain House[8]. At first my mother had some idea of joining the long expedition through the wilderness, but that has been given up on account of the many nights camping. We still hope to visit the two peaks of the Twins and perhaps camp one night. It is hard to decide what you want to do until you are face to face with the weather and other circumstances. Of course you shall hear of all that your humble servant does. But shall we meet you among the Apes?

I suppose in the matter of weather our experiences of the past two weeks have not differed greatly, though I doubt if it was cold enough in North Woodstock, on the night of June 30, to blacken the cucumber vines as was the case, they say, between here and Jefferson. Thundershowers have been many and grand, but we have had no heat to make us think they could be suffering ninety-seven degrees in New York, as my aunt writes.

Enough for this time, I have at least cleared the decks for the AMC meeting "in our next".

With kind remembrances, in which my mother joins me, to Dr. and Mrs. Stone, believe me always,

> Your sincere friend,
> Marian Pychowska

* * * * * * * * * * * *

Edith Cook writes a postal card to Isabella Stone.

> Ravine House
> Randolph, N.H.
> July 18, 1883

Dear Miss Stone,

Do you receive my *Echo*, for I receive yours, my copy coming addressed to Miss I. Stone, Russell Cottage, Randolph, N.H. I suppose yours comes E. W. Cook, Ravine House, North Woodstock, N.H. Lillie has written to the *Echo* office to have the mistake at this end rectified. My identity

---

[8] Built in 1869-70, the Twin Mountain House was located in the Ammonoosuc River Valley five miles west of Bretton Woods, in the town of Carroll. Enlarged over time to a fine and grand hotel, it remained in operation until 1959 and was torn down in 1960.

is much mixed this summer. My New York paper comes to me addressed to "E.W. Thomas". At our Randolph post office I am, for the present, Thomas, Stone, and Cook.

I reached here on Saturday with my brother after a pleasant journey from home. Yesterday, Lillie, Marian and I went up Durand Ridge, my first mountain climb of the season, and had beautiful clouds drift over the peaks and down into the ravine and exquisite summer color in the sky over the hills and valleys.

Randolph paths are as charming as ever, as Marian has already written you.

Edith W. Cook

* * * * * * * * * * *

Marian Pychowska writes to Isabella Stone.

Ravine House
Randolph, N.H.
July 27, 1883

Dear Isabella,

Was it not a strange thing for the *Echo* man to transport you and "Russell Cottage" into Randolph? I think that would be a very good arrangement, but I hope he may leave the "Ravine House" where it is for the present.

I will give you the Appalachian chronicle that I promised, hoping that you and your mother are in such good health and spirits that the recital of our playtime will not be an impertinence.

My uncle and aunt arrived on Saturday, July 14. The former set to work early last week on the two paths he is interested in, to the Pond of Safety and to the Gulch. The first of these is inaugurated today. My mother and Miss Barstow, my uncle, Mr. Peek and Reverend Mr. Butler of Michigan are making the trial trip.

My mother astonishes me. She took but one day's rest after the fatiguing Twin Mountain excursion, not willing to let this superb weather slip by unemployed, and roused us up yesterday to climb through King's Ravine. The crawling and scrambling among the boulders had no terrors for her, and she climbed unwearied the long slide to the Gateway. We had it all our own way for there were no gentlemen in the party, Edith and Miss Barstow being our companions. This time we visited Star Lake, on the Glen side of the Madison-Adams Col, a big rain pool girdled with green moss. As we sat by the water, the rising edges of the plateau shut us off from all but a little glimpse of the lower world northward, the barren symmetrical truncated cone of Madison rose before us with nothing but the sky beyond. It was a view that art could not reproduce, for there was no object, not even a stunted tree by which to measure things. Our path home was by Durand Ridge.

My aunt and I were glad to have rest and dinner today, but the two indefatigables could not resist the attractions of Safety Pond. But I must go back to the beginning, and you will see that "extremes meet" on Durand Ridge.

It was there we took Edith for her first walk. She wanted to make some pencil drawing of rocks and peaks, but this plan was frustrated in a most beautiful way. At noon, when we emerged from the woods, the clouds were beginning to roll over "John Quincy" and pour down into the ravine. Nowell's Ridge and the lower end of Durand were in brilliant sunshine, while the east wind drove the fog over the crests, sometimes shrouding and then revealing them, and out past us in long streamers only to melt in the dry, pure air. How you would have delighted to watch the continually changing play of sun and cloud!

Last Saturday morning, a little before six o'clock our wagon load of Appalachians and their allies set out for the meeting. The Ex-Councillor of Improvements, Mr. W. G. Nowell with his little girl, Gracie, his son and two other boys under his care were our companions. The members of this party had been "hardening themselves" by camping several nights at Lowe's Camp in spite of the cold. When we'd passed over the ever lovely way to Jefferson, the rest of our drive had the spice of novelty, for we took the road through to the Carroll Post Office on the west side of Cherry Mountain. As we neared our journey's end, the views of the Franconia and Twin Mountain ranges were very fine.

A few minutes before ten, Mr. Watson drew up his four lively steeds before the Twin Mountain House, the festive strains of the hotel band greeting our arrival. A number of AMC acquaintances came forward to help us and our bundles out—Miss Whitman, Miss Knowles, Mr. Scott, Mr. Edmands, Professor Fay, greeting us so cordially. Having settled our things in the comfortable room próvided for us, we went down into the large parlor which was beautifully ornamented with growing ferns and pond lilies. The meeting was most interesting and enjoyable. As you will see the accounts in the mountain papers, I will pass over the particulars.

After dinner my mother and aunt joined the Cherry Mountain excursion. Some energetic leading Apes had sent a gang of men to make a clearing near the summit with the special view of studying thence the Twin Mountain Range so soon to be traversed. My sightseers report this view and that down the Notch and to the mountains beyond as very grand. Some of the party, my two among them, continued along the ridge of Cherry Mountain to "Owl's Head", the bare knob overlooking Jefferson. The wagon met them at the foot of this path. It was a good deal to undertake for an afternoon stroll, and they did not get back to me and supper until half past nine. Such unwonted dissipation and the pleasant company they had been in had put them in high spirits. You will wonder why I was not one of the dissipated this time. I was busy dosing and coddling myself against Twin Mountain on Monday.

You may remember what decided signs of a coming storm there were on Saturday and Sunday. When we interrogated Mr. Lowe he promised us "nice weather", even "something extra" (with a twinkle). Who would have thought his ambiguous prophecy was to be so pleasantly fulfilled. Sunday we passed in quiet. At the meeting, Mr. Edmands had asked for volunteers to aid his topographical work on the Twin Mountain excursion, explaining how ladies and gentlemen of no scientific training could be of great use in making rough sketches and recording angles read by the observer. I thought of course that when the topographical section was called together on Sunday evening there would be a goodly array of eager assistants. What was my disappointment, being the only lady present, to see the small gathering of men, and most of these so hampered with the care of ladies, etc. as to be unable to promise much help. Our Councillor was much disappointed.

We were unable to find any others who wished to make the Twin excursion according to our plan, so we concluded to do it without escort. Mr. Scott gave us every encouragement and help in his power, explaining the complications of logging roads. The hotel people were also very obliging, supplying us with three sorts of cold meat for our three meals in the woods. Thus well provisioned and trusting in Mr. Scott's instructions, we three ladies started off at a quarter past eight Monday morning.

My uncle went our way as far as the railway station, whence he made straight for Mt. Hale. This pathless and undescribed summit had more attraction for the explorer than the Twins, so soon to be overrun by a whole army of Apes.

The distance to the peak of South Twin has been roughly guessed as eight miles, but it seems to me nearer seven. Mr. Scott had provided a large number of signs to be placed along the road at doubtful forkings, but they had not been taken out of the car, and he had been telegraphing right and left in search of them. They finally came in time for him to put them in place on Monday afternoon as he came up to camp. Not having these helps, we followed Mr. Scott's directions, as I thought, choosing a logging road within sound of the Little River, after we had crossed to the west bank. I travelled on confidently for a mile or more, following recent tracks of horse's hoofs (which I had been told to expect to find along the correct road) until we suddenly were brought up to the bank of the river, the road crossing back to the east shore. This was not part of our programme. Leaving the others I went in search of our lost way higher up the bank. Fortunately, though we had been out of the true way for a long distance, we had been traveling parallel to it and found it within a hundred yards of us. Thankful to have lost no more time, we sped on till we came to a sign, "PATH", where the beautiful new trail left the dubiousness of wood roads to make its own clear way to the mountain summit.

A mile more (making about four from the Twin Mountain House) brought us to the fresh and substantial camp where we were to pass the night. Here we gladly unburdened ourselves of extra wraps and provisions and made a new start, at eleven, to climb the mountain in earnest. It is a model path, of which all Apes should be proud, an easy grade and through beautiful woods. Two or three times we startled up game birds, and once came upon a dear little brown rabbit crouching just beside the path, his ears laid back and his pretty eyes intently watching us. He did not move in the least while we all passed within about three feet of him. I even suggested to Edith to put out her hand and stroke his back, but all thought it would be too bad to startle him. I wonder whether he trusted us or was playing dead, as the safest course.

At last we began to get lovely glimpses through the ever shortening trees toward Mount Washington and company. The broad summit of the North Twin is mostly overgrown with "scrub" from about five to ten feet in height, of such impenetrable character as to make one wonder how Miss Ricker ever did get through it. Now, thanks to Mr. Scott, there is a broad avenue connecting the outlooks. The first of these, toward the east and south, gave us perhaps the most beautiful view we obtained that day. The shining white shoulders and peak of Chocorua are seen between the steep sides of Carrigain Notch. From the north and west lookout all the Franconia region is to be surveyed. Hooket seeming near at hand and below. Here we enbottled our names. Among our few predecessors was Mr. William Sargent of Thornton, employed on the path work, I think. It lacked a few moments of one o'clock when we reached this point. We did not linger long, as we knew the South Peak would afford us a more comprehensive view. The distance along the col is about a mile. On the way we had a refreshing drink from a small spring filled by Sunday night's rain. A little before two we gained the rocky, wind swept peak of the South Twin, and here at last there was time to rest and enjoy.

Looking down the valley of the East Branch it seemed no very great way to North Woodstock, and I wish we could have transported you into our company. I will not go through the catalogue of familiar mountains. Loon Pond and Kineo did not escape notice among their grander neighbors. The great charm, as you may imagine, was the wide stretch of wilderness east, south and west—the high mountain walls of the Franconias and the Willey Range shutting off all traces of man's passage in the two great notches. The extension of our range, Mounts Guyot and Bond, with their immense flanks sweeping out into the forest, lay southward. These great shoulders and intervening valleys, together with ridges and valleys of the two parallel chains, were to be the chief study of Mr. Edmands and his assistants.

Shortly after three o'clock we crossed to the North Twin, admiring on our passage the picturesque views of the two peaks between which we were traveling. At the first lookout, where my aunt intended to make a drawing of Chocorua and Carrigain Notch to have as a reminiscence of our trip, we found Mr. Edmands just beginning his topographical work. Edith's skilled hand was immediately put to work drawing the outline of Mount Hale and the Little River Range with its hitherto unmapped connection with Mount Guyot. I was glad she could be useful, but I regret that lost view of Carrigain Notch. Presently arrived Mr. Edmands' companion, Mr. Mann[9] and their woodsman. These three were going to camp on the col in order to have more time for observations.

It was now quarter to five, and the mountains were clothed in all their late afternoon beauty of local color and strongly shadow-marked folds. When Edith's drawing was finished, we reluctantly left our newly conquered mountain and descended leisurely to the forest camp. When we got there we found the guides and a few gentlemen making sad havoc of the surrounding trees in order to supply us with fires and beds. We took up our position on a commanding root to watch the preparations and the arrival of our fellow campers. They straggled in, in small parties. Mr. Scott and his efficient lieutenants, Misses Whitman and Knowles, bringing up the rear as darkness settled down. The large and lofty bark shelter was made almost untenantable by smoke from the fire, so a slight shelter was put up on the windward side, and appropriated to the ladies. The carefully packed lunch boxes were now opened, chocolate brewed over the coals and everyone made as comfortable as circumstances permitted. Mr. Scott kindly reserved for us a corner of the rather crowded camp, in which all the ladies settled themselves, if not luxuriously at least good humoredly. At any rate there was no danger of our suffering from cold or damp in front of the large well tended fire. If I had the gift of describing people, I could spoil a few more sheets with picturing the funny scenes of that night, but I will spare you and myself the attempt. Sleep did not rob my mother or myself of any of those swiftly passing hours, but my aunt succeeded in losing one or two very pleasantly. For the wakeful ones there was plenty to see and enjoy, firelight and moonlight playing in the surrounding forest.

About 3:00 A.M. my mother and I left the shelter and perched on our commanding root where we could see all and still be near the fire. It was hard to believe that day was breaking, the sun coming back so soon. The gray light from the east touched the spruce spires behind camp and gradually overpowered both moon and firelight, while the Swainson Thrushes sang softly about us.

Before five all but the sleepiest were aroused. We three independents then exchanged good wishes with our kind friends Messrs. Scott

---

[9] George C. Mann of Cambridge, MA, was a founding member of the AMC. He served as President(1890), Vice-President, and Councillor of Natural History.

and Fay and Miss Whitman, and made a beeline for breakfast at the Twin Mountain House. The logging roads had been wet enough the day before, but at this early hour the grass, especially when we got down into the foggy valley, drenched our feet and skirts. At half past seven we entered the hospitable hotel and fully appreciated the comforts of the dry clothes and a hot breakfast. My uncle joined us at the table and told of his successful exploration of the various heads of Mt. Hale, his aneroid barometer setting up the highest considerably over 4,000 feet, and of his comfortable return to supper. My aunt, having had some sleep in camp, took upon herself to support the credit of the family by appearing on the porch with her knitting and saw a flash of the heliotrope signal when our company reached North Twin, while mother and I got a short doze in our room.

At 1:17 we all took the train for Jefferson. At Whitefield, where we changed cars, there was an hour and one-half wait, but this was no hardship for we could survey the mountains from Lafayette to Starr King, including our new conquests. Moreover we had pleasant company, a gentleman of decidedly clerical appearance who by degrees was drawn into our mountain talk. He had come from the valleys of the Mad River and Pemigewasset and told us much about the new slides. The Waterville mountains were familiar to him and he passed a night at North Woodstock (perhaps in your house) on his way up. Soon we found that he knew a great deal about Randolph, in fact he was bound for the Ravine House, at which he had passed one or two seasons some years ago. This gentleman, the Reverend Mr. Butler, is the namer of Triple Falls, and I remember reading his description of them in the *Echo* the summer we spent at Goodnow's. How things interweave! You will find a well written letter of his signed "A Prairie Parson", in the last *Echo* July 28. I think you would find it pleasant here in the midst of such a company of enthusiastic mountaineers as we have now at the Ravine House.

Mr. Watson and our two young ladies from Portsmouth were waiting at Jefferson Station, and on the way home we picked up Mr. Peek who was sketching by the roadside, so we had a gay drive, as pleasant and as beautiful as any part of our excursion. What was our pleasure at being able to identify some distant mountains which come in between Cherry and Deception and about which we had never been certain before, as the veritable North and South Twins and Mount Hale.

I have a dim remembrance that you wrote me last summer that you had employed, or were about to employ, as guide William Sargent of Thornton. He is a great favorite with Mr. Scott and Miss Whitman, and the latter told us some touching stories about him and the wonderful little girl who takes care of his poor house. He was employed as one of the guides on the Twin Mountain trip, William Pollard being the other.

Now just suppose I had gone on the five days trip, what hope would there have been of a termination to this document? May the *Echo* give us a full account of the travellers during those four other beautiful days.

Ending as I began with best wishes for your health, and adding the wish that we may one day be united in the contemplation of the One Supreme Beauty in Truth, in comparison of whom all created beauty and pleasure are toys, I remain always,

Your sincere friend,

M. M. Pychowska

* * * * * * * * * * * *

Isabella Stone writes to Marian Pychowska (draft copy).

Russell House

North Woodstock, N.H.

August 1, 1883

Dear Marian,

...On July 17, a party of nine of us spent the day in visiting Georgiana Falls, riding to and from the entrance to the footpath. The recent heavy rains had swollen Harvard Brook so that the Falls proper, as well as the picturesque cascades above and below, and the "new" waterfall, were in splendid condition, fuller than I had ever seen them. We walked nearly five miles in all, spending eight hours, with lunch and rests and "paddling" in the stream, gathering fungus brackets and birch bark. I found the spot from which my stereoscopic view of the Falls was taken, and recognized its likeness. It is a cascade nearly one-third of the way below the highest fall.

You may remember that last year our party had a long climb through a tangled mass of burnt fallen timber to reach the head of the Falls. I begged Mr. Russell to hire a man to cut a passable path through this, offering to pay part of the expense. This has been done. The lower part of the path is badly overgrown in places and encumbered with logs. I wish Mr. Sargent could be put on to it with his axe, authorized to extend the path to Bog Pond, thence a trail might be made by AMC some time to the summit of one important peak of the Kinsman Range, "Nameless", which must afford a fine view into Kinsman Notch, and over the Blue Ridge to Moosilauke. From my observation and Mr. Russell's information, it seems as if the map places Bog Pond far too near the summit of Mt. Pemigewasset. Certainly the map ignores several mountains between Moosilauke and Pemigewasset. I noticed them from Loon Pond Mountain, and hoped to study their intricate relations from the summit of Moosilauke this season.

The Georgiana Falls Expedition was pronounced by all to be very delightful, but also exceedingly arduous and fatiguing (!), rather beyond the "reasonable limits" above mentioned, and I am teased to "propose some nice excursion, you know all the lovely places." "But is it as hard as Georgiana Falls?", is immediately asked. Fortunately for me Mr. Russell is a sober family man of over fifty years, who never touches tobacco or liquor, thoroughly trustworthy, kind and attentive, and though a plain farmer with toil-worn hands, he shows in many little ways the instincts of a gentleman. We are so well acquainted with him that father and mother are willing to have me, a middle aged spinster, go alone with him as guide on an occasional expedition otherwise impossible of accomplishment by me. I find Mr. Russell more companionable and appreciative of mountain scenery than strangers would suppose, and sometimes quite ready to kindle with exploring enthusiasm. Feeling assured of my friendly interest, he talks freely of their homely life, past trials, and future plans, etc. Are you shocked at the above?

Tuesday Eve, July 24

Today the Apes are on the Twin Mountains. What unusually fine weather for the excursion! Are you camping with them? Had I been sure of the weather, of my mother's favorable condition (she is gaining slowly but steadily) and of my own health, I might have attempted to meet the Club, but on an uncertainty, it was rather too expensive and fatiguing a trip, and the excitement would probably, to use Jane Welsh Carlyle's frequent expression in her published letters, "have made me go off my sleep."

Instead, today, with a pleasant party of seven, all but one whom spent last summer here, I have ridden to the Flume House[10] (greatly enlarged and improved both inside and out, since last year), ascended Mt. Pemigewasset (for the second time this season, each time obtaining a fine clear view) and visited the Flume. O, the wonderfully changed and utterly transfigured Flume[11]! A description is impossible. Come on the wings of the wind and see for yourself. Before passing the covered bridge on the toll road nothing is altered, after that nothing is the same. Then a saddening scene of devastation meets the eye: acres of barren sand and rocks from pebbles to enormous boulders, mixed with uprooted trees of all sizes, denuded of their bark to the smallest twig, stripped of foliage, dead and desolate. The Flume Brook appears half choked with all the hideous debris of the avalanche ten to twelve feet deep around it. In the middle of the waste, a broad piece of new plank walk slants upward in perspective against the sky, apparently going nowhere, or so it looked to me from our wagon.

Walking upward into the Flume one is bewildered by the greatly increased width of the entrance—five times that of the former one—and looks behind to behold with amazement the broad side of Mount

---

[10] This was the second Flume House. It was located in Franconia Notch near the base of the Flume Gorge and was built in 1872.

[11] On June 20, 1883, an avalanche, caused by heavy rains on the peaks above, crashed down through this famous canyon.

Flume House

Pemigewasset, then part of Kinsman, and a goodly portion of Moosilauke with the house on its summit. Here and there portions of the old smooth granite ledges are left bare, and the brook comes rushing and tumbling over them with more turbulence than in the old days when it slipped and glided along down this part of its course. The beauty of the Flume is gone, but its grandeur is increased. That is speaking broadly of course. Its dark weather stained walls coated with the mould of years, and beautiful with the dripping moss, lichens, waving ferns and tendrils of creeping vines, the slippery ledges on the left hand whose every niche was familiar to me from frequent clamberings to the mossy log that bridged the chasm above, the dark boulder[12], so delicately poised and yet presumably fixed for centuries, are all vanished. I seem to be walking along a new and mighty chasm freshly riven through the heart of some mountain, but it must be a hundred miles from Franconia Notch!

The granite walls still rise on either hand to the height of seventy

---

[12] This huge boulder was suspended between the walls of the narrowing upper part of the Flume and was a principal natural attraction of Franconia Notch before the devastating storm.

Flume, above the Boulder, before the avalanche

feet and more, but the rocks are light gray and red, scraped clean from top to bottom, exposing the cracks between the gigantic layers and the dip of the strata in the original upheaval. The pavement beneath the crevices on the sides are encrusted with a glistening red loam, the remnants of the fine powder into which rocks were ground in the crush of the mighty avalanche. It occurred in the midst of a heavy thunderstorm on Wednesday, June 20, after two days and nights of heavy rain. Some persons maintain that it was caused by the bursting of a water spout, others that a big rock on Mount Liberty was struck by lightning. At any rate the slide began on the steepest part of the southern side of Liberty, apparently about a quarter of the way down from the top, starting a mass of rock and earth which widened and deepened as it descended leaving a channel fifty feet wide and thirty feet deep. From the top of Mount Pemigewasset an excellent view is obtained of the entire winding course of the slide, its upper part in profile, and even of the Flume where people can be counted walking up and down beside the brook! Last year from Pemigewasset we could not look into the Flume or at least we never noticed it. Pemigewasset also affords a good view of the great slide on Flume Mountain, occurring at the same time, the scarred channel of which is much wider than the other and of a grotesque shape. This was prevented from entering the Flume, by a little hill east of the Flume.

The damage in the Flume was caused by the slide from Liberty which entered the stream nearly three-quarters of a mile above the old Flume. Torrents of rain had fallen and were then pouring from the inky clouds hanging low over the Notch. An ominous crash and awful roaring, deeper than the voice of the tempest and lasting forty minutes, alarmed the inhabitants of the Flume House, and was heard at Bethlehem sixteen miles distant! Flume Brook became a raging river, and this tremendous mass of mingled water, rocks, earth, overturned trees and boulders, rushed with resistless force down the Flume, sweeping everything before it, ripping off great slices from the solid walls, scratching deep furrows in the rocks, and bevelling out immense grooves in the lofty grottos newly formed. Huge battered logs afterwards found stranded on top of the ledges indicate that the whole Flume must have been dammed for some time before The Boulder was carried away. What a sight to have witnessed! But no human eye saw it. The length of the Flume is increased by (they say) five hundred feet. It certainly seems one-third longer than formerly, and, except in the central part, six or seven feet wider, and more impressive. In the upper part are two splendid waterfalls, one of which must be fully forty feet high surrounded by immense promontories of solid rock fifty feet high, jutting out into the bed of the stream, indented with ledges like giant's stairs.

On the top of the chief of these cliffs, not more than two feet wide, I perched close to the plunging waterfall separated from me by a chasm extending deep down in sheer vertical descent to the bed of the stream, and lined in the upper part with a rock resembling slate. Kneeling down carefully I looked over and watched the leaping waters strike the brook which divides at the foot of this promontory, rushing away in two beautiful foaming currents that unite in another waterfall farther down. The latter is hidden and marred by the new broad plank wall and bridge, which, though well made and commodious, were unfortunately not located by a person with eyes open to the picturesque. Mr. Russell, perceiving me from below, made earnest signs to me to go back to the main shore above, where others of the party were sitting, which I presently did by the same safe way I had come. The frequent ledges and projecting crags, over which the water now falls in the Flume, break it up into the most luminous spray sparkling over sheets of whitest foam, sometimes dashing out in ten thousand separate drops like globules of molten silver.

We followed up the slide for a short distance above the Flume, walking beside and in the brook, comparatively now but a winding thread of water in a wide chaos of sand and pudding-stones. I walked into the cave roofed with enormous slabs of granite laid on in this way; the floor slants up at a steep incline, and there is a hole in the roof. With inward reluctance, though with outward cheerfulness, I acquiesced in the party's desire to turn back, though myself longing (you will know) to continue even as far as the slide was traversable. My estimate of heights above given is based on the supposition that the Flume walls at the deepest point measure seventy feet up, and allows for the elevation of the bed of the stream above that point in the upper part of the Flume where the waterfall is, but I do not pretend to possess accurate judgment. The *Echo* makes the fall much higher.

This letter is long delayed, and must be sent without a description of my Moosilauke trip accomplished at last, of which you shall receive an account later. Hearty thanks for your long letter of July 27 about the AMC Meeting and your walk over the Twins with mother and aunt. My kind regards to them both.

Ever yours,
Isabella Stone

* * * * * * * * * * * *

Charles Fay writes to Isabella Stone.

College Hill, Mass.
August 4, 1883

My dear Miss Stone,

I imagine that you have already heard from Mr. W. F. Dusseault and Mr. Sanborn much more concerning our trip to Mt. Moosilauke than I could put upon paper. I will therefore only say that we reached the Tip-Top House[13] on the summit shortly after seven o'clock having left the Smith Farm just after 11:00 A.M. We gave an hour to our lunch and so were about seven hours in making the same number of miles. There were so few outlooks and so many zigzags that our ladies were quite glad to reach the summit. We found the western sky very unpromising for the morrow, and so decided after a hearty supper to descend by the carriage road that night, rather than wait for the promised rain. Just before dark we set out again and with the light of a lantern, kindly furnished by Miss Woodworth[14], were able to make the five miles very comfortably in two

---

[13] The Tip-Top House on the summit of Mount Moosilauke opened on July 4, 1860. The original stone building received wooden additions in 1872 and 1881, enlarging the operation of the boardinghouse substantially. The Tip-Top House remained in business for over eighty years.

[14] Miss S. F. Woodworth was the manager of the Tip-Top House on Mount Moosilauke.

Tip-Top House, Mount Moosilauke

hours, arriving at the Breezy Point House just after ten.

Our anticipations of rain were justified, so all the party but Messrs. Dusseault and Sanborn and myself went around to Campton by regular conveyance. We took to the wet path between Cushman and Kineo. An hour was lost in making sure of the beginning of the trail. So that it was noon before we were fairly under way upon it. The Appalachian portion we found quite agreeable, but so much could not be said of the part that has been obliterated by the logging road. Well down toward the Thornton end we waded long distances in quagmires. It was about four o'clock when we reached the road. I rejoined my party at the Campton Village Station, and we spent Sunday at Sanborn's. The party broke up Monday, although my sister and I remained there until Tuesday P.M. I shall hope to give you more particulars of our trip when we meet.

Please give my kindest regards to your father and mother. We shall long remember your kindness in providing for us so generously on the night of our stay in Woodstock.

Hoping to meet you at one of the autumn meetings in the city, if not, indeed at the North Conway field meeting.

I am with great respect,

Cordially yours,

Charles E. Fay

* * * * * * * * * * * *

Marian Pychowska writes a postal card to Isabella Stone.

Ravine House
Randolph, N.H.
August 6, 1883

Dear Isabella,

Many thanks for your long and interesting letter with its careful description of the slides, and also for the *Echo*. I am delighted you have been to Moosilauke and by such a charming new way, and wait with interest your conclusion. You ought to prepare an account of that new path for the AMC.

Since I wrote you we have been through Evans Notch from Gilead to Chatham and on Mounts Baldface and Royce. In time you shall have details.

Yours always,
M. M. P.

* * * * * * * * * * *

Isabella Stone writes to Marian Pychowska (draft copy).

Russell House
North Woodstock, N.H.
August 6, 1883

Dear Marian,

Perhaps the most enjoyable trip since my last letter was the ten-mile ride in a buggy through the ever charming Franconia Notch to the Profile House whence Mr. Russell and I made the ascent of Cannon Mountain, where he had never before been, so that, as he laughingly said, I was "guide" that day. It was that beautifully clear Thursday, July 26. We went up easily in an hour and twenty minutes, greatly enjoying the rocky mossy path (which you will remember), every rod of which was to me associated with you and yours and our pleasant trip from "Goodnow House". We arrived on top at 12:30 and left at 4:30 P.M.; four good hours, which would have been dismally tedious probably for a large party, were happily spent in the restful abandon of gazing at the superb view, clear in every direction, except during the last hour towards Jefferson where it was slightly obscured by the rising smoke of pestiferous brush fires.

After lunch (during which I rattled my tin cup for water in vain) I studied the view down the Pemigewasset Valley in such contrast with the grand stern colossal forms of Lafayette and his brothers directly opposite us. Then we went down and sat on the Cannon and I welcomed the dear old northern friends, Green Mountains, and Percy Peaks, a magnificent landscape, in the foreground of which lay Bald Mountain, Echo Lake, and Profile House. Most of this view was obscured, was it not, the day you ascended?

Wandering about promiscuously on the top, towards the true summit, we were simultaneously seized with a desire to go down to the edge of the cliff above the Profile and look over on to Profile Lake. Mr. Russell gave utterances to the wish first, our watches said quarter to three, there was no one to hinder, and away we went, leaping over the rocks, scrambling through the low bushes, passing down one great ledge or plateau only to see another stretched before us more slanting with bigger boulders. Guided on our way by a rude short ladder and low staff bearing a cotton streamer, we went on careless of the steep hillside rapidly rising behind us, up which we must soon retrace our steps. It was impossible to tell how far above and back of the Old Man's helmet we were at the final pause, where the slope became very precipitous, the entire lake was visible, and the view of Lafayette and Lincoln indescribably grand and impressive, probably a long way off. Back to the old path where (according to the guidebook) we had left flying a handkerchief, which is not necessary. We descended in three-quarters of an hour and at twenty-five minutes of six the horse was harnessed and we were tucked up in warm robes driving rapidly homeward.

Sitting in the parlor that evening in the midst of a merry company I was informed by a lady that a gentleman was in the hall inquiring for Miss Stone. Stepping out, what is my surprise and pleasure to discover our mutual friend Professor Fay, in knickerbocker tramping costume. After an exchange of cordial greetings, he reveals himself as a beggar for a night's lodging not merely for himself but for three ladies, Miss Lincoln, his sister-in-law, and Misses Alice and Carrie Congdon, and also Mr. R. F. Curtis[15], our former AMC Secretary, who are in a wagon outside with their baggage just down from the Profile House. They came out from the East Branch Wilderness Wednesday P.M. and spent that night at Pollards, having separated from the rest of the AMC camping out party who had gone on up Thoreau Falls to the Crawford House. Knowing me to be at Russell House, Professor Fay aimed for it, but supposed it to be located considerably north of Pollard's. "We gentlemen will sleep anywhere, even in the

---

[15] Rest F. Curtis of Cambridgeport, MA, was a founding member of the AMC. He served as President(1891), Vice-President and Secretary.

barn, if only, Miss Stone, you can prevail upon Mrs. Russell to take in the ladies." The house was full and several applicants had been refused. It seemed a hopeless case, but finally we arranged for father to give up his room and go to sleep with mother for that night and the sister of a lady who is away visiting consented to allow the latter's room to be occupied. Mine is a narrow single bed, almost a cot and therefore useless in this emergency. It was 10:30 by the time supper was served for them. Both then and in the morning we had much interesting talk with map and compass, observations from the plateau, etc.

I heard of your movements on Twin Mountain, the smoky camp, and the route of the party. They were all much pleased with North Woodstock, this house, and hearing a little about the excursions possible from here, they agreed with me that it would be a charming place for a little AMC party to locate for several weeks some season.

Professor Fay made particular inquiries about the new Moosilauke path which he supposed to be less than five miles. I told him that my estimate of times and difficulties would be no criterion for him (and presumably not for his party) as I am only a novice in mountain climbing; which is certainly true though he declares he is satisfied that I am "well on towards taking the second degree."

Joined by two gentleman acquaintances who happened to be passing the night at the next house (Mr. Sanborn, tutor at Boston Institute of Technology and Mr. Dusseault, Universalist minister), Professor Fay's party actually made the ascent of Moosilauke on Friday, planning to return the same way that I did, by the Thornton-Warren (AMC) Path and spend Sunday in Campton at Sanborn's, sending their trunks by railroad. The usual vexatious delays prevented their starting until nearly as late as I did on July 18. It was a great temptation for me not to acquiesce in their cordially expressed wish and make the ascent again with so nice a party. But it was impracticable, fortunately so as it proved. The bright morning of Friday settled into a dull cloudy afternoon and Saturday was a day of pouring rain. Mr. Sanborn and Mr. Dusseault, being on a walking tour through the mountains, stopped here a moment in their dripping overcoats on their way to Guernsey's[16] by way of the Flume House Saturday P.M. They reported that the party reached the Tip-Top House after seven o'clock. Fearing to be stormbound there, they marched down that evening to Breezy Point House by the carriage house, reaching there at 10:30. Dear me! How tired the ladies must have been! Mr. Sanborn calls it a hard tramp, but he is not an Ape. The ladies rode from here to C. A. Smith's, the gentlemen walked. We noticed the peculiarly graceful, light, and agile gait of Profes-

---

[16] The Guernsey Farm was located about one mile south of the Flume House in Franconia Notch. Mrs. Jessie Guernsey is credited with discovering the Flume while fishing the brook in the notch.

sor Fay. By-the-by he and Mr. Curtis succeeded in obtaining a garret room in an old farmhouse across the road for Thursday night. Their advent made quite a breeze of pleasurable excitement for us here.

Good night, dear Marian.

Your friend,
Isabella Stone

* * * * * * * * * * * *

Isabella Stone writes in her diary about a trip from the Russell House in North Woodstock to Franconia Falls and Black Pond.

August 13, 1883

We leave home at 6:30 A.M. with others going fishing. Arrive at Pollards at seven o'clock. Walk to Clear Brook, estimated two miles, 7:35 A.M. Cross Clear Brook and go on to Hancock Branch coming in on opposite side of river four miles from Pollard's. On our return Mr. Russell makes three slashing blazes on a young white birch on the side of the path nearest the river at a point opposite the mouth of Hancock Branch. Here is the place to cross the East Branch to continue on the nice path which runs upon the east bank.

Behind us is a fine view of the three peaks of Potash Mountain. On our right is Black Mountain and behind it Scar Ridge and good views of Mounts Huntington, Upham, and Hitchcock. We walk through a mile or more of waist high brakes and then through the "burnt district." From Hancock Branch at 8:20 A.M. to Franconia Branch at 10:30 A.M., five miles in two hours and ten minutes in all. The path is much poorer and at times somewhat obscure. We pass on our left the brook outlet of Black Pond. We follow a side path down a few yards to Franconia Branch and sit down, drink and christen the spot "our morning drinking place."

At twenty minutes of eleven we start up Franconia Branch by a rude path on the west bank which we soon leave for the bed of the stream. We go down a steep bank, across a divide on an island and another divide to the Branch. About one mile up the stream are the falls, twelve to fifteen feet high spouting out and around the ledges of rock worn smooth by water, resembling Agassiz Basin. About to leap a chasm over the foaming torrent, I slip and but for Mr. Russell seizing me, I should have gone in and down to a deep huge basin and been drowned. We climb on up to a noisy cascade over which is stretched a huge log denuded of bark. We pass on our left a cave and higher up on our right is a great slanting rock, overhanging the stream so as to make a large cavern, and darkening the water which is a deep placid pool extending into it from which pours out a cold damp atmosphere.

We lunch by the big log at 11:30 A.M. Attempting to spread my gray shawl to dry on this log —Mr. Russell having dropped it in a pool we crossed below—a rock under my foot rolls away and I fall heavily striking again the lower part of my spine (as at Walker Falls in 1882) so as to make me faint for a minute or two. It aches and stings terribly and deprives me of my appetite for lunch. Mr. Russell rushes to the rescue and looks very sorry and sympathetic, afterwards offering, in the most delicate manner, to retire and let me bathe my back, which I decline. Every step on the way home hurts me especially springing over logs.

At five minutes to one o'clock we start downwards through the woods past the falls, keeping on the right bank of the stream as in ascending. On our left we pass a bark camp low down while our path is on the terrace. We go down and examine it, then we go back to the point where we left the path and follow it up a steep little hill until we find it forks with the right hand path leading to the falls, about forty rods, and the left hand to Black Pond, one-half mile. Mr. Russell blazes two trees and I mark the signs with a pencil as above. This at two o'clock. Then we travel to Black Pond which deserves its name. We stand on the eastern shore. A rough path runs on our left down to the outlet, but we have no time or strength to follow it. We return to our signs, arriving at 2:45 P.M., having taken forty-five minutes to do the pond. Repassing the bark camp, we hasten on our way through the rain. We reach the East Branch at Franconia Brook at three o'clock. One must be very careful not to get off the track, which is at times very plain, but occasionally quite obscure. The woods seem interminable, bushes are dripping wet and so are we soon. My old gossamer is soaked in half an hour. We arrive at Pollards at 6:20 P.M. and we are so wet, feet and clothes, that we do not dare wait for our team which Fred was ordered to bring at seven o'clock. So we pack our heavy wraps left at Pollard's into my big shawl bag which Mr. Russell carries. I've donned a gray shawl so as to disguise somewhat my wet and shaggy appearance and condition. We walk rapidly homeward meeting our carriage after half or three-quarter's of a mile, before reaching David Dearborn's house about 7:30 P.M.

* * * * * * * * * * * *

Isabella Stone writes in her diary about a trip from the Russell House in North Woodstock to Jefferson Highlands.

August 16, 1883

I leave North Woodstock at 7:40 A.M. with Miss Mary Collins of New York in the big wagon with my two trunks and my medicine box. Mr. Russell drove looking pale and sleepy having been ill the day and night before. We find that the trees and bushes around the Basin have been cut down so as to show the Basin and waterfall and the upper cascades quite plainly from the wagon in the road. We water the horses and ourselves at the spring by Mrs. Dolloff's who is just sweeping out her store and has not yet spread out her stock. We pause at "Half Way Place"[17] and I take a last look of admiration and awe. (Between the Basin and Mrs. Dolloff's, Mr. Russell and I notice the tree we blazed to mark junction of Cascade Brook with Pemigewasset River last summer.) Miss Collins talks a great deal, I some, Mr. Russell none. We pass Profile Lake, and pause to gaze again at the "Old Man of the Mountain" while Mr. Russell and I speculate as to the point we went down to above his head. I bid farewell in my heart to the grand face and beautiful lake.

It is bright, sunny and breezy, but towards noon, as we drive down into Franconia, the sky clouds over to a dull uniform gray, and the mountains grow hazy, threatening to rain by night. We arrive at Profile House at ten o'clock where we leave Miss Collins, and I take off some of my wraps while her trunks are removed.

Then Mr. Russell and I make a fresh start at 10:20 A.M. on our last ride together, the last for the season only, I trust. We water the horses at Echo Lake Spring, this being the first time this year that I have been there. Mr. Russell grows at once communicative and we keep up our usual pleasant, friendly, confidential conversation all day; agreeing that we no longer feel merely like landlord and border, but like old friends. As we turn up the road to Bethlehem, I eagerly recognize and hail the dear familiar peaks and the various boardinghouses, especially Goodnow House. From Echo Lake past Bald Mountain and down the long hill towards Franconia. How dear and welcome it all seems with the familiar vistas and mountains seen before this summer. All hail the Goodnow House and Sugar Hill of Blessed Memory!! For a few minutes I feel a desire well nigh irresistible to ride directly to Goodnow's and stop. But we go on over the old stage road to Bethlehem, every yard of which is familiar to me. How grand the view is! Goodbye to Liberty Peak as it peeps up away down the Notch. This ground is new to Mr. Russell and me together having no associations with it until today's ride forms such. His lunch has been forgotten and he tries to buy crackers at two houses. Just before reaching the crest of the hill near the Mount Agassiz Carriage Road Tollhouse and in full view of the Franconia Range near a white house on the right, we stop for our lunch and to bait the horses at 12:15 P.M.

Mr. Russell goes for water to the spring, while I get over the stone wall and find a good place in the field back of the barn where we spread the heavy blanket robe and sit down together. Mr. Russell first presenting me my tin cup of water; "One more cup of cold water for you." The residents of this house have evidently locked up and gone away. I share my lunch with Mr. Russell—plain bread and butter being all he dare eat.

We have been talking about Fred Russell's future and his lack of aim

---

[17] Known today as Lafayette Place.

Sinclair House

and perseverance. Now we talk of their winter life, rooms they occupy, their plans for alterations in the house, etc. Mr. Russell says several pleasant things about our excursions together and we exchange invitations to correspond. At one o'clock I carry dipper back to spring, Mr. Russell harnesses and we drive down into Bethlehem at Sinclair House[18].

Mr. Russell leaves me at the office of the *Echo*, but the editor is gone to dinner so I can't see him. Mr. Russell goes up the street to the cafe, at my earnest desire to eat crackers and have a cup of hot tea. I walk up there and we drive down Bethlehem Street taking the first road on the left just beyond Maplewood[19]—same as in going to Whitefield—which leads to Bethlehem Hollow. We inquire our way thence to Wing Road Station, and take the left hand road following close to the river which is on our left all

---

[18] Originally a two-story home, the Sinclair House was opened in 1859 as a stage tavern with rooms for boarders. Over the years, it was developed into a huge and commodious hostelry, becoming the leading establishment of Bethlehem Village.

[19] In 1871 Isaac S. Cruft came to Bethlehem from Boston and purchased the Maplewood Farm. He remodeled the farmhouse and opened a small hotel. In 1876, on the same property, Mr. Cruft erected a spacious and elegant hotel known as Maplewood. Business flourished and the hotel was ranked among the best in the White Mountains. Some of the buildings remain today on the grounds of the Maplewood Country Club.

E. A. Crawford's Boardinghouse

the way. It is about four miles from Sinclair House to Wing Road, where we arrive at 2:20 P.M. My train for Whitefield leaves at 3:17 P.M. I ask the ticket-master to "help my driver get off my baggage" which he does. Then Mr. Russell and I bid each other a cordial "good-bye" with a hearty grip of ungloved hands (and!) both sorry to part. The ride has been very delightful to me, though feeling sad to leave North Woodstock and the Franconia Notch where I have enjoyed so much this summer. As Mr. Russell swung me out of the wagon, a strange feeling came over me for a moment or two that it would be the last time forever, and struck a pang in my heart! But I shook off the presentiment as mere fancy, and hopefully said good-bye with its old meaning, "God be with you." Mr. Russell drove away at 2:30 P.M.

I checked baggage and bought ticket for Jefferson via Whitefield where I need not change cars, if I get into a particular car, which I do.

This Wing Road depot is very bewildering. I arrive at Jefferson at 4:15 P.M., no team to meet me from E. A. Crawford's[20], so I wait till ten minutes of

---

[20] Crawford's Boardinghouse in Jefferson Highlands was established in 1874 by Ethan Allen Crawford, Jr. Shortly thereafter, Ethan Allen Crawford, III became the proprietor. The house burned down in 1905 and subsequently the property was sold to Mr. James Carter. In addition to being an innkeeper, Ethan Allen, III was also the builder of the Jefferson Notch Road (completed in 1902) which runs from Bretton Woods to Jefferson Highlands through a mountain pass. This nine-mile road reaches an elevation of 3,008 feet, which remains today the highest point of any through road in NH.

six train, when Miss Beatrice Crawford comes down for the mail and I ride up to the house with her and the pet spaniel Brownie on a buckboard, five miles, arriving at seven o'clock. My baggage is brought by the Mount Adams House team. Miss Hattie Crawford insists that I wrote I was coming Wednesday, August 15, and she was down to the depot for both trains.

* * * * * * * * * * *

Marian Pychowska writes to Isabella Stone.

Ravine House
Randolph, N.H.
Thursday, August 16, 1883

Dear Isabella,

So you have deserted the regal house of Franconia and placed yourself under the shadow of the Presidents. It is strange that you should have left Liberty behind you, but that Liberty wears a Phrygian cap and is after all only a freed slave!

I thought to have a message of welcome awaiting you when you arrived at Ethan Allen's, but when, with this view, I questioned Mr. Crawford last night, I learned that probably you had already come. At all events, it is not too late to prepare a hearty welcome for you at the Ravine House, whenever you find it convenient to come and spend the day with us. My mother, uncle, and aunt, Mr. Rockwell (the New Haven Ape), Mr. Peek and others have gone on Mt. Adams today to put up the distance signs. Three of us finished the measurement of our new path via Durand Ridge last Saturday. The path is four and one-half miles long, Lowe's is just under four miles. Mr. Sargent is expected next week, and then I suppose will come off the two days trip to Moriah and Carter Dome. Mr. Rockwell's stay is reduced to two weeks, so my uncle is putting him through a fearful course of sprouts—the Gulch, King's Ravine to Madison, and Mt. Adams on three successive days.

You have probably already made the acquaintance of some of the Crawfordites. Mr. William H. Ladd and Miss Frothingham we met on the Twin Mountain excursion. The latter is a famous little lady for tramping. We have seen her more than once on Mt. Adams with Mr. Lowe, and it was only last Tuesday they came round from the camp and down Durand Ridge. Do you not feel inspired to try some of these high climbs again, when there is not a bitter east wind like that of September last?

Thanks for the end of the Moosilauke account. What a pity the loggers and barkers are always upsetting our paths. Mr. Currier[21], one of the Twin Mountain party, sent my mother a printed account of that expedition written by him which would interest you, if you have not already seen it.

---

[21] S. E. D. Currier of Boston, MA, was a founding member of the AMC.

Thanks too for your last kind letter. The opening quotation is beautiful and, as is often the way with genius, holds a more practical truth than Mr. Ralph Waldo Emerson (whose I take it to be) could know. It is only those who love God "with all their heart and all their soul, with all their mind and all their strength" who can be united in a true friendship in Him. Hoping to see you soon, I remain always,

Yours very sincerely,

M. M. Pychowska

* * * * * * * * * * * *

Marian Pychowska writes a postal card to Isabella Stone.

Ravine House

Randolph, N.H.

August 23, 1883

Dear Isabella,

I was sorry not to be able to speak to you yesterday evening being deep in preparation for tea, after our day's tramp. It was a delightful day and the walk to Mt. Jefferson easier than we anticipated. Today the others go to Pine Mountain. Tomorrow I expect to join them on the Castellated Ridge expedition. I will tell you about it when we meet. The between days I must occupy with finishing the paper on Evans Notch and Royce which is wanted for the Conway Meeting of the AMC on September 4. You shall see a copy.

We do not at all care to keep the Twin Mountain account, so will turn it over to you. I am glad you had such a lovely day at the Glen. Did not know when we looked down at it between the great knees of Adams and Jefferson you were looking up at the same mountains. Hope we can arrange a meeting sometime next week. Mr. Sargent has come. Mt. Carter will be in order as soon as circumstances permit.

Yours, M. M. P.

* * * * * * * * * * * *

Marian Pychowska writes a postal card to Isabella Stone.

Ravine House

Randolph, N.H.

August 24, 1883

Dear Isabella,

Tomorrow morning, unless rain is or threatens seriously, my mother and I will be at Mr. Lowe's at 9:30. If you have no other plan for the day, feel well and it be agreeable to you, join us there at that hour and we will spend the day in King's Ravine. If this seems too much of an undertaking we can plan something milder at our tryst. You have your things here, so can either spend the night or return with Mr. Crawford after tea. If anything interferes with your joining us do not feel at all distressed, for we shall not be inconvenienced and can plan for some other time.

The Castellated Ridge is indefinitely postponed. The Carters are resting in preparation.

Yours,
M.M.P.

* * * * * * * * * * * *

Lucia Pychowska writes a postal card to Isabella Stone.

Ravine House
Randolph, N.H.
August 27, 1883

My dear Isabella,

I find I am much wanted to go at least as far as the top of Moriah on the coming expedition. As the party starts tomorrow or Tuesday according to the weather, I shall not be able to go to the Pond of Safety on Tuesday. As soon as I can, I will write again to let you know when we can go, when I hope you will be able to accompany us. I am sorry to change my plans, but several reasons make it seem best for me to do so.

Affectionately yours,
L. D. Pychowska

P.S. They are off, but not I. Will write again when we can go.

* * * * * * * * * * * *

Lucia Pychowska writes a postal card to Isabella Stone.

Ravine House
Randolph, N.H.
August 29, 1883

My dear Isabella,

Mr. Peek, Marian and I went to meet the party (Mr. and Miss Cook, Miss Barstow, Mr. Sargent, Mr. Lowe and his son[22]) as they came out on the top of Carter Dome. They appeared at five minutes before three o'clock P.M., in excellent condition, the ladies unwearied, and with scarcely a rent in their garments. They found the distance from Moriah, over the ridges of Imp Mountain and the various heads of Carter, to be not over eight miles with less than one mile of bad scrub. The same party and Marian go tomorrow up the Castellated Ridge of Jefferson. (Mr. Lowe and his son not included.) When you are ready for the Pond of Safety send a line to say so. It was well that both sides recently were prevented at the same

---

[22] Two of Charles Lowe's sons, Thaddeus and Vyron, were notable guides in their own right.

time. Did you see the parhelia and other curious cloud phenomena this morning? Marian and Mr. Peek were both prevented from accompanying the Carter-Moriah party. Explanations when we meet.

Truly Yours,
L. D. Pychowska

* * * * * * * * * * * *

Lucia Pychowska writes a postal card to Isabella Stone.

Ravine House
Randolph, N.H.
August 31, 1883

My dear Isabella,

Should Monday be a good day, I see no reason why we should not go to the Pond of Safety. The path goes from our house, and if you will be here about nine o'clock, that will be ample time to start. The smoky atmosphere need not interfere with that walk, but I advise you not go to Mt. Adams until the air is clearer. There is no difficulty at all in your going alone with Mr. Lowe, a most respectable man, father of a family, and an excellent husband. He will be as careful of you as if you were his own daughter. We can talk it over when I see you. The excursion to Castellated Ridge turned out fine. All were well repaid.

Very truly yours,
Lucia D. Pychowska

* * * * * * * * * * * *

Marian Pychowska writes a postal card to Isabella Stone.

Ravine House
Randolph, N.H.
September 5, 1883

Dear Isabella,

Your note received. We took it as certain you would not go on Adams today, so were quietly at work in the house when the bundle came. I cannot yet tell what will be done tomorrow. Wildcat is a possibility, but if Mr. Watson is disengaged, he will go with my uncle to help cut the trail toward the Castles[23]. If this be done, we, my mother and I, may see you on some part of Lowe's Path. Do not look for us certainly.

Hope the weather will be favorable for your trip. If we should by any chance not be at home when you come down Adams, go to our room and make yourself comfortable. Your things are on the shelf in the closet.

M. P.

---

[23] The Castle Trail.

Isabella Stone writes in her diary about a trip to Mount Adams.

Thursday
September 6, 1883

My guide and sole companion, Charles E. Lowe of Randolph. Why attempt to describe the indescribable? I will not. I will merely endeavor to construct a skeleton, a memorandum of times and distances, which my own memory can clothe with flesh and blood.

Wednesday is a cold windy day with heavy lowering clouds on the mountains which are swept clear by the hurricane of a northwest wind, so that Thursday morning dawns crystal clear and absolutely cloudless, cool and calm and bright and sunny, after a frosty cold night.

I rise at 5:15 A.M., dress in a kersimere suit with a little knit shirt under my old Park Street Union Flannel, and cotton flannel drawers. Breakfast at 6:15 A.M. Lunch put up. Leave Crawford's at seven o'clock and drive to Mr. Lowe's arriving at 7:20 A.M.

Into his big basket Mr. Lowe puts my worsted jacket, mother's blanket and shawl, my old hood, my rubber shoe bag and his own lunch. I put on rubbers to go through the meadow and cross the Moose River on stones and a board. At 7:30 A.M. we start on to the path from Lowe's house, Mr. Lowe and his yellow dog, Rover, and I. Mr. Lowe straps his basket on his back and I don my skeleton knapsack holding my gray flannel wadded sack. I walk ahead.

At 8:20 A.M. we reach the point where a path diverges with guide board, "King's Ravine" on our left. Thus far our route has been the same as that followed by Marian and I when we went into the King's Ravine. Today Mr. Lowe and I keep on upon the regular "Lowe's Path" up Mt. Adams via Nowell's Ridge. We have reached this "King's Ravine Path" (one and one-half miles) in fifty minutes from Lowe's. The usual time allowed is one hour and thirty minutes, so we are forty minutes ahead of average walking time for ladies.

We reach Lowe's Camp at fifteen minutes to nine o'clock and record our names in the AMC metallic bottle with date and time from Lowe's— one hour and fifteen minutes. Here is a spring (the only one on this path) where we drink from my Moosilauke tin cup. This is our first fine outlook northward and Mr. Lowe begins to exult in the wonderfully clear day we are having. Our path continues on past the camp which is at our left hand as we resume the trail, while on our right hand diverges southwest the path with its sign "to the Ravine of the Cascades," which is the ravine on the eastern side of Castellated Ridge between Adams and Jefferson.

Our path is excellent, but very steep, and the small trees left growing on either side are of great assistance in pulling oneself up. The air is damp and cold in these dense woods, not yet penetrated by the morning sunshine, and after the exertion of climbing it makes my lungs and bronchial tubes ache to breathe it. Remember that after crossing the Moose

River and entering the woods, rubber shoes are not necessary until you are ready to leave Lowe's Camp when, there is a short interval of mud. After that there is no wet, and leaky rubbers are just as serviceable for clambering over the rocks above timberline, but this work wears out rubbers sadly, especially walking over the dead roots of the scrub which has been chopped through. I ruined one nearly new pair of rubbers. Lowe's Camp is about two miles from Lowe's house and if it can be so easily reached in one hour fifteen minutes, I cannot imagine why any one should go there and camp over night in order to ascend Adams, but many do consider it necessary.

We mount through evergreen growth and ever dwindling trees. At our left we pass one of Mr. Peek's signs, "Monte Video"[24], a blazed trail leading out perhaps fifty rods to a separate little peak affording a good view, a peak which Mr. Lowe afterwards points out to me from our higher station.

At fifteen minutes of ten o'clock we emerge above timberline, and what a glorious view bursts upon my excited eyes! Just before this, however, as I am hurrying on to follow the path curving round to the right of a rocky bluff[25], Mr. Lowe calls me to observe the view behind me. Here we discern Lafayette to the extreme southwest. We pass through an interval of low bushes, and then emerge as above. The wind begins to feel very cold and piercing and I put on my capuchin and also tie on my hat at the next rocky bluff or second viewpoint[26]. Soon I don my worsted jacket and wear it constantly till we reach the woods on Durand Ridge coming home.

Following the cairns, we clamber over rocks of all sizes lying at every conceivable angle. Mr. Lowe seats me in a sheltered nook to admire the northern view. From here he points out Monte Video. Up again and on we go hand in hand over the rocks. I get out of breath very quickly and have to stop very often to rest. The wind is very cold and blows hard, giving me, with the exertion, a terrible pain in my head, which is relieved by sitting down, or even standing still in sheltered spots. I have to put on my hood over my capuchin and tie my hat over all (my pansy shade hat).

We come out on the head of Nowell's Ridge, whence I think we get our first view of the true summit of Adams with its signal staff of the U.S. Coast Survey. Here Mr. Lowe leaves me to rest with Rover and carries off my cup to get water to drink for himself out of a little hollow in the rocks which I do not like. From this point I get a fine view of the grassy col into which our route descends by a rapid incline, passing by the western peak

---

[24] Mountain viewpoint.
[25] The Quay
[26] Gray Knob

called "Sam Adams" on our right and making straight for the main peak of Adams. Here for the first time I comprehend the relation of the several peaks to one another and understand that one need not pass over "Sam Adams Peak" to reach our summit, as I had supposed. The air is so clear that every rock and every tree stands out in startling distinctiveness, and the various near knobs and shoulders of Adams, and even Madison itself, seem near enough to be touched! Mr. Lowe takes me to the top of Sam Adams and enjoys my delighted astonishment when the whole glorious sweep of Mount Washington with the Great Gulf, carriage road, and houses on its summit, charms our vision. Adams from here appears as a perfect cone, a majestic pyramid, and Madison is only second in imposing beauty. Wind blows a pretty stiff breeze and my thermometer registers forty degrees! Time is 11:00 A.M.

We descend towards Adams, hurrying over the rocks in the intervening hollow[27], casting backward glances of admiration on to Washington and Jefferson as we mount the cone of Adams proper. We reach the summit at 11:30 A.M. which is four hours from Mr. Lowe's and excellent time for the ascent. The usual time for ladies is five and often six hours. We stay here two full hours, eating our lunch and admiring the view and identifying various peaks. We record our names, date, and time in the AMC bottle, and Mr. Lowe sets his heliotrope and flashes to his own house and the Ravine House, plainly visible with the road in front of them, away down northwards at the foot of our mountain. He also flashes to the Glen House and east to Mount Washington. But no one replies to us from either point. All my wraps are needed. Thermometer now reads forty-four degrees.

We leave at 1:30 P.M. descending the steep northeastern slope of the cone over the roughest rocks with sharp edges. Short as is my skirt, it catches and throws me forward, once in a dangerous manner. Endeavoring to recover myself, I fairly knock Mr. Lowe down. No one is hurt, fortunately. We find a large and beautiful specimen of rock containing small but exquisite quartz crystals. We pick up several other stones as mementoes for me.

We then ascend John Quincy Adams, sit down and look over into the grand Madison Ravine, Star Lake and the Glen Ridge[28] running down from Madison. Then we go up to the tiptop and Mr. Lowe puts me—or helps me put myself—on to the very highest point of the huge top rock where there is room for only one person. Hurrah! Down again, and we turn gradually towards the left reluctantly leaving Madison on our right looking so near and alluring! There would be time enough to climb it, really, but I prudently refrain to please mother.

We pass the sign at the head of the "new" path marked four and

---

[27] Thunderstorm Junction.
[28] Known today as Osgood Ridge.

one-half miles. By this path we go home over Durand Ridge. We arrive at
the Gateway of King's Ravine at 2:15 P.M. Part way down the wall of the
ravine, before reaching the Gateway, we discover two fellows eating their
lunch, who inquire the way and distance to Mt. Washington. We go on in
a delightfully leisurely way, Mr. Lowe frequently taking me to the edge
for fine views into and over King's Ravine. I step down the Gateway a
few yards and returning, catch the beautiful view of the cone of Madison,
about which Marian wrote me. Mr. Lowe points out to me, at my request,
the grotto or natural camp discovered by Professor Fay and himself in
their famous climb up the wall of the Ravine from the bed of Cold Brook.
Coming on down I am not quite sure which is the huge pile of rocks on
Durand Ridge where last autumn I was obliged to halt and wait while
Marian and Mrs. Pychowska went to the Gateway.

At 3:15 P.M. we reach timberline again, and taking one last fond lingering look at all we love so well, we say "good-bye," having enjoyed five
and one-half hours of unobstructed mountain views since we got above
timberline on Nowell's Ridge at fifteen minutes of ten o'clock.

I took off hood, capuchin and jacket. We tramped on a much rougher
path than Mr. Lowe's of the morning, abounding in moss which Mr. Lowe
admires. At one of our rests before reaching "Bruin Rock," two lovely
hermit thrushes come quite near us, on the branches hopping, and with
querulous notes answering my "peep, peep." Rover scares them away.
We reach "Bruin Rock" at 4:00 P.M. where we rest and notice the slide far
up above us at the right and across Snyder Brook, whose music tantalizes
us with its water far below, for we are very thirsty, having drunk no water
since we left Lowe's Camp at 9:00 A.M. We go on down to Upper Salmacis
Falls, drinking from its great basin, forty-six degrees by my thermometer.
Here we rest some time, being two and one-half miles from the road. Then
on to Lower Salmacis, more picturesque than the Upper because the water turns when halfway down and does not fall in one straight slope from
top to bottom, in other words the granite ledges are broken and curved.
There is so little water compared with the amount last autumn that I
scarcely recognize the falls. We reach the Ravine House at 6:05 P.M.

How pleasant to come out of the woods on to the meadow of the
Moose River, into the late afternoon sunshine, and look back up to the
heights we have left suffused with a golden saffron tint in the light of the
setting sun. Mr. Pychowski greets me with effusion, calling for three cheers
and a tiger for me. Mrs. Pychowska and Mr. Thompson[29] have gone to
Carter Dome #2 today, in the Glen, while Mr. and Miss Cook, Marian, and
Mr. Sargent explore Mount Wildcat.

Mr. Crawford, Senior drives me home, where we arrive at 7:30 P.M.

---

[29] Mr. Leonard Thompson, Jr. of Woburn, MA

Postal Card

Ravine House Sept. 7th
1883.

My dear Isabella, We were sorry not to be able to meet you
yesterday on Durand Ridge, but
delighted to hear that you had
had so successful a day with
so little fatigue. Mr Cook, Miss
C—, Marian, Mr Sargent, and Mr
Mathews went yesterday over
Wild Cat; and Mr Thompson
and I went over Carter Dome
and the new path to Carter's
Dome, No 2 —. We did not get
home until nearly half past
eight. Marian flashed to you
from the cliffs on Wild Cat
to the top of Mt. Adams, about
2 P.M., but probably you
had left before that time.
The top and the view from
Carter D— 2 are superb. We
had 1 3/4 hours on the summit,
and got down to the Glen House
over Carter Dome and the North
path by 5. 40 P. M.. Mr Peckham
represented you as looking not in the
least weary. Affec. L. D. P.—

Lucia Pychowska writes a postal card to Isabella Stone.

Ravine House
Randolph, N.H.
September 7, 1883

My dear Isabella,

We were sorry not to be able to meet you yesterday on Durand Ridge, but delighted to hear that you had so successful a day with so little fatigue. Mr. Cook, Miss Cook, Marian, Mr. Sargent, and Mr. Matthews went yesterday over Wildcat; and Mr. Thompson and I went over Carter Dome and the new path to Carter Dome, #2. We did not get home until nearly half past eight. Marian flashed to you from the cliffs on Wildcat to the top of Mt. Adams, about two P.M., but probably you had left before that time. The top and the view from Carter Dome #2 are superb. We had one and three-quarter hours on the summit, and got down to the Glen House over Carter Dome and the Notch Path[30] by 5:40 P.M. Mr. Pychowski represents you as looking not in the least weary.

Affectionately,
L. D. P.

* * * * * * * * * * * *

Lucia Pychowska writes a postal card to Isabella Stone.

Ravine House
Randolph, N.H.
September 9, 1883

My dear Isabella,

Thanks for your note. The party went yesterday to cut the path to Castellated Ridge—path not finished yet.

I advise you to accompany the party to the top of Mt.Starr King. It will interest you and be very easy. We shall not go again on Carter. The path from Carter Dome #2 is all cut. The distance from Carter Dome #1 is about three-quarters of a mile making the distance from the Glen House about five miles or a little over. It is an easy walk. Mr. Nowell, yesterday or the day before, saw in the distance a bear eating berries on the top of Carter Dome #2. He and Mr. Lowe were on the top of Carter Dome #1 putting up an observatory, so that one can now see over the scrub.

We have no plans as yet for this week—perhaps Safety Pond again tomorrow for the benefit of Miss Tompson, who could not go when you went.

Affectionately yours,
L. D. Pychowska

---

[30] The Nineteen-Mile Brook Trail.

Marian Pychowska writes a postal card to Isabella Stone.

Ravine House
Randolph, N.H.
September 10, 1883

Dear Isabella,

Today the gentlemen went to Moriah with barometers, leaving me home to observe one instrument for comparison.

Four ladies went to Safety Pond. Go to Starr King by all means. I will write you tomorrow what is arranged for Wednesday. It will probably be Pine Mountain. If so, would be glad to have you join us.

Always yours,
M. P.

P.S. Our arrangements are so uncertain, do not let slip any other opportunity you may have to employ the good weather.

* * * * * * * * * * * *

Lucia Pychowska writes a postal card to Isabella Stone.

Ravine House
Randolph, N.H.
Tuesday afternoon
September 11, 1883

My dear Isabella,

I am desired by Mr. Nowell to say to you that he proposes camping tomorrow night at the camp on Mt. Adams with Gracie and Mr. Lowe. Miss Barstow and her niece will probably join him and if you like, he would like to have you join the party. This might give you an opportunity for going on to Mt. Jefferson.

We propose going tomorrow on Pine Mountain if the weather be suitable. If you care to go we shall be glad to have you. We expect to start at 9:00 A.M., but we shall wait ten minutes later to give you time to arrive if you should be on the way. Do what you like best. I fear a little the weather.

Affectionately yours,
L. D. Pychowska

P.S. Postal received. Part of the way to Pine Mountain is without path. The distance from the house is about eight miles there and back. In going to Mt. Jefferson one may leave Lowe's Path on Nowell Ridge or go on to Sam Adams.

Marian Pychowska writes a postal card to Isabella Stone.

> Ravine House
> Randolph, N.H.
> September 14, 1883

Dear Isabella,

Thanks for your parcel and your notes received. Thanks too for the very kind renewal of your invitation to my aunt and me. I am sorry not to be able to fix a time for our little visit. I would gladly make it tomorrow, but cannot get any decision from my aunt. As our movements are so uncertain, do not expect us at all and do not let the thought of our possible coming interfere with any of your doings.

Yesterday, my mother, Miss Trask[31], and I finished the measurement of our "shortcut"[32] to Lowe's Camp. The distance from here is a very little over three miles thus saving one mile in comparison with the way by road to Lowe's and thence to the camp.

The camping party got in about eight last night, having been to Adams and Jefferson and down by the new Castle Trail. Miss Barstow left camp very early and had time to include Mt. Clay in her day's trip. They report the new path excellent. I hope you will be able to corroborate their testimony next week.

With all best wishes for these last mountain days when the leaves are changing under our very eyes.

> I remain always yours,
> M. P.

* * * * * * * * * * * *

Marian Pychowska writes a postal card to Isabella Stone.

> Ravine House
> Randolph, N.H.
> September 15, 1883

Dear Isabella,

Here I am again to tell you the plan which has developed itself for my mother and me regarding the employment of the early part of the coming week. Tomorrow afternoon we propose to walk down to Gorham where we shall spend the night. Monday morning after we have been to church, we plan to walk on to Gates' Cottage and pay the visit we wished to make last year.

I look forward with pleasure to the walk down the north side of the

---

[31] Susie C. Trask of Beverly, MA.

[32] This trail was known as Chicago Avenue, named in honor of Chicagoan William H. Peek. The lower portion of this trail is known today as the Amphibrach.

river and to being once more in those old haunts.

We expect to be back here on Tuesday for dinner. My aunt, I believe, has no plans yet, and the gentlemen have a number of crazy things on hand. If anything should bring you Randolphward again before you leave, I hope we may meet once more before the scattering time. If this is not to be, good-bye and may you find your parents well and Goodnow's as pleasant as of you.

M. P.

* * * * * * * * * * * *

Marian Pychowska writes to Isabella Stone.

Ravine House
Randolph, N.H.
September 19, 1883

Dear Isabella,

My aunt and I drove over to Crawford's this morning, thinking we might find you at home packing for today's transit to Sugar Hill. What was our surprise to find you already gone, and our regret to hear that your departure was hurried by the illness of someone (Mr. Crawford could not tell us who) at Goodnows. I hope we may have a card from you soon to tell us that nothing serious is the matter and that you and your parents are getting the benefit of these beautiful <u>October</u> days.

Providence blessed our Gorham and Shelburne excursion in every way. We met a kind reception from the Miss Larys with whom we passed Sunday night. After an early visit to church on Monday morning, we held a consultation in regard to the weather and decided to trust the lowering sky. In spite of the murky air we enjoyed our walk by the familiar path and byroad to Gates' Cottage. Here again we were met with open arms by Miss Sara and her mother, though we were entirely unexpected, my mother's card announcing us not having arrived. All their boarders had left and Miss Sara was deep in the wash tub, but all was put aside to entertain the surprise party and prepare for the hungry tramps a most appetizing dinner of tender meat and delicious white and sweet potatoes, corn, and tomatoes. While we were sitting in pleasant converse with these good people, a regular "Shelburne breeze" swept down out of Baldcap and cleared the smoky air like magic, so that all the familiar hills looked at us with clean faces. We were pressed hard to stay over night, but my mother thought that, as we had reached there so early in the day and paid our visit, we would best get back to Randolph to tea. So after dinner we were comfortably wrapped up and tucked into the two seated wagon and drove back to Gorham through the beautiful rain. Alighting at Lary's, Miss Ruth ushered us into their sitting room where we toasted by the open fire until the showers passed over and we could set out on the home tramp. No one expected us, but we were allowed to take our places at the supper table as usual and to have our share of the sunset. It was well we had not delayed our return, for Tuesday proved to be the very day we had been waiting for to take Miss Tompson on Mt. Adams.

Everybody wanted an early breakfast that morning, for the Raviners were to scatter in every direction from Mt. Washington to the forsaken Mt. Pliny. We made our climb very slowly and enjoyed old Durand more than ever in his gorgeous autumn dress of crimson and gold. Up near the Gateway we found quite a quantity of blossoms on the alpine rhododendron, one of the flowers that stirred our botanical hearts on our first ascent in June. Miss Tompson was too tired by the unusual exertion of climbing to attempt the last pull from the Gateway to the summit, so we let my mother and aunt go on to the top, and we two ate dinner and rested at the ravine head, and then crossed the base of "John Quincy" to Star Lake. Here we stretched ourselves out in a soft, sunny spot and lazily studied Washington and the steep rocky sides of Adams and Madison and the deep gulf below us with the Carters and Wildcat beyond.

The home returning was very gently taken, but I think we may flatter ourselves that Miss Tompson has received no harm from the trip, and she certainly enjoyed it greatly, in spite of her fatigue. My aunt sent flashes to Mt. Jefferson thinking you might be there. That will be for another year. Mr. Crawford told us today he meant to have a path and camp[33] of his own on Mt. Jefferson. How they are all getting stirred up!

My mother and aunt join me in regards to you and Dr. and Mrs. Stone and wishes for the health of all. We shall scatter next week. I do not know whether my parents and I shall join the rest at Bartlett next Thursday the 27th or stay here till the following Monday and go directly home.

Yours always,

M. M. Pychowska

P.S. Please remember us to Mr. and Mrs. Goodnow and any old acquaintances who may be at Sugar Hill.

---

[33] Camp Crawford and the Camp Crawford Path were built shortly hereafter by Fred Crawford, who was the brother of Ethan Allen Crawford, III. The path began at a point approximately four miles up from the northern end of the future Jefferson Notch Road and ended near the summit of Mount Jefferson. The camp was located next to a brook at nearly 4,000 feet on this path. At first, it was only a small, enclosed log cabin. In 1897, a cook house and a little terrace were added. It fell into disrepair during the massive lumbering operations of 1910.

Marian Pychowska writes a postal card to Isabella Stone.

Hoboken, N.J.
October 22, 1883

Dear Isabella,

Thanks to the wonderful birthday memory and to the kind heart that prompts it. The card is a beauty. One side is like Sandy Hook, and the other like the Shrewsbury Heights of my native Jersey.

When this busy time has passed by, I have much to tell you of the days at Bartlett and how my aunt and I actually did reach the top of Carrigain. For two weeks our house has been a mill for the grinding out of *Appalachia* articles. My uncle has had his report to write, together with accounts of some of his solitary rambles. Where he had companions in his explorations he has turned the work of historian to my mother, aunt and me.

We had a call last evening from Mr. Trask, whom you remember on the Pine Mountain walk. Miss Barstow and Mr. Watson made an exploration of the Imp face of which she has written for the AMC.

Hoping you and yours are well,

Always your friend,
M. P.

* * * * * * * * * * * *

Marian Pychowska writes to Isabella Stone.

Hoboken, N.J.
December 16, 1883

My dear Isabella,

You must think me a very remiss Miss in regard to my promise of writing you about our adventures in Bartlett. Do you not think that nearly three months should be sufficient time to regain my breath after the arduous ascent of Carrigain? For ought I know, you may be in no condition to care about last seasons trifles, burdened as you are perhaps with sickness or anxiety, yet I will venture to open my store of nonsense, trusting it will be received with your usual benevolence.

I need not say much of our journey by wagon to Fabyan's[34], and our first ride through Crawford Notch by rail, for you know the route and what weather we had. The great object my mother had in view was that my father (infatuated with Randolph as he is) might see once more the beauty of Jefferson, and be introduced to Bartlett. In this respect our way

---

[34] Located on the site of the former "Giant's Grave" (an immense mound of gravel that was situated just above Crawford Notch), The Fabyan House was another of the grand hotels in the town of Carroll. The Fabyan House opened for business in 1872 and remained in operation until it burned in 1951.

was a continual triumph. My father had never cared to extend his walk beyond Mr. Lowe's and I suppose, thought it was mere inborn restlessness that made us look for anything better than the views just above the Ravine House. When, however, we drove out on the Bowman meadow and he saw that majestic Mt. Jefferson crowned with snow, he was ready to turn round and take us to task because we had not made more fuss about it. How pleasant it was to hear him repeat: "Next year this shall be my favorite walk."

You can imagine how we were all eyes during that all too rapid flight through the Notch. It immeasurably surpassed my expectation. It is certainly the grandest half hour I ever spent among the mountains, such the advantage of position, like a bird in the air, with the height above, the depth below, and the continual variety. My father was again the most enthusiastic in retracting past animadversions on the Portland and Ogdensburg Railroad. We have now only one crow to pick with it, and that is the defacement to the Gateway of the Notch by the piles of debris and wooden sheds which it seems a little art might disguise. After all, I fear that it is more by good luck than good management that the railroad has proved an advantage to mountain lovers. On the platform at Bartlett was my aunt and we soon learned the story of the advance guard.

Tuesday's fierce storm had prevented my uncle and the young men from coming down from Mount Washington by the Crawford Path, and driven them to make use of the railroad[35], a comfort not to be despised on this occasion. Wednesday, while we were watching the snow lying way down into King's Ravine, they were looking into the great Oakes' Gulf from Mounts Langdon and Parker. Thursday was devoted to visiting Mount Nancy. Perhaps before you get this you will have read Mr. Matthews account of these mountains in the forthcoming *Appalachia*.

After so many days of jaunting and lunching, the gentlemen were presumably tuned down more to our female capacity. Accordingly my aunt and I prepared ourselves to be of the Carrigain party on Friday, while my mother paid a morning visit to renowned little Langdon. Our grand, deceitful, old mountain gathered his clouds and veil of smoke about him, but we were not to be scared off by a shower nor even by the prospect of

---

[35] The Mount Washington Cog Railway runs from the foot of Ammonoosuc Ravine, on the western side of the mountain, to the summit. It was the first railway of its kind in the world. The projector of this new enterprise was Sylvester Marsh, a native son of New Hampshire. On June 25, 1858, the NH State Legislature granted Marsh a charter to build what one Legislator satirically called a "Railway to the Moon," a nickname that has been with the Cog ever since. Construction began in May of 1866 (after a delay brought on by the Civil War) under the direction of Walter Aiken of Franklin, NH. Aiken had also engineered the design of the Cog's locomotive. The railroad was completed in July of 1869. One hundred and twenty-six years later, it remains in operation today.

Cog Railway

seeing nothing when we got on top. A lovely drive up Sawyer's River ending at the strange mushroom mill village, and here our walk began.

There was a fine trunk logging road for about one and one-half or two miles and then we confronted a sign, "Carrigain", pointing across the road into the brush. Here my uncle had been thrown off the scent once before, but was now prepared for the blind way. It had been a road once, through a district where the large timber was largely cut out, and the way was principally distinguished by its thick growth of cherry and maple saplings. Once my aunt's quick eye saved our missing the track, but another time when I thought to do likewise, my advise led the party off in a wrong trail and we had a long troublesome time regaining it a mile or more beyond. Here the way was clearer, and we were cheered on by the frequent signs pointing to the mysterious mountain. At last we saw the large board, "Path of the American Institute of Instruction", and we sat to rest before the long breathless climb.

The men, released by us, gauged their own gait, and we kept on slowly and steadily up the steep well marked path, till we came out on the narrow Durand Ridge-like crest of Burnt Hat Ridge[36], (who will disburden it of its unworthy name?). We looked at the big cairn crowning the rocks that look so like an alpine summit, and then we followed the ridge down some distance, and from this hollow climbed the big, overgrown head of the mountain. The men had not been there long and our natural elation at reaching the much desired top was increased at what they had to tell us. The old sprite of the mountain had been found out in an unsuspected trick. When my uncle and Mr. Sargent had climbed the mountain in wind and cloud last year, they had not been on top as they supposed! They were on Burnt Hat Ridge, where the big cairn and the glass record bottle, the whole aspect of the place, assured them they were on the summit, the clouds not letting them see there was anything beyond the hollow down into which my uncle went part way. Now this time, in deference, doubtless, to the ladies, the party was permitted to reach the true top. The tops of the higher mountains were in the clouds, but as the day wore on the dirty smoke cleared and there was more than enough to satisfy geographer and artist during our stay. What was my pleasure, in the process of identification, to light on a little spot of shining water over beyond the Loon Pond ridge. Sure enough, little Peaked Hill Pond, and I remembered to have seen the tip of Carrigain when we visited that nook of Campton.

On our way down we stopped awhile on the Burnt Hat crest. This is by far the most impressive view, being clear of trees. You are just on the edge of a slope so steep that the stunted trees can hardly grow among the broken rock which covers it, and plunging down into the gorge of Carrigain Notch. Vose's Spur juts out boldly to your left, and opposite is the still steeper face of Lowell, whence part of the earth has fallen away exposing curiously wrought and brightly tinted cliffs, reminding one faintly of Yellowstone pictures. Our descent was rapid, the way kept throughout, and we were housed šoon after dark. When the path has been remade through the bad part, as Mr. Matthews reports is intended to be done, it will be an easy and delightful excursion for you.

The next day my parents and I were obliged to leave for home unexpectedly, finding it to be the last day we could make through connection by Fall River. Thus we had a peaceful Sunday here, my aunt and uncle having two more days in Bartlett. Mr. Sargent held out bravely (and perhaps rashly) with his lame foot, and moreover had a fall from a high tree

---

[36] Burnt Hat Ridge is known today as Signal Ridge. Mount Carrigain later had both a fire lookout tower and a warden's cabin as its location offers one of the most expansive views of the White Mountain region.

on Nancy but he returned alive to Boston and we hear he is busy with his studies at the medical school.

On Thanksgiving day we had a pleasant call from Mr. Matthews, coming on by way of the football match between Harvard and Yale. He was at the AMC meetings and heard of the Ravine House productions. He was not known to be there, so had the pleasure of hearing his papers well read by Miss Hale. Mr. Sargent did not so escape, being called up to do his own reading. We had the hope some Boston friend would send us a newspaper account, but none came.

Mr. Nowell wrote he meant to breathe the Appalachian Air of Hoboken, but has not yet done so. Lately we had an alpine walk across the Brooklyn Bridge to see Miss Barstow, who has lovely trophies of her last days at West Bethel in the snow. I have not much room left to tell of ourselves and present doings. As to the former, we are all well, and the latter I will leave for next time.

My mother joins me in love to you and kind regards to Dr. and Mrs. Stone,

As always, your friend,
M. M. Pychowska

1884

"Indeed, do we not enjoy the beautiful things about us, and do they not make a much deeper impression on us, when we must take them slowly and a little at a time, as an invalid is obliged to do, instead of skipping from viewpoint to viewpoint, greedily doing and seeing all and forgetting to say grace after our feast?"

Edith Cook writes to Isabella Stone.

Hoboken, N.J.
January 10, 1884

Dear Miss Stone,

At an early opportunity I seek to prove that I will not withdraw from my correspondence with you so long as it gives you pleasure to hear from me, and you feel like keeping up the double pen intercourse between your-self and our Hoboken household. It might be something of a tax on you to write to both Marian and myself, and so I thought, perhaps, you had found it and in this way have accounted for your long silence. I intended writing you last evening, having spent the morning with my brush at Madison Spring, but a friend came to tea and spent the evening and so my talk with you was postponed.

I was very sorry to find you gone that day I drove Marian over to Crawford's, that perfect day whose sweet atmosphere of idleness and soft happy autumn warmth was perfectly fascinating to my dreamy soul. I enjoyed intensely our drive over in the buckboard with the quiet mare that had no desire to make time and I was perfectly willing to haul up by the roadside and let everything pass us that cared to, feeling chiefly the desire to keep on driving indefinitely and no desire whatever to walk. The air was too soft to disturb with the persistent energy of climbing and my lazy hands didn't care to grasp anything less obedient than the light reins that rested so easily on my lap, but my eyes were in active service.

From Marian you have heard of our active days after that perfect day on Durand Ridge when Marian got Miss Tompson over to Star Lake and I took my last look from Mt. Adams. Though that was the day before you left, we imagined you on Mt. Jefferson and flashed a mirror and directed an opera glass over to the unresponsive peak.

The next week came the bright beautiful days at Bartlett when the Councillor and his companions scoured the hills so successfully and continuously, and, when I was alone in the valley, my comrades being off, I spent such perfect hours on gray rocks under golden oaks and blue skies or by the rapids of the Saco River with the daintiest of verse to read and a golden summer to think over and set into golden resolutions for the winter. The lovely mountain atmosphere of last September, like our present after glow, stretched far into the late autumn and the winter now with us. I even dreamed of golden oaks and birches while I was stirring my grape jelly over the kitchen range and the jelly wasn't burnt! I was more to the manner born than King Alfred.

I have seen Booth once during his present engagement in New York. Lillie and I went to see him in *King Lear*, a part in which she had never seen him and the impressive simplicity and pathos of which you know. I had a somewhat distracting subinterest when I saw *Lear* in watching the Regan of the night, who was Miss Bartlett, the Portsmouth girl who has been at the Ravine House both years we have been there and whom I helped to write album verses for Mr. Sargent.

Have you ever seen Joseph Jefferson? To me he is the most charming of actors, the most perfect, one who holds you so particularly on the verge of a smile or tear, or rather in that deep region of the heart that is their common fount. Lillie and I went to see him this fall in the *Cricket on the Hearth* and it was delightful. Of course it was not Shakespeare, but the actor's simple compassion and twinkling humor were a great treat. His voice was so sympathetic.

I have heard nothing of how the AMC winter excursion came off. Just before it was to take place, Mr. Sargent wrote me to urge our joining the party, especially he wanted me to use my eloquence with Eugene. Mr. Sargent, Mr. Matthews and Mr. Clark proposed accompanying the expedition and they wished the assistance in this pleasure of the Councillor. The excursion was a tempting one with its perspective sleigh ride up the valley of Pemigewasset, a possible ascent of Moosilauke, with a visit to the Flume and the vision of the afterglow among the sunny mountains. But Eugene was not tempted and I have since heard from Mr. Sargent that neither he nor the other two gentlemen went on the excursion and so I have heard nothing from it, of either success or failure. Mr. Sargent is busy studying this winter at the medical school in Boston.

We are patiently waiting for *Appalachia* with its record of so much of our last summer. I found the writing of the account of our exploration on the Carter Range a mighty undertaking. I had no notes, save Eugene's times and heights to work from and I was so afraid my memory might play me false. I do not feel a veteran in topographical writing. It is more easy to measure Durand Ridge in verse than to survey Carter Mountain in prose.

If I can muster sufficient courage to call on a stranger whom I cannot in any way help, I will, sometime, go to see your artist friend. I am now so out of art circles, that among the artists, I only visit one or two old friends and feel myself entirely apart from the actual life of that world. As if to atone for my art idleness of last summer, though the work was in fact an outgrowth of that idleness. I was very busy for a while making pen and ink drawings illustrating certain of my verses, these combined labors of the pen being scattered at Christmas time, a sowing of seed that brought in to me a rich golden harvest of thanks. Mr. Peek has sent me a charming water color drawing of Mt. Adams from Durand Ridge, one of the noblest of our Randolph views and one of the very best of Mr. Peek's drawings. Mr. Peek sent each one of us one of his drawings leaving the selection of the pictures to ourselves, but we thought we could detect his intentions with each one through some personal association, and on this plan, Durand Ridge fell to its singer.

So far we have lost sight or hearing of few of our Raviners of last summer, one after another turning up from time to time. We are expecting a little visit from Miss Tompson in a week or two and I am looking forward with pleasure to trotting her about. If I could only trot her once up the road from Watson's to Charles Lowe's!

Marian sends love and thanks for your letter which she will duly answer. Please remember me kindly to your father and mother and believe it always gives me pleasure to hear from you.

Yours sincerely,
Edith W. Cook

* * * * * * * * * * * *

Edith Cook writes a postal card to Isabella Stone.

Hoboken, N.J.
January 13, 1884

My dear Miss Stone,

I find I forgot to answer a question in your letter which was certainly a wholly unpraiseworthy deed on my part, especially as the question was of a most practical nature. You asked me the name of the builder and projector of the Mount Crescent House at Randolph—it is Mr. Ingalls Leighton.

I suppose you have seen that Eugene has been reelected your Councillor of Explorations.

Edith W. Cook

Mt. Crescent House,

THE HIGHLAND HOME.

LEASANTLY situated on Randolph Hill, commanding from its broad piazzas one of the finest mountain views in New England, it being one of Starr King's favorite resorts. Will be open to the public

ABOUT THE MIDDLE OF JUNE, NEXT.

Said House contains the largest and best ventilated rooms of any house in the White Mountain region; size of sleeping rooms, 12 x 16 feet, height, 10 and 9 feet. Said House is newly built, and will be furnished with good sets throughout, and supplied with both spring and well water of excellent quality.

Choice Milk, Butter and Vegetables fresh from the farm.

Teams furnished on short notice to all points of interest in the White Mountain region, at low rates.

Regular boarders will be carried to and from the station for half price.

Satisfaction guaranteed.

Mail daily.

For further particulars address the undersigned,

R. I. LEIGHTON,
Box 60, GORHAM, N. H.

"*Come all ye who love o'er Nature's vast wilds to roam,*
Please give us a call at this highland home."

Mount Crescent House Advertisement

Edith Cook writes a postal card to Isabella Stone.

Hoboken, N.J.
February 2, 1884

Dear Miss Stone,

Do not trouble yourself to return the newspaper slip. If you care to possess it, keep it. I should probably only put it in the fire as I have only kept it so far because I cut it out to send to you and had not done so until now.

The councillor is very well pleased with the printed appearance of his summer labors and those of his lieutenants, and much of next summer's work is already planned. Some of last year's aides have already volunteered their services—one of them if only one leg remains to him to stand on.

Edith W. Cook

* * * * * * * * * * * *

Marian Pychowska writes to Isabella Stone.

Hoboken, N.J.
February 10, 1884

My dear Isabella,

Here I am at last with a Sunday afternoon in which to answer your letter of December 26. It does not take much distracting care to make me imagine I am very busy, but such as they are, these cares have for some weeks been more multifarious than usual in my quiet life.

In the first place, part of my time has been given to a sick neighbor. It is the mother of our church organist, a most interesting old lady of eighty-seven, who, when I go to sit with her, does much more for my entertainment than I can ever do for hers. Her hearing and sight are good, her mind bright and active and full of memories of her long, varied life which she tells with a vivid simplicity. Her parents narrowly escaped from Bordeaux in the French Revolution. Within her own recollection and personal experience are the great earthquake in Caracas, the insurrection in San Domingo, and yellow fever in Havana. As a young married woman she lived a few years in New England, first at Portsmouth, N.H. and later at Salem. These were happy years, and she corroborates all we ourselves know of the hospitality and cordiality and kindness of you cold-blooded easterners! She paints glowingly the gaieties of the Portsmouth Navy Yard more than fifty years ago, the long drives to church from Salem to Boston, the dinners with Bishop Cheverus, renowned in the story of Boston town in the time of President John Adams. You can imagine it is no hardship to sit a couple of hours with a dear soul who has for the least of her attractions such a wealth of old-time memories. Her daughter, on whom most of the care of the old mother falls, is a very successful public school teacher and these duties of course claim much of her time.

Another pleasant distraction has been a visit of nearly three weeks from Miss Tompson whom you remember at the Ravine House. She is a belle in Portsmouth, so I felt much flattered by her accepting our invitation to stay in such a quiet corner of the earth as our house. One of our wildest gaieties was a little lunch at Miss Barstow's, after which my uncle, Miss Barstow, Miss Tompson and I went skating on one of the Brooklyn ponds, while Edith watched us sympathetically from the grandstand. The weather has been very unpropitious for much going about, but this did not seem at all to distress our young friend.

Randolph people and things have continued to make an occasional pleasant excitement for us. Another picture (Mt. Washington from a view on the side of Mt. Hayes) and literary communications of various kinds arrived from Mr. Peek. He is now much interested in the genesis of the English people and language, and has much to say against the time-honored, but apparently doomed to destruction, "Anglo Saxon" theory. Mr. Matthews has paid another flying call, and Mr. Sargent writes of more wrenches in the gymnasium as a preparation for next summer's pedestrian feats. In one letter, when congratulating my uncle on his re-election as Councillor of Exploration, he speaks in his comical style of his willingness to assist again in exploration and, if he have any leg left to stand upon, to point it in the direction of the required mountain.

My aunt is arranging a little plan for an Appalachian excursion of limited character, to take place during the Easter holiday, which falls in the middle of April. The objective point would be the Dunderberg, the southernmost of the river highlands, on which none of us has ever been. The above two young men may come on for the occasion and Miss Barstow, Mr. Thompson and one or two others are possible additions. If Framingham were not so far away, I think I could tempt another Ape to be of the party. If it be anywise possible for you to come on, my mother joins me in asking you frankly and cordially to come and stay with us and help us enjoy our North River trip. It will probably be strictly AMC, with the exception of Edith, who ought certainly to be made an honorary member on account of her services to the Club. She laughingly assumes the title of "recruiting sergeant to the Club". Her last recruit was gained by sending a copy of *Appalachia* to an old friend, a lawyer, in Poughkeepsie. Apropos of Mr. Sargent and the Dunderberg trip, Edith dreamed last night that the aforesaid gentleman had arrived on crutches to go on the excursion! Even her dreams are to the point.

In reading over the last number of *Appalachia* does it not occur to you that a paper from your pen on some of your Woodstock explorations, would have fitted very well among the Randolph and Bartlett descriptions? There is yet time to prepare something for the June number in which you will have for company Edith's account of the Carter Range with accompanying illustrations. My mother's botanical notes have brought her more work to do. Mr. Ridler (the same, I believe, who is announced to have a paper at next meeting) has written to her for information and specimens of plants. So, the more we do, the more is expected of us.

There are two questions in your letter. In answer to the first, Friday, September 28, was the date of our ascent of Carrigain. As to the second, I think you left Jefferson on Wednesday morning. The day before, which is the Tuesday you mean, I suppose, the Ravine House pedestrians were dispersed thus: Mr. Peek had gone to Mt. Washington to make a comparison of barometers, the young men went to dine at Glen House via summit of Madison, my uncle was exploring Mt. Pliny and we three women with Miss Tompson climbed Durand Ridge, and imagined to ourselves you and Mr. Lowe speeding on to Mt. Jefferson. So you see there was no place for Mr. Lowe with any of the Raviners that day.

Take the Dunderberg into consideration and come if you can. With kindest remembrances to Dr. and Mrs. Stone I am always sincerely your friend (not merely "summer acquaintance").

M. M. P.

* * * * * * * * * * * *

Marian Pychowska writes to Isabella Stone.

Hoboken, N.J.
March 23, 1884

My dear Isabella,

Perhaps I should begin by an apology for answering your welcome letter so soon, but we will not call this an answer, it is only to clear the decks.

Let me begin with what you say about writing for the Club. In what dream did you see the editor of *Appalachia* sitting surrounded by "heaps of riches" which embarrass his choice? I think he would laugh. The very fact that our party cuts such a figure in the exploring department of the last issue, shows how little trouble others take to send in their reports.

I have read what you wrote about your plans for the next summer to my uncle. He will be delighted to have you explore Mt. Waternomee, and also, if convenient, Cushman and the Blue Ridge. An account of the new Moosilauke path would also be acceptable. We all request that these reports may not be buried in the *Echo*, but may be sent to the head of the department so that the Club may profit by the work of its members. I judge, by what you plan, that North Woodstock will claim part of your summer. I can appreciate its attractions, Mr. Russell included. Is not Jefferson the other point "d'apprise"? Mr. Crawford, you know, was going to have his path and camp on Mt. Jefferson. If this is not completed, remember that the Hunt-Watson-Cook and Company (Castle) Path is waiting for you to test it.

Our rooms at the Ravine House are engaged. Thus we intend that Randolph may be the base of operations, the "happy valley" where the traps and the squaws may rest while the warriors are out on the war path in various directions. Miss Tompson has made her arrangements to be with us. She has been banished from home for many weeks, her sister having gone through scarlet fever meanwhile.

The subject of early English history is indeed interesting. Following Mr. Peek's recommendation, my aunt got out of the library John Payn

Yeatman's *An Introduction to the Study of Early English History*. Of course he is not the only writer who opposes the generally received theory of the making of the English people, but he is perhaps the most ardent and indeed fanatical in his opposition. I did not myself read the book, but give you the ideas I found from hearing it discussed en famille. Yeatman contends that historians have generally taken as their authority on early Anglo-Saxondom, chronicles which he considers to be of doubtful authenticity. The view which he tries to uphold is the following, I believe: The Saxons (taking their name from their weapon) were banded together rather by their common marauding interest than by unity of race and, coming in upon the Britons, they found a people possessing a much higher civilization than their own. They could not and did not exterminate the Britons, who continued to form the bulk of the population and exercised a considerable influence upon their savage rulers. In fine, he maintains that English law, English speech and English blood are essentially British, though more or less affected by the successive invasions of Romans, Angles, Saxons, Danes and Normans. Mr. Yeatman's theories are interesting, though some of them are wild. If you enjoy intellectual dynamite, read him. My feelings say to him—"Stand up for our ignored and despised Celtic ancestors, but leave us our Alfred too". Moreover, if I want a proof that there were high capabilities in those invading savages, I have only to read the long list of Saxon saints, persons who have practiced virtue in an heroic degree. In his little dissertations Mr. Peek has well maintained the reasonableness of a middle course between the British and the Saxon partisans.

Another book that you would find very interesting is one that my mother and I read together some years ago, *The Development of English Literature, Old English Period* by Brother Azarias (of the Christian Schools) published by D. Appleton and Co. It "traces the growth and development of Old English Thought as expressed in Old English Literature, from the first dawnings of history down to the Norman Conquest". It is intended to be used as a class book, but in both style and matter it is apart from the beaten track. This author proves the Celtic influence in early literature, quoting Morley and Matthew Arnold among others, but does not run into any of Yeatman's extravagances. If you care to read the book, I think my mother would be glad to send her copy for your perusal.

This 23rd of March our crocuses are open to the sun. With kind regards to your parents and believe me always,

Sincerely yours,

M. M. Pychowska

Marian Pychowska writes to Isabella Stone.

Ravine House
Randolph, N.H.
June 29, 1884

Dear Isabella,

The heroic practice in medicine is, as my uncle says, to reduce your patient, like your equation, to the lowest terms first, and after this he will be easier to treat. Up to a certain point I believe in this theory. Let me proceed to illustrate. Until your equation was reduced to B.E.D. you were doing the work of one and one-half well women with the strength of half of one or less. By the first of August I dare believe you will be in better health for having been obliged to own your collapse and take care of yourself, than if you had succeeded in making believe you were able-bodied. The rest and mountain air always do so much for you, I do not despair of receiving, before the summer is over, reports of new finds about North Woodstock and of standing with you on some mountain top in this region.

While you were so fully occupied with your spring work and subsequent illness, things progressed about as usual in Hoboken. My father and mother have been and are now, well. It is my aunt this time who has astonished us all by showing signs of sharing our poor mortal frame. Frequent headaches, loss of appetite and chilly fits suggests that she had that which our doctor says is called a "bilious attack", but which is treated with quinine. In spite of her discomfort and debility, she had the energy to organize and carry through a delightful excursion for Decoration Day. Again there were ten in the party, including the three constant Brooklyners, two young ladies from our town, and Mr. Butler who was here last summer, but who is no longer the "Prairie Parson" having been called from the Bay City to a small church in New York City.

First of the day's pleasures was the thorough good nature and mutual enjoyment of all hands. Again we patronized the West Shore of the Hudson, passed the scene of our Salvation Army labors, and on up through the Highlands to Cornwall. Here we left the train and piled (eleven bodies, including driver) into a not over large nor over strong three seated wagon. The valiant pair of animals pulled us up the two miles to the hilltop where lies our ten acre lot with its beautiful view of Highlands, river, and Catskill Mountains, blue in the north, its well grown trees planted so carefully by my mother and grandmother in bygone years, its thriving crop of blackberry vines covering the neglected ground.

Having inspected our property, we set out on foot to cross the mountains, southward to West Point. It was gloriously cool and exhilarating, the air very clear, so that nothing shrouded the distant Catskills except a passing shower on the mountains, which was probably snow. The lonely mountain road keeps very high, skirting the edge of Black Rock Glen, down which you get a real fairyland view, then crossing the back of Storm King to "old Cro Nest" of Culprit Fay fame. We diverged from the road and followed a path to the top of the Nest. How different from these same little mountains as seen in their shroud on April 5. The great delight all day was that we need give no thought to time and could linger and linger, almost as long as we wished. It was the witching time of day, with shadows lengthening on the abrupt slopes and in the high sequestered valleys and across the broad blue river.

After leaving the top, we sat again for some time at the head of the steep face that dips into the river, looking down on the "Point" with its roomy plateau, as if made expressly for a drill ground bordered by the military buildings and tree embowered dwellings and commanded by the height of old Fort Putnam with its crown of dark cedars. At last we climbed down the slope into Washington Valley and met the road once more. It is such a beautiful road through the open forest full of dogwood blossoms just shedding their snow and laurel about to burst into pink and white glory. We made a little detour into the burying ground and Mr. Thompson left his bunch of wild blossoms on the monument which commemorates two of his family. Thus we earned the name which was given us later as we passed a group of West Point urchins—"The Decorators". We had planned to be on time for the evening parade, but we had lingered so long by the way that we saw only the close, and the trot to barracks. It is always a beautiful sight and one full of meaning, this graceful perfectly timed and ordered movement of so many hundred men, but to my mother and aunt it brings up old memories of the days when my grandfather used to bring them to the Point. This was a fitting end to such a day.

July 1

My aunt had a refreshing two weeks in Portsmouth with Miss Tompson, which did her much good, and came home the 23rd in time to take charge of the house on our departure, the 24th. Up to that time there had been but few days when our town deserved the name of "frying pan" for a sea breeze was frequent, but the noise and dust of a horse railroad which has lately been laid in our street made open windows a doubtful luxury. The journey hither was pleasant and not over fatiguing, so we are ready to begin at once to profit by the mountain change.

Randolph is looking up in the world, and place and people deserve to be appreciated, but I am glad we have known it before it becomes a popular resort. Mr. Watson began the work on his new house[1] in the early

---

[1] Soon hereafter named "Durand Hall," this building was the former dry house of the starch mill located on Carlton Brook and was moved westward down Durand Road during the winter of 1883-84. The third floor was used for a few years as a public meeting place to hold annual town meetings and social functions until the Randolph Town Hall was erected in 1888.

part of May and in a few days it will be as far completed as he intends this season. It stands thirty odd feet from the old house (toward the east) and a little back from the road, a fine gallery on three sides, and a platform (still in progress) connecting the houses. Within, the rooms are large and airy and will be well furnished, many provided with facilities for being heated. Twelve rooms are to be finished at present, six on each floor, then comes the mansard roof story which is now left all in one as a hall, but will later probably be divided into bedrooms. Still above the mansard, there is a deep, peaked roof which will serve as an air chamber for coolness to the rooms beneath. You will see this is quite an imposing building, and rather casts in the shade the little familiar gabled Ravine House, but as far as my uncritical judgment goes, it is in good taste and very comfortable. The Watsons seem to be in no doubt of filling it. Mr. Peek came only two days after us, and shortly the Nowell family, the Wares, who were here two seasons ago, the Tompsons, and Miss Barstow are expected. There is new Watson baby, Ralph.

On Friday, my mother and I visited the Mount Crescent House. They are hard at work finishing it, carpeting and furnishing, in expectation of having it ready by the 10th of this month. It is a very attractive place both within and without. We met our friend Hubbard Hunt there at work at a carpenter's table, and had a pleasant talk with him. He has had no time for the path finishing promised in Castellated Ravine and elsewhere, but is very enthusiastic in his intentions for such work when the time presents itself. Perhaps you suspect a little sarcasm in this last sentence, but if there be any, I assure you it is very benevolent, for Hubbard Hunt shows to be a very worthy man and an excellent woodsman, moreover, appreciative of natural beauty.

We have not heard whether young Mr. Crawford has made his contemplated path to Mt. Jefferson. Mr. Ethan Allen Crawford, Jr. is still our mail carrier. The old Grand Trunk Railroad is getting so very lively in its old age, that it brings its evening train to Gorham an hour earlier than last year, consequently our mail arrives about tea-time.

The town of Randolph has met with a loss in the person of Mr. Lowe. However, he has not gone very far. Having, in company with Mr. Libby[2] of Whitefield, purchased the Canton Stream Mill, which as you know, is near the divergence of the upper and lower roads from here to Jefferson. He has gone to live by his acquisition. Thaddeus Sobieski Lowe is left in possession of the old place, so neatly arranged last year and he is expected to step into his father's guiding shoes. We cannot but be sorry that Charles

---

[2] Nathaniel W. Libby and Charles Lowe's Canton Stream Saw Mill was employed primarily for producing clapboards. Later this same year, it was lost to fire, but was soon rebuilt and operated until the local supply of suitable lumber was exhausted.

Lowe should have withdrawn from the old congenial occupation. How can he ever be so happy or succeed so well in anything else?

My mother and I have had two good walks since our coming. On Saturday we went by Chicago Avenue to Lowe's Camp on Mt. Adams and over Nowell's Ridge, and I kept on as far as Peabody Spring in search of alpine plants. Finding nothing considerable in that quarter, we visited the big snow patch at the head of King's Ravine. We were in the very nick of time, for the most beautiful of the plants were in their very prime, and the grassy slopes of the gully whence the snow had lately receded, were fairly tapestried with the perfect pink, purple and white bells and stars. This time my mother saw all herself, and climbed down to the head of the snow arch. The day was so warm and our mouths so parched, even on these heights, that we were glad to get the snow for refreshment.

We came home by Durand Ridge, finding the paths in good condition, with the exception of a few wind-fallen trees on the lower part of the mountain. Neither of us felt very energetic for the long climb, so we simply made a long saunter of it, consuming between ten and eleven hours in the tour, never travelling fast enough to get overheated or out of breath, and so escaped any over fatigue. Since our visit, the snow patches have been shrinking rapidly, and in a few days all will have disappeared.

Our other trip was to the Pond of Safety. A most delightful day we had, for the woods were fresh and cool and the pond in fine condition with the water so high as to cover the lily pads. Botanizing had some success, since there were sufficient remains of blossoms on the plants we desired to identify. Rhodora was very plentiful about the lake though only a few faded purple petals told of its late beauty. Black flies and mosquitoes are of course rampant, but when we are armed with our blue tarlatan Appalachian headgear, we manage to be comfortable enough. We do not look for my aunt and uncle before the 15th.

When next I hear from you, I hope you will have good news to tell of your own health and of that of Dr. and Mrs. Stone. My mother joins me in kindest remembrances to you all.

Very sincerely yours,
M. M. Pychowska

Mount Washington Summit House

Marian Pychowska writes to Isabella Stone.

Mount Washington
Summit House[3]
July 31, 1884

Dear Isabella,

Here we are, stormbound in this comfortable Summit House, which we have abused so heartily as usurping the broad top of the dear old mountain. Twelve of us left the Ravine House this morning about seven o'clock, defying the threatening streaks in the sky. Ten drove to Glen and

---

[3] This was the second Mount Washington Summit House. The new hotel opened for business in July of 1873 and continued to operate for thirty-five summers until it burned in 1908. The large wooden structure, which accommodated one hundred and fifty guests, was anchored down with bolts and cables and withstood winds measuring up to 186 miles per hour.

Mounts Adams and Madison from the Mount Washington Carriage Road

up the mountain on the carriage road[4] while my uncle and Mr. Sargent footed it bravely.

At the five-mile post Miss Barstow alighted with me and struck across the rocks to Huntington's Ravine. Reaching the edge after a short easy jaunt, we found ourselves somewhere near the middle of its length and in a very favorable position to view the grand headwalls. Thence we climbed the steep slope to the peak that dominates the northeast corner, always in view of the ravine. We left our wagon at noon, and spent two hours looking and sketching, before we settled down to dinner behind a sheltering cairn, in view of Mounts Adams, Jefferson, and Madison.

From there we turned once more to the ravine and skirted the headwall round to the further side. The wind, which was strong from the southeast, blew up the ravine with tremendous force so that we could hardly crawl along the edge in some places. Miss Barstow said it blew her eyelids down and I was fairly choked sometimes. The views were won-

---

[4] The Mount Washington Road Company was chartered July 1, 1853, with the intention of constructing a well graded carriage road from the Glen House to the summit of Mount Washington. Surveying began in 1854 and by 1856, the first four miles were completed to the ledge just above the Halfway House. By the end of 1856, the first road company went out of business due to the overwhelming cost of construction. The Mount Washington Summit Road Company was subsequently incorporated a few years later and finished construction of the road in 1861. The road is eight miles long and makes an ascent of 4,600 feet. Over a period of more than one hundred and thirty years, it has been vastly upgraded and improved and is today commonly known as the Mount Washington Auto Road.

derful and grew more so as we reached the westerly side. The depth is certainly much greater than at King's and exceeds anything I have seen yet as a hole to look into. Some of the cliffs are positively fearful to look over. Certain very sheer and solid smooth masses jut out over the immense depth, offering grand foreground. We climbed down to the top of one of these points[5]. A sharp angle formed by the ravine wall and this long overhanging knife blade of rock, made a gutter for a stream of clear water which rises in the Alpine Gardens above. The magnificence of rock architecture and the fairy delicacy of the waterfall and rich beds of vivid alpine green and blossoms are not describable, but you can easily visit this district the first time you come here again. It is a short and easy walk from the road near the seven-mile post. Clouds had been sweeping over the mountain top from time to time, but now they were beginning to sprinkle us, so we gathered some handfuls of rare and lovely alpine plants from a corner of the noted garden, and soon reached the road. Clouds, rain and wind were fierce in our faces up that last mile, but we soon dried our things by the steam pipes and were in fine feather. Mr. Sargent and Mr. Lyon[6] had visited the snow arch in Tuckerman's after dining on top. They also came in safely just before we did.

Our object in coming here was to walk over the peaks tomorrow. Miss Tompson is the queen of our party, she having climbed Madison last Friday with us and suffered no harm thereby. My mother, aunt, Miss Barstow, her friend, with your humble servant are the other ladies. Shall we have weather for our purpose? Shall we have a sunrise? The rain that pelts through the windows seems to answer—No! But there is always a chance of clearing and besides we have had so much on our way up, and it is good to be so high—and the much abused house is so comfortable— we are content.

I have read Isabella Stone's letter in the *Echo* and consequently know all about the Flume, old and new.

> Yours always,
> Marian Pychowska

---

[5] Known today as the Pinnacle.
[6] Mr. John E. Lyon was the owner of the Boston, Concord and Montreal Railroad. Lyon was also instrumental in the building of the Pemigewasset House in Plymouth, the Fabyan House and the Mount Washington Summit House.

Marian Pychowska writes to Isabella Stone.

Ravine House
Randolph, N.H.
August 3, 1884

My dear Isabella,

It will not do to let you wait long for the continuation of the Mt. Washington story, of which I sent you the first installment last Friday. You will have guessed already what the upshot was. The sunrise, of course, was not forth coming, but the sun, once risen, shone encouragingly through the driving mist, giving us to understand that there were no thick storm clouds between it and us. At eight o'clock the nine sallied forth and gaily faced the brisk west wind, down the railroad toward Clay. As we neared the edge of the Great Gulf the fog was torn and opened by the wind, giving us fine glimpses into the depths, and assurances that we were on the right way. I understand that the thermometer was in the neighborhood of forty degrees, but the cold and the wind were just enough to be exhilarating, without nipping even my chilly mother.

The most voracious mountaineer could hardly have regretted the clouds that swept over us, for they grew more and more ragged, and the views through the ever widening rents were more beautiful and more impressive than an uninterrupted sight could have been.

Now it was the Carter Range, an intense deep blue in the morning light, beyond the green shoulder of Mt. Washington, and then came a rift on the other side, showing the bare, rounded crests of the southern range leading off to the Notch. Mt. Clay is made of fine solid rock masses with even, alpine lawns between, and has thus a special beauty of its own, and affords very easy walking. As we climbed Jefferson, the clouds dispersed and left even Mt. Washington clear. My aunt, Miss Tompson and I lingered behind the others and strayed over the eastern slope, gaining better views down on the great pale green knee, which separates the Jefferson Ravine from the Gulf. While we sat in a warm sheltered nook "taking it all in" our eyes wandered out into the clear distance, and there to the left of Sebago Lake, on the very horizon, were two shining silver bits with a small rise between them, Portland Harbor without a doubt. We are so seldom on a mountain top in the morning hours when the light is best for bringing our distance and color, that it seemed to me in great part a new experience. Before eleven, we all gathered about the crowning cairn of Jefferson, and the AMC bottle was given to our recorder, my aunt. The record was in a sad condition, soaking wet and unmanageable.

At noon we had reached Peabody Spring and settled ourselves to lunch. Thence to the peak of Adams is not much over half a mile, so we were soon gazing down from that well known pinnacle, on the familiar pathway of Durand Ridge. You can imagine Miss Tompson's delight when she stood at last on the long desired peak. Just a week before, that other beautiful Friday, she had been on top of Madison, and now she was on the most commanding of the northern peaks, and the only one that was lacking to her.

We were now at home, so the party broke up into groups of twos and threes according to caprice. Mr. Sargent and Mr. Lyon completed their tour by including Madison. Durand Ridge was the way chosen by the others. As we left the summit, there arrived a party of "Jefferson Highlanders" from your Crawford's, including Miss Frothingham, with Mr. Lowe as guide! They too patronized our Ridge on the home way.

In parting from my father before our trip, we had invited him to come up and meet us on Adams. What was our delight as we neared the lower ledges, to see him with Mr. Peek coming toward us. Yes, he has actually looked down into King's Ravine from our dear Durand!! This committee of reception did not leave the Ravine House till toward noon, so my father was very warm and weary with the continuous and unusual exertion, but he was nevertheless charmed with the beauty of our path. My uncle, of course, was the first to reach home at about four o'clock, the rest of us straggling in as we pleased, until all were housed in time to dress for supper.

I am sure I have inspired you with a renewed desire to get to Mt. Jefferson and perhaps to follow in our track from Mt. Washington down over the range. Indeed, I think there is no doubt that our latest trip is a much easier thing to do than to visit Jefferson and return. You have not the labor of climbing your mountain, and you have much more time to look and enjoy by the way. It is a whole long day on the crests, in the pure high air, a day of delight, and the labor is not felt because the rests are many.

The Apes are complaining that there are no papers for the September meeting. Will you not help them? I am sure they would appreciate what you will give. Hoping to hear good news soon.

Yours always,
M. M. P.

P.S. We have a friend at the Mount Crescent House, who says it is very comfortable. Her only complaint is that the table is too hotel-like in variety and profusion for the price asked in board. This is owing to the cook, who has held this position at the Crawford House, and is used to big hotel ways. I think you can safely recommend the house.

Marian Pychowska writes to Isabella Stone.

Ravine House
Randolph, N.H.
August 10, 1884

My dear Isabella,

Your long and welcome letter has been read and reread and pondered over. I had hoped to hear of a more rapid improvement in your health since your writing from Laconia, but if it is slow we may hope it will be sure.

The description you give of your surroundings as you lie in your hammock on the plateau, certainly holds elements enough of delight and profit. Indeed, do we not enjoy the beautiful things about us, and do they not make a much deeper impression on us, when we must take them slowly and a little at a time, as an invalid is obliged to do, instead of skipping from viewpoint to viewpoint, greedily doing and seeing all and forgetting to say grace after our feast? Appalachiandom belongs to the spirit, the devouring and never reposing spirit, in the age of "partial exploration" of many mountains.

But generalizing is dangerous, and I can give the lie to myself by producing an example of persistency at one thing on the part of my uncle, the very leader of giddy exploration. He, with Mr. Peek, has spent many beautiful days of two seasons, unraveling the labyrinthine ways of Mounts Crescent and Randolph, following lot lines north and south, east and west hunting the trees which mark the corners, being prey to legions of mosquitoes, and often plunged in a chaos of cutting new and old where all landmarks failed and all this in order to locate the famous Ice Gulch. Yesterday they returned in triumph as they had identified an important corner which settled the much disputed point.

While they were thus "sacrificing themselves in the cause of science", five ladies, Miss Barstow and her pupil, and three whom you can guess, climbed once more the steep but pleasant ways to Mt. Madison, and, skirting eastward, below the crest, descended upon the most prominent peak of Howker's Ridge, "Hamilton Howk" as we have agreed to call it, in memory of Madison's partner in the composition of *The Federalist*. We had to pass through two delightful short (or delightfully short, perhaps I should say) patches of scrub in order to reach our destination. It is like a small Chocorua cone of rock, rising out of the dwarf forest, and from its top you look down on a whole nest of similar prominences, a half dozen or more points of patches of rock partly clothed with pale green moss, the steep gullies between filled with dark spruces. The view through the Carter Notch is of special beauty. Miss Barstow worked hard with her brushes during our hour's stay, but my aunt reposed and possessed herself of the place in another way—in your way.

Last Friday a large party, chiefly novices in the art, gathered from here and Mount Crescent House and attempted Adams. At the time of their 6:30 breakfast the weather promised well enough, but the day grew more and more smoky and cloudy, until afternoon when the rain came down and soaked them. What with the heat and the clouds and various mishaps, they got no farther than Durand Ridge. However that was something to see, and no one is the worse for the exposure. Some of the ladies will try again. The Mount Crescent House people have not been fortunate in their attempts. In a previous one, they were driven by the weather from the top of Adams after a stay of ten minutes, and spent a night of pouring rain in Lowe's Camp. Also, two of the ladies, along with the clerk of the house, tried the Gulch, but lost the trail (and no wonder) and had another drenching.

The best that the Ravine House has to boast of in walking line this year is the exploit of Stanley Tompson (aged fourteen) and Fred Nowell (a little older). These sturdy boys left here about five o'clock last Monday morning, went to Lowe's Camp by Cold Brook and "Chicago Avenue", thence by Nowell's Ridge to the col[7] and over Jefferson and Clay to Washington, which they reached at 10:45 A.M. Returning by way of the carriage road and the Glen, they walked up to our house just ten minutes inside of twelve hours from the time they set out in the morning. The distance made by road was sixteen miles and the climb to Mt. Washington between eight and nine miles, I think. If there are any lazy boys in your house give them this bone to gnaw on.

Our little house seems to exert all the fascinating influence of former years on all occupants, old and new comers. Even the ladies who cannot walk far are delighted with the new piazza and small rambles. Mr. Watson is as energetic as ever in the making and keeping up of paths.

Did I write you that there is a new bit of path up Durand Ridge from near the old two-mile post to just above the old three-mile post? The new bit saves the going down to Salmacis Upper Fall, is more gradual in ascent perhaps, and saves enough to bring down the whole distance to Adams peak to four and two-fifths miles. If you regret the fall which is omitted on this route, be content that it has a beautiful outlook from a cliff near the two and one-quarter mile mark. This has been cleared out by our gentlemen, and commands a lovely view over Gordon Ridge to Androscoggin Valley and beyond, and also up the Glen to Madison, John Quincy, Adams and the Gateway rocks. This is a place I hope we may spend a day at together, if you gain so much strength. We owe this lovely spot and its appropriate name "Durand Scar" to Mr. Peek. Thus you see I have begun planning for those lesser, but no less pleasant jaunts which we may hope to share.

Now for the Lafayette business. My uncle has never walked over to

---

[7] Known today as Edmand's Col.

the sierra in question, and has not, I believe, had reason to give it any careful observation. After pondering your letter and the guidebook, and comparing my own meager recollections and lights on the subject, I agree entirely with your interpretation of the profile. As a new confirmation of this view, I will show you when you come, a drawing of Lafayette from Moosilauke in my aunt's sketch book. In this drawing there is a small definite tooth between the main and south peaks, corresponding exactly with that little hitch in your outline. Evidently there are two ways of naming these peaks, according as persons choose to ignore this small "hummock" and give "Lincoln" to the south peak, or to let all the names stand. Evidently also, the guidebook is not consistent and wavers between the two methods. Possibly it gathered its information from a number of authorities who did not all take the same view.

My aunt's sketch book does not extend far enough to include Mt. Liberty, so I cannot form any idea as to the character of the ridge running thence to the south peak. Is it not possible that from the commanding height of the south peak (which, whether they call it Lincoln or not, I believe they were on) your people should not have noticed any striking prominence on the ridge below them, and yet, seen from below, the mountain ribs, as shown in your drawing, might isolate a small prominence into a majestic "Haystack"? Perhaps too, as they were all called "Haystacks" in the old days, and then the distinctive names of Lafayette, Liberty, Flume, etc. came in, the old name may have been transferred to the only point which remained to bear it. If Bethlehem had a Haystack, must not Woodstock have one too? The guidebook is in great danger of making a jumble of local and map usage, thus giving no very clear result. It is a wonder to me that Mr. Sweetser, with such a field to cover, has preserved as much accuracy. I fear I have not given you much light, but what thoughts have come, I give you the benefit of.

Mr. Lowe, as you expected, has several times been led off into the old ways of guiding. He and Hubbard Hunt occasionally stop here and have a good talk with my uncle and Mr. Peek. The Castellated Ridge Path is done, even to being signed at its entrance.

I believe my Washington missive enclosed some purple heath from the Alpine Garden, Harebells from the turn of the road near the seven-mile post (gathered by my aunt), and a bit of Labrador Tea being probably from slopes below six thousand feet.

I am glad to think we shall see you so soon. We are all ready for whatever sort of trips you want to take for the last bit of views. Mr. Sargent has laid himself up with a lame leg, done on the tennis field.

With kind remembrances to Dr. and Mrs. Stone, in which my mother joins me,

Yours,

M. M. P.

Alpine House

Marian Pychowska writes a postal card to Isabella Stone.

Ravine House
Randolph, N.H.
Wednesday
August 20, 1884

Dear Isabella,

Your note received yesterday, and am glad the hammock is no longer necessary. I hope to walk over some morning soon and return with Mr. Crawford in the afternoon. I cannot say what day it will be, so do not expect or wait for me.

Seventeen Randolphians improved this warm day by visiting the Ice Gulch and found it an excellent refrigerator. Perhaps you have heard that the AMC meeting is to take place at Alpine House[8] in Gorham the first week of September.

Yours,
M. M. P.

---

[8] This was the second Alpine House in Gorham, the first falling prey to fire in 1872. Opened in 1876, it was in operation for twenty-nine years, closing in November of 1905.

Charles Fay writes to Isabella Stone.

College Hill, Mass.
August 28, 1884

Miss M. Isabella Stone
Dear Madam,
Your favor of the 23rd has come to hand and it will give me pleasure to forward it at once to Mr. J. R. Edmands, the Chairman of the Committee for the Gorham field meeting. Their circular of information is just issued, and while some four papers are mentioned as on the program for the indoor session, I should think opportunity might still offer itself for the presentation of your interesting communication. I will ask Mr. Edmands to communicate with you directly.

I exceedingly regret that I am not likely to be present at the Gorham meeting, a disappointment made the greater by the fact that side of the mountain is comparatively unfamiliar and also because I shall miss enjoying its attractions with the Appalachian friends who are likely to be there.

If the two events had happened to occur together, that you should unfortunately be detained while my kind stars led me to the meeting, you surely might have counted on me for the acceptance of the complimentary invitation to read in your place.

I cordially hope, however, that those who are so favored as to go, may have the pleasure of listening to your paper from your lips and that we who must stay at home, may hear it when read again later at one of the regular meetings of the Club.

With assurances of respect, I am,
Yours sincerely,
Charles E. Fay

* * * * * * * * * * * *

Marian Pychowska writes to Isabella Stone.

Ravine House
Randolph, N.H.
Saturday
August 30, 1884

Dear Isabella,
It is delightful that you have come out unscathed from last Monday's walk. Are you not ready to try something else?

My uncle and Mr. Peek returned with Mr. Hunt early in the afternoon of Tuesday. They had a very satisfactory time, doing even more than they anticipated, in spite of the rain. After one day's rest, the two indefatigables were off again, on Thursday, through the Evans Notch to Chatham to remeasure Baldface and explore Speckled Mountain. Probably they were stormbound yesterday so we do not look to see them here before Monday. My mother and I have merely taken afternoon strolls during the week. If you find the weather suitable and feel otherwise inclined, come over on Monday and we will go to Durand Scar or any other place you may prefer. I am entirely at your disposal since I trust you will not propose anything very terrible.

You poor persecuted "Ape" in the midst of such an unsympathizing household! I suppose the ladies there enjoy threading their worsted needles more than threading the forest ways. Let us give them all our stockings to darn! But no, as you say, they are probably very nice people, though not mountaineers.

I did not notice what costume Miss Frothingham's companion wore, having only seen them pass here but Miss Tompson tells me it was something of a "bloomer"—I know not the derivation of the word nor its spelling.

Looking to see you again soon, I am always,

Yours sincerely,

M. M. Pychowska

* * * * * * * * * * * *

Marian Pychowska writes a postal card to Isabella Stone.

Ravine House
Randolph, N.H.
September 15, 1884

Dear Isabella,

My mother and I got ready early to start with the party for Moriah, but Mr. Lowe and the other weatherwise were so sure it would storm, that I backed out. But if they were wise, they (campers and all) went on the mountain.

As my mother is not expected before mail time, I opened your note thinking it might need an answer. If you will cut open the curious growth you sent, you will find in the center a small grub, for whose sake the whole thing seems to be formed. Gray's Botany merely says that certain species of willow "often bear cones on the ends of the branches, formed of closely imbricated leaves, probably occasioned by the puncture of insects". I believe my mother knows nothing more about it.

We have no plans yet. They may crystalize tomorrow so that I can inform you. If your ideas are more definite, take the initiative and perhaps I can hitch on.

Yours,

M. M. Pychowska

Lucia Pychowska writes to Isabella Stone.

Ravine House
Randolph, N.H.
September 18, 1884

My dear Isabella,

I am grieved to learn that your Randolph Mountain cold has taken so deep a root. I trust that ere this, the proper coddling has relieved its most distressing effects and that you are really better.

The camping party returned last evening in high spirits—everything delightful—except of course the loss of sleep, which a full rest last night will have made good. Marian and I were going with the advance guard on Monday as far as the top of Moriah, but the day seemed unpropitious, so Marian remained at the Ravine House while I went down to Gorham to do anything pleasant that might turn up. There, the weather having improved, Mr. Spaulding proposed that he and I should accompany the party as far as Mt. Surprise. We did so to our great profit and pleasure. Mr. and Mrs. Nowell, Miss Barstow and Miss Thallon, Mr. Cook with Mr. Lowe and two choppers and pack bearers were the party that went to the top from here. From the Alpine House went Miss Robinson, Messrs. Edmands, Lawrence[9], Potter, Parris, Curry or Currier, and Lindsey, with Hubbard Hunt and one or two more pack men. The camp was well made and the company jolly so they did not mind the rain of Tuesday morning. My brother and some of the gentlemen went over to the peak of Carter and Mr. Lowe guided all the ladies except Mrs. Nowell and the rest of the gentlemen to the top of Imp Mountain. The air was clear and they had fine views.

On Wednesday morning Mrs. Nowell and Miss Robinson with some of the gentlemen came down Moriah to the Alpine House, while my brother guided the rest of the men folk, Miss Barstow and Miss Thallon over the heads of Moriah, down the Rattle River, to the Lead Mine bridge where Mr. Watson met them and brought them home (those that belonged here) about half past seven in the evening. All are well and say the excursion was charming. Eugene says it was delightful except for the lack of sleep. The usual noises in a populous camp prevented sleeping except among those who can sleep anyhow, no matter what the commotion. The third day was smoky, but nevertheless they enjoyed the climbs and saw some things, if not all that ought to have been seen. Mrs. Nowell kept house while they were off on Tuesday, and had a good hot supper for them on

---

[9] Mr. Rosewell B. Lawrence was an active member of the AMC and participated in recreational mountaineering on a year-round basis. He was the head of the AMC "Snowshoe Section" whose purpose was the advancement of winter excursions. On February 22, 1889, he and Laban Watson made the first recorded winter ascent of Mount Madison.

their return. Mr. Lowe went over the Moriahs with that party on Wednesday, and Mr. Hunt came down with the weaker members and his share, or more than his share, of luggage. He had guided the day before to Carter; my brother always steps aside when a professional guide is present, unless the route be one not known to the guide. He considers any other course as taking the bread out of honest men's mouths. This much may entertain you of what I have heard from the campers.

Tomorrow we go up Durand Ridge to replace the signs in accordance with Mr. Peek's new cutoff.

Trusting you may soon be well again. I remain yours affectionately,
L. D. Pychowska
P.S. All greatly praise your paper read at the meeting.

* * * * * * * * * * * *

Marian Pychowska writes a postal card to Isabella Stone.

Ravine House
Randolph, N.H.
September 22, 1884
Dear Isabella,
I am glad you are on the war path again.
Tomorrow does not promise well. If it suits you, let us say Ravine of the Cascades for Wednesday. I will be at Mr. Hunt's at 9:30 Wednesday morning. If you prefer, we can go by the "old reliable route" from Lowe's.
My mother and I have been on Mt. Adams again today and seen, handled and eaten snow and ice. Some ice still five inches thick. Got on top at 12:30, stayed ten minutes, and then came down to treeline where rain overtook us. We reached home before four o'clock.
Yours,
M. M. P.

* * * * * * * * * * *

Marian Pychowska writes to Isabella Stone.

Ravine House
Randolph, N.H.
Wednesday
September 24, 1884
Dear Isabella,
I expected to answer your question en route for the Cascades, but as that was not permitted, I will give you what satisfaction I can now. Mr. Watson charged my mother two dollars for carrying us both, but Miss Thallon was heard to say that he had charged her two dollars for herself alone. Perhaps he thought the lateness of the return entitled him to an

advance on the usual price, and perhaps he charged my mother less than others because she obtained his entrance into the AMC. However, these are only conjectures. Miss Tompson has not paid any bill since then, and I believe the same is the case with my aunt.

I enclose a bit of the fabric sent by Mrs. Muir from Montreal. You will see there is a large proportion of cotton in it. If it suits you, my mother will gladly let you take five or six yards of the piece sent. It cost twenty cents a yard in Montreal, but with the custom-house charges, it amounts to thirty two cents a yard.

Last night Miss Tompson and I arranged to rise before five to see a dawn and sunrise this morn. The storm fairly surprised us. What weather is in store for us tomorrow? Who can say? I hope you will get a satisfactory trip with Mr. Lowe. That will be something to remember. If tomorrow proves a Ravine House day, that is, one which you could not use with Mr. Lowe, we shall expect to see you. I may help Mr. Peek with some of his surveying in the morn, but with the expectation of getting home early after dinner.

Always yours,
M. M. Pychowska

P.S. *Appalachia* arrived and thanks also for the circulars.

* * * * * * * * * * * *

Marian Pychowska writes a postal card to Isabella Stone.

Ravine House
Randolph, N.H.
Thursday
September 25, 1884

Dear Isabella,

Your last plan is excellent—sufficiently elastic to suit all happenings. I am at present the obedient servant of an ulcerated tooth, but I hope my obsequiousness will win my release and a permit for one or two more walks.

Are not the golden birches and the flaming maples superb? There is to be no work done on the Pilot Range this season. Mr. Sargent has gone home and yesterday my uncle left for North Woodstock intent on demolishing Mounts Blue and Cushman.

Hoping the many times planned farewell meeting will be realized.

Yours,
M. M. P.

Marian Pychowska writes to Isabella Stone.

> Ravine House
> Randolph, N.H.
> Monday
> September 29, 1884

Dear Isabella,

Last bulletin received. We were afraid that the weather did not declare itself yesterday in time for you to use the day. Nevertheless, I gazed up at the heights, thinking you might possibly be up there. We drove to church in the morning and after dinner I went on Randolph Hill to join Miss Tompson on her way home from a meeting. It was wonderfully beautiful, but the gray bank in the west suggested the return of the storm. Saturday we did nothing more than stroll to Cold Brook.

This is packing day for us. Tomorrow my aunt and Miss Tompson are off early by way of Jefferson and my mother and I hope to have one more wandering—whither I know not. She is very tired with today's packing—more so than after any walk this season.

Edith, Miss Tompson and I have just come from a stroll up Salmacis path. I have never seen the woods in such glory, golden leaves waving above, strewing the ground, and sailing down through the air. The rain and the wind have begun to strip the bright maples in back of our house.

> Adieu,
> M. M. P.

* * * * * * * * * * * *

Marian Pychowska writes a postal card to Isabella Stone.

> Ravine House
> Randolph, N.H.
> Tuesday eve
> September 30, 1884

Dear Isabella,

Letter received and entirely understood. I thank you very much for thinking it worth while to write it. Excuse haste and postal—it is the only thing at hand. I came in just before tea from my farewell walk to the Bowman place and found letter waiting for me. This morning I went with my mother to Lookout Ledge.

We go tomorrow by Gorham, so cannot even wave adieu to you. Will write from home. Mr. Crawford has come for the mail. Goodbye.

> M. M. P.

Marian Pychowska writes to Isabella Stone.

Hoboken, N.J.
October 5, 1884

My dear Isabella,

Let me begin by thanking you again for your letter of September 30, and for thinking us worthy of such a detailed explanation. Explanations are good things where the parties are reasonable. We certainly had no right or reason to judge your inquiry about the charge to be strange, after what we had told you. Still, I am very glad to understand all the circumstances which led to it, and which, not by any right of ours, but out of your kind heart you have made known to us. Not to my knowledge did any of the Watsons say anything about the matter nor would it be like Mr. Watson to do so. Neither did my mother speak to him about the charge of two dollars. I fancy that some other of those who rode down may have made some representation to Mr. Watson in consequence of which he reduced the charge to the usual one dollar and being an upright man, extended this alteration to all.

Not long since, my mother had a long talk with Mr. Leighton of the Mount Crescent House. He does not see how Laban can make anything at his prices, and thinks another season he must raise his own so as to range from eight to fourteen dollars a week. But Mr. Leighton is a raw hand at hotel keeping, and was ridden this year by a first class cook who insisted on big hotel ways. My mother tried to explain to him that Mr. Watson succeeded because his boarders came early and stayed late, and that people who were willing to pay high prices were not generally those who made a long stay. I hope Mr. Watson has really had a successful season, for his house was steadily filled and his teams in almost constant use. I suppose you have heard that some of the rooms in "Durand Hall" were ten dollars to single occupants.

You, I suppose, are still in the midst of the autumn beauty of the hills, to which we have bade adieu. Our last ride to Gorham was delightful, the beautiful clouds heightening the charms of the familiar mountain forms and the sun breaking through in patches of glory on the bright foliage. The thirteen hours in the car were wearisome of course, but on the much abused Norwich Line there is at least no fear of being left, everything is bound to wait for one. At 10:30 P.M. we took possession of our comfortable, airy staterooms and got some hours of refreshing rest. A little after six A.M. my mother and I were out breathing the salt air and watching the schooners bearing down "wing and wing" over the gray waters of Long Island Sound toward New York. About eight we landed, and were soon at home, where my aunt and uncle had arrived the day before. My aunt and Miss Tompson went down through the Notch on Tuesday, that splendid day, but were detained owing to a collision of other trains near South Berwick. Thus Edith was too late arriving in Boston to take a steamboat train, so she and my uncle came through by the shoreline.

My uncle had an altogether delightful time at North Woodstock. He is charmed with the views, with the Russell House, its inmates, and its table. The little eight-year-old who waited on him quite won his heart. The evening of his arrival, Mr. William Sargent called on him, and they laid their plans. Mr. Sargent was anxious that my uncle should let him carry his camp equipage so that they might spend the night in the woods, but my uncle preferred to travel lightly laden and depend on the hospitality of the summit of Moosilauke.

That beautiful Friday they visited the Agassiz Basins, and thence on up the future bridle path, whose twistings were duly admired for their easy grade. My uncle sends word to you that Mt. Blue could easily have been added to your conquests, as its top is only about fifteen minutes walk from the path, but the views obtained from tree tops show that a clearing would not be worthwhile. Returned to the path, they ate their lunch at a fine spring with a tin basin (the one you told me of?). It was still so early in the day that Mr. Sargent proposed they should gain distance and economize as well, by going over Moosilauke and down to Merrill's on the road, before putting up for the night. So they spent some time on the mountain, during which Miss Woodworth showed them an elaborate large panorama of mountain profiles with the names attached and also imparted some recent pocket level measurements of Blue, Jim, Waternomee concern. When they were nearing Merrill's Mr. Sargent again suggested camping, but my uncle did not bite. He was much pleased with Merrill's.

Saturday morning after eight o'clock they set out for Mt. Cushman, following up a wood road. Several times they flattered themselves that the top was reached, and a blaze was made and names inscribed. Finally, two or two and one-half miles from Baker's River, they gained the true top. Here the trees were scanty enough to allow something of a view, but on the way down they came upon a very fine outlook toward Mt. Washington and Franconia Notch. Mr. Sargent suggested they should strike for Elbow Pond, which proposition chimed in exactly with my uncle's views. They walked, and they walked, and they walked, meeting logging roads and afterward cattle tracks, fancying they might have passed on the right of the pond until finally they struck it just by the narrow connecting channel. On the farther side lay a raft, which Mr. Sargent fished over and they sailed northward over the water, enjoying the beautiful views both ways. Again Mr. Sargent was ready with a good suggestion, that instead of following out the usual road, they should strike for an old trail which connected Woodstock with the Mt. Silly Farms. This was most pleasantly accomplished and they came out finally on the Moosilauke Brook Road near where they had started. This day they travelled about 12 miles. Of course Mr. Sargent's knowledge of all these by-ways was invaluable, and my uncle was exceedingly pleased with him and reports him to be a real "Natty Bumpo", a thorough woodsman and lover of the woods. My uncle also visited his home and saw his famous little girl. Some day you will probably read the whole account in *Appalachia*, but I knew you would be interested in any scraps I could give you now.

After spending Sunday at Russell's, my uncle went down for Monday to our dear old Blair's and received the heartiest welcome from those good people. He also found a few friends still lingering in their cottages in the neighborhood, and everything very flourishing. He says no bad word of the railroad through the valley.

Please thank your parents for the kind message sent by your last letter, and give our responsive good wishes to them. When will you be all together again in Framingham? Believe me ever,

Sincerely your friend,
M. M. Pychowska

* * * * * * * * * * * *

Charles Fay writes to Isabella Stone.

College Hill, Mass.
November 17, 1884

Miss M. I. Stone
Dear Madam,

In his report as Councillor of Exploration, Mr. Cook refers to your paper on Waternomee, which I had not the good fortune to hear.

Would you kindly allow us to print it, in whole or in part, as the exigencies of the number may require as an appendix to the Councillor's Report in the forthcoming issue of *Appalachia*?

Very respectfully yours,
Chas E. Fay

* * * * * * * * * * *

Eugene Cook writes to Isabella Stone.

26 Hudson Terrace
Hoboken, N.J.
November 20, 1884

Dear Miss Stone:

Your note of yesterday came this morning. Your lucid and interesting account of Mt. Waternomee was of course spoken of by the Councillor of Exploration as he expected it would appear in the forthcoming number of *Appalachia* with his report.

The heights of Mounts Waternomee, Jim and Blue as set forth in the record book on Moosilauke are respectively, 4,096 feet, 4,218 feet, and 4,533 feet. These measurements I suppose are recent. My own measurement of Blue was but a foot or two different, so I trust the figures are very near the truth. I have forgotten whether or not you mentioned "Nameless Mountain" upon which the Moosilauke Path first ascends. Mr. Sargent so called the mountain. It might however be considered a part of Waternomee, I think. The sign indicating the way to the top of Waternomee had better be moved further along the Moosilauke Path as it runs for some distance at only a slightly diverging angle, and as a shorter branch would be more easily kept in order. A clearing upon the top of Waternomee would be a gain, for the reason you have set forth. The fund for "Improvements" is rather limited, so some circumspection is required in making the best use of the money on hand.

My excursion over the Moosilauke Path and over Mounts Blue and Cushman was in every way enjoyable. I was greatly pleased, too, with my companion, Mr. Sargent.

Since I have been home I have been very busy. Among other employments, I have been practicing assiduously upon my violin so as to take part in duets. Herr Steinitz, the great chess magnate, has settled in New York, and is going to edit a chess magazine which will commence with the new year.

With kind remembrances to you father and mother, and with most friendly good wishes.

Yours truly,
Eugene B. Cook

* * * * * * * * * * * *

Charles Fay writes to Isabella Stone.

College Hill, Mass.
November 29, 1884

Miss M. I. Stone
Dear Madam,

Pardon my delay in acknowledging the receipt of your manuscript of the article on Mt. Waternomee, but I must beg indulgence by reason of the stress of work. I find the editing of *Appalachia* no sinecure when added to my professional duties.

I hope the disposition of the article, which circumstances seemed to render necessary, will prove satisfactory to the author. It seemed advisable to publish it in the present issue with Mr. Cook's report in which reference is made to it. The number of special articles is already over large, so that I fear some one of the number will have to remain in type until another issue. Your paper was not so lengthy as some of the appendices we have printed, and therefore in consideration of all circumstances it seemed best to print it in this category with some slight cuttings. The profile will accompany it, though reading that your copy was "from memory", I wrote to the Reverend Mr. Dusseault to ask if he chanced to have a view from North Woodstock of the range in question. In case he has, it will be very helpful. In view of the treatment of other summits than the title role, I have taken the liberty to change the heading to "Mt. Waternomee and the Blue Ridge".

Your second manuscript came to hand today, and has been forwarded to the printer. I trust you will see the latest number on your table by the 18th of December. I was sorry to learn of your illness and hope that you are now entirely recovered.

> Yours very truly,
> Charles E. Fay

* * * * * * * * * * * *

Marian Pychowska writes to Isabella Stone.

> Hoboken, N.J.
> December 2, 1884

Dear Isabella,

A part of last Sunday was to have been spent in writing a letter to you, but the anticipated time was not at my disposal. I will not wait now until I am able to write you a document of length, but will take this bit of twilight merely to say, "How do you do?". We certainly wrote to one another often enough during those last two weeks in the mountains, to cover a long period. Still, that is hardly a satisfactory way of arranging correspondence.

Your communication to my uncle reassured me as to your well being, yet I have some doubt as to whether you ever received the letter I wrote you early in October and sent as you directed me to do, to the Bay View House[10]. I did not know you intended returning thither to finish the season. When the AMC notices came announcing the Winnepesaukee excursion, I anticipated a long letter telling me how you had climbed Mt. Belknap with the Apes and seen sights of autumn beauty as no mortal ever enjoyed before! But it never came and I am afraid that you did not add this mountain to your list.

Do not think I am complaining of your silence. We understand one another well enough not to feel bound to write when we are busy or have nothing special to say.

I have no news to give. My mother is very well and full of energy as ever, the rest of us about as usual. Excuse my hasty scrawl, and believe me as ever,

> Sincerely yours,
> M. M. Pychowska

---

[10] A boardinghouse overlooking Lake Winnepesaukee in Laconia, NH.

Marian Pychowska writes to Isabella Stone.

Hoboken, N.J.
December 21, 1884

Dear Isabella,

I see with surprise that your welcome letter bears the date December 5. These days of preparation for Christmas seem to fly with wings. I would have been glad to get a more definite account of your health, but it is good that you can tell me at least that you are mending.

Our household has been enlivened of late by the presence of a favorite cousin with her Spanish poodle, a thriving puppy, rather troublesome, but attractive to dog lovers. This evening while we were at supper, "Sir Isaac" was left in my cousin's room as usual. The villain signalized himself this time by getting up on the table and demolishing two of his mistresses carefully thought out Christmas gifts!

A whole gallery of pictures has come to us from Chicago. Mr. Peek has distinguished himself. He was not satisfied with copying the sketches which he made us select last September, instead he adds his own selection, sending us two apiece all round. My choice was an excellent study made that rainy time when Mr. Peek camped with my uncle and Mr. Hunt on Carter in preparation for the AMC excursion. Chatham, Baldface and distant hills seaward come in between the characteristic trees of Carter's top. Mr. Peek's choice for me is a glimpse down the Moose Valley from "The Sightable Place", otherwise known as the "Huntable Place", a secluded spot back of Hubbard Hunt's. Mr. Peek had never been to this locale until my very last day in Randolph, when I had the pleasure of taking him there. He stayed and painted, while I wandered vagrantly on to the Bowman Place for a last good look at Mt. Jefferson. Another good thing in the gallery is one of the cliffs in Evans Notch, sent to my uncle.

We have not seen much of Randolphians lately. Life goes on with its changes. Miss Barstow's father has died since her return. Mr. Sargent is really hard at work with his medical studies and appears thoroughly interested in them. Miss Tompson announces her engagement to Mr. Rollins, a relative of Mr. Kennard, our Club Treasurer. He has been attached to her ever since they were children together. Edith, who is a good judge of young men, pronounces him a very worthy and attractive person. She saw him often last June when she was staying with Alice.

My uncle got a notice the other day from Mr. Lawrence concerning the postponement of a Council meeting, on account of the death of Miss M. F. Whitman. When I asked after her last summer, I was told she had finished her medical studies and was resident physician in some institution. I have most pleasant memories of this good lady.

Please give our most cordial wishes for the New Year to Dr. and Mrs. Stone, and believe me always,

Sincerely yours,

M. M. Pychowska

1885

"The mountains speak to us with our own voice—they may have other speech for us, indeed they do have in a certain sense, but, after all, they are only echoes."

Edith Cook writes to Isabella Stone.

Hoboken, N.J.
January 18, 1885

My dear Miss Stone,

It was very pleasant once more to receive one of your letters, though I feel sure in your case that you often think letters when you do not write them, but however far one trusts the unwritten assurance of friendship and interest, its spoken renewal is always welcome and one cannot satisfy one's thirst solely by the sound of the stream that is hidden deep under the rocks. I am very glad to have given further pleasure with the speech I have given to the mountain path. I should be very willing to publish what I have written in book form, but its need is doubtful and I suppose one ought first to make a name in the magazines, that such unsalable ware as verse may find a profitable market.

It will interest you to know that a poem of mine has been accepted by one of the Boston children's magazines, *Wide Awake*, and will appear therein in due time, how soon I do not know. The subject is an Indian one, a charming story told in Leland's *Algonquin Legends* that I read with so much interest this fall. This story of Wasis the Conqueror has a delightful humor in it, as well as the tenderness of our common human nature, that one is not apt to look for in the typical Indian of romance and New England history. I have not read *Ramona* though I have read of it and have heard of it through a California cousin of mine who dines with Mrs. Jackson lately in Los Angeles. It is a dreary question, the Indian one, and as nations cannot be judged or punished, as such, in the court of eternity, they receive their chastisement here. Do you remember that couplet from the German? "The mills of the god's grind slow, but they grind exceeding small."

I am going to send with this letter my copy of *The Catholic World* which you need be in no hurry to return, as we have another copy in the house. I think you may be interested in the description of the Catholic Indian settlement of Wikwimikong on Lake Huron as showing how the work begun so long ago by the old French Missionaries is still carried on today among the native tribes of Canada. I think too it may interest you to read the article on George Eliot. There are still other things in the magazine to interest one who cares at all for the social questions of the present time.

I intend to copy for you and send a poem of Father Labor's that expresses some of my ideas with regard to the influence of the mountains, especially with regard to the point that the mountains give us what we take to them, restful for our spirits in a certain way, ministers to our physical restlessness, but, at best, they are temporary consolers when we are weary hearted. As a poet one may ascribe many things to the mountains and they may be very true things, but they may not be all the truth, only one phase of it. Perhaps the very fact that you find what you believe of the mountains in what I have written is only proof that I took it with me to the mountains then, but they cannot give it back to me now. Sometimes the mountain paths seem very easy to our tread, but at other times, when we are tired, our clumsy feet knock the stones about our heels, and we walk bruised where we have trodden with light unflinching step. The mountains speak to us with our own voice—they may have other speech for us, indeed they do have in a certain sense, but, after all, they are only echoes.

I wish I could give you some counsel or wisdom in the matter you ask of me. Of course the impulse of charity is always to disbelieve, to think no evil, but sometimes for the sake of a greater charity, we may have to do that against which all our impulses cry out and in each case one must be guided by its special circumstances and the abiding law of one's conscience.

The symphony concerts are the only public entertainments I have been to this winter, and to these only because of the kindness of the friend who sent us four season tickets. And my most mountain-like walking has been my various transits of the Brooklyn Bridge which lifts in an exhilarating way above the cities to the upper air that would be difficult to analyze and seems a little absurd on the face of it. Perhaps it is a sense of physical freedom that makes the charm. Marian sends her thanks for your letter and the message that she will answer in the course of time. It is very possible that I shall go down to Washington for the 4th of March. You know I have a host of cousins down there and they want me.

Remember me most kindly to your father and mother,
                              Sincerely and affectionately yours,
                              Edith W. Cook

Marian Pychowska writes to Isabella Stone.

Hoboken, N.J.
April 4, 1885

Dear Isabella,

Ere you get this, my aunt's bunch of daffodils will have told you that we are as usual. My tame prose bulletin can scarcely add to the information carried by her Easter remembrance. But then, I am not so afraid of boring you with tame prose bulletins, as you seem to be in my regard! Why should we be brilliant? Let us have our tallow candle, or perhaps a good steady kerosene lamp (with a bit of red flannel in it by way of decorative art) alongside of our hearth fire of logs, and leave the flashy electric lights and stifling furnace heat to the great world which does everything by wholesale, even to the entertaining of its friends. Modern improvements are good in their places, but they need not invade our homely ways. How much better is a little kindness and love than ever so much cleverness. Let us be done with the fear of boring one another so long as we feel there is anything good in mutual kindness.

You have had a hard winter for mind and body. I hope your efforts in behalf of your friend will be crowned with a blessing, and that these matters that have been weighing on you so, will have an end, so that your summer may have a chance to set you up permanently.

Our arrangements for the summer are the same as last year. As far as we can tell, the last week in June will find us at Randolph with the prospect of staying there the usual three months. There has been no suggestion of mutiny from any member of the family. In fact, all take the Ravine House for granted. My uncle has heard from Mr. Chubbuck[1], the new Councillor of Improvements, in regard to the proposed path over what Mr. Peek calls "Moriah-Carter-Kettle-Dome". The money is forthcoming for the work, Mr. Chubbuck and my uncle will probably both be on hand to superintend it. The Pilot Range, and the airiest line[2] up Durand Ridge, by which the distance is to be still farther reduced, also attract the Dux Explorationis. My uncle wishes me to tell you that if you visit North Woodstock again, the Kinsman Notch offers itself for your exploration. Mr. William Sargent last fall intended extending a hay road in that direction. Be sure we shall be very glad to have you for a neighbor if you can make it convenient to come our way. I believe all our trysts have been very successful with the exception of that cold day on Randolph Mountain when you took such a cold.

My uncle, (probably as being an officer of the AMC) received today a circular headed "Canoe Expedition to Great Lake Mistassini, under the pa-

---

[1] Isaac Y. Chubbuck of Roxbury, MA was AMC Councillor of Improvements from 1885 to 1887.
[2] Still in use today, the Air Line is the most direct route from the Randolph Valley to the summit of Mount Adams.

tronage of Colonel Rhodes of the Quebec Geographical Society. Important to Scientists, and Sportsmen, Tourists and Invalids". They expect to be gone from June 10 to September 1. The route is up the Saguenay and then by canoe route through various lakes and rivers to the mysterious great water. Quite an attractive programme for such as have five hundred dollars to invest in travelling.

Have I read *Appalachia* yet? No. But I did not speak of this neglect in my last letter in order to boast of my business, but rather as an example of how apt are the Apes to omit reading their own organ. More than one stupid mistake would have been spared some of the writers therein, if they had read up their back numbers. But how can we expect busy men to do this? Only let them not be quite so positive in their assertions.

If you were inclined to be green-eyed, you would envy me something which I found hanging on the back of my chair when I came down to breakfast this Easter morning. Edith, with her usual kind forethought had prepared an Easter gift for each one. For my mother, a growing hyacinth; for my uncle, a specimen of German confectioner's art, a sugar rabbit, sitting up on his hind legs singing to the accompaniment of his guitar. Hoboken cake and candy stores are full of bunnies and eggs of all sizes at this time, just as at Christmas time "Santa Claus" and "Horsey cakes" reign supreme. I believe the Germans have a legend for their children, that at Easter, rabbits lay eggs! This must be the origin of the present display. But, to return to my enviable acquisition, perhaps you remember the basket carried by Mr. Thompson that day you went with us to Pine Mountain, year before last. This is asking a good deal of your memory, but I found it a model packbasket and wanted one like it. Edith's sharp eyes discovered its mate in New York not long since. It is woven of palmetto, flat when empty, pliable and weighs almost nothing. We have not seen Mr. Thompson for several months. He is engaged to a young lady from Denver and is probably too happily busy to keep up with other friends.

Two other friendly Apes have dropped in during the last ten days; Mr. Matthews, whose health seems to be improving, though he still looks very pale and thin, and Miss Barstow, who is in excellent training for the summer's work and play. She ascribes this restoration in part to the private skating pond which she made for herself in her back yard. First she had the exercise of carrying the water, bucket by bucket, to the freezing ground, and then she would snatch the spare moments between work, to practice engraving with steel on the surface so laboriously prepared.

I send a Booth item which had been lying in my writing case, waiting until I should write you. If you do not care for it, the stove will soon dispose of it.

Remember me most kindly to Dr. and Mrs. Stone and believe me as ever,

Yours,
M. M. Pychowska

Isabella Stone writes to Isaac Chubbuck (draft copy).

Framingham, Mass.
June 17, 1885

Mr. Isaac Chubbuck
15 Georgia St.
Roxbury, Mass.
Councillor of Improvements, AMC
Dear Sir,

Although a stranger I take the liberty as a member of the Club to address you in your official capacity, introducing myself as the lady by whose efforts the path was made to Bridal Veil Falls on Coppermine Brook in Franconia in 1880 and the path to Georgiana Falls in this vicinity last summer, as was described in *Appalachia* December 1884 in the appendix to your predecessors report. Perhaps it would be better however to refer you to our Councillor of Explorations, Mr. E. B. Cook and his family who have been for years personal friends of mine.

For two summers or more I have had much at heart one special improvement in the North Woodstock area and have done what was possible towards its accomplishment which would be desirable to achieve before the field meeting at The Flume House next month. To finish the path, residents and others will contribute work or money. Mr. William Sargent is ready as heretofore to take the practical charge, and I write to entreat from your department a small contribution without which it will be impossible to proceed. We need $10.00, but would be delighted to receive a smaller sum. It is so nearly the hour for the departure of the mail (only one per day here) that time forbids my writing details, as I am anxious to hear from you as soon as possible whether we can depend on assistance and how much. So I can only assure you that this is a bit of work in a direction where the Club has already done a great deal.

Respectfully yours,
M. Isabella Stone

* * * * * * * * * * * *

Isaac Chubbuck writes to Isabella Stone.

Roxbury, Mass.
June 19, 1885

Dear Miss Stone,

I was very glad to hear from you, and I appreciate the work you have done on the paths you mention.

I thank you for the aid and assistance to the department of Improvement. I will contribute the amount you mention ($10.00) and am very glad to do so. If that is not enough, please let me know. Also let me know when you are ready for it and in what manner to send it.

I would like the address of Mr. William Sargent as I would like to correspond with him in relation to the Waterville-Livermore Path. Something has got to be done in that direction this summer.

Very truly yours,

Isaac Y. Chubbuck

* * * * * * * * * * * *

Mary Low Stone writes to Marian Pychowska (draft copy).

Laconia, N.H.

June 28, 1885

Dear Miss Pychowska,

Doubtless you will feel surprised to receive a letter from me, but Isabella is not able to write. She has long been wishing and hoping thus to do, but for the last few months has been growing more and more ill from nervous prostration, a disease with which she was threatened a year ago, but which seemed to be checked by the bracing and exhilarating air of the mountains and the exercise which she so much enjoyed. It has now assumed a more serious form, accompanied with loss of appetite and sleeplessness and general debility which prevents her from anticipating even the enjoyment of long walks as in previous years.

The physician forbids any excitement or mental effort at present. When stronger he desires she should walk all she is able on level ground, so that physical fatigue may induce sleep if possible. We hope much from change of air and scene for her. She has taken two short rides.

She had engaged her old room at E. A. Crawford's and it is a bitter disappointment to her to be obliged to abandon her plans for Jefferson, the pleasure of her walks with you and yours and "not to see the dear Pychowskas, how can I give that up!" she exclaimed. Finding herself really unable to attempt going to Jefferson, she agrees with us that I must write immediately to Mr. Crawford canceling her engagement. I shall do so today.

These nights of wearisome restlessness with little, often no sleep, produce an exhaustion hard to bear and naturally cause great depression. Isabella has surprised us in keeping up so bravely, striving to do, but there comes a limit to everyone's power of endurance. She would be very glad to hear from you and any friends who would be kind enough to write when she cannot answer. Her address will be Russell House, North Woodstock, N.H., till you are informed otherwise.

Give my love to your dear mother and say to her I know it would delight and comfort daughter to receive a letter from her. I know she will give us her sympathy in these hours of anxiety.

With kindest regards to your father, aunt, and yourself, believe me,

Truly yours,

Mrs. H. O. Stone

* * * * * * * * * * * *

Lucia Pychowska writes to Mary Low Stone.

Ravine House

Randolph, N.H.

June 30, 1885

My dear Mrs. Stone,

We owe you many thanks for your kind letter to Marian. I need not tell you how sorry we are to learn that Isabella is still so far from well, and that we shall not have her near us this autumn. I have myself gone through a tolerable siege of a malady similar to hers, and, having come out with renewed strength, I can but hope that she may do the same. The lack of sleep is one of the most wearing symptoms, one that must be gotten over before much good can be hoped for.

To look at the matter medically, is there any cause beyond the prostration of nervous strength which enters as a factor in the sleeplessness? One possible cause of such disturbance, I know to be constipation, a trouble from which many suffer. That will produce much headache. The best cure for this trouble that I have seen employed is "Schiffelin's little pill of Aloes, Strychnine and Belladonna", one taken at night, and an enema used in the morning, if the pill does not produce a natural effect, at least after breakfast. Some very obstinate cases require two pills, one at night, and one on waking up in the morning, to bring about a change in habit. Of course, the procedure must be persevered for months to produce a radically good result. Pardon my speaking of this. I know that Isabella has the best of scientific advice, but sometimes one may be able to suggest something that has not yet been tried, and we feel so desirous that she should regain health and strength that every straw should be turned to account.

I fear your long anxiety will have a trying effect upon your own health, already not strong.

Mr. Pychowski, Marian and I are already established at Randolph. My brother and sister will be up about the 14th of July. Marian and I are waiting for this long, though greatly desired, rain storm to clear away so we can go up to the snow patches at the head of King's Ravine in search of the delicate alpine plants of the season. Tell Isabella that Marian will write to her an account of this, our first walk on the great mountains for this year, when we have succeeded in accomplishing it. Meantime, give her much love from us, with best wishes for a radical recovery. With renewed thanks for your letter, and the kindest remembrances to Dr. Stone and love from Marian and myself to you. Believe me,

Very truly yours,

L. D. Pychowska

P.S. Has Isabella ever tried any of the excellent preparations of pepsin now in use? They are useful adjuncts to the pills in cases of constipation and feeble digestion. I mention these things in ignorance of Isabella's malady, merely at a venture. Pardon me for doing.

* * * * * * * * * * * *

Charles Fay writes to Isabella Stone.

Flume House, N.H.

July 5, 1885

My dear Miss Stone,

It was very kind of you to take so much trouble about my umbrella. I discovered my loss before reaching here, and regretted my carelessness, yet knew that it was safe under Mr. Russell's roof. Please accept my cordial thanks for your kindness with the earnest hope that the added effort of writing the note did not add to the discomfort which I fear my visit inconsiderably occasioned.

Mr. Edmands and I now propose to start for Kinsman by 7:30 A.M. tomorrow. With good success in finding an easy way, we hope to be there by noon or one o'clock. I will try and indicate our presence there in the afternoon by a fire, which I hope you will see from North Woodstock.

With expression of high regard and sense of great obligation, I am,

Most truly yours,

Chas. E. Fay

* * * * * * * * * * * *

Charles Fay writes a postal card to Isabella Stone.

Flume House, N.H.

July 6, 1885

My dear Miss Stone,

The weather did not favor our ascent of Kinsman today and it is postponed until Wednesday.

Tomorrow I hope to traverse the range from Lafayette to Flume

Mountain and Mr. Edmands expects to spend the day in topographical work on the Flume.

If fires are seen on the range, they may be considered ours if not too extensive!

Very truly yours,
Chas. E. Fay

* * * * * * * * * * * *

Lucia Pychowska writes to Isabella Stone.

Ravine House
Randolph, N.H.
July 10, 1885

My dear Isabella,

We have had two walks since I wrote to your dear Mother. In both of which we were caught in the heavy thunder storms which have been lying in wait for us during the past two weeks. Marian is very busy writing up our first excursion, and she will send you a copy of the same when it is finished to her satisfaction. Both were botanizing excursions, the first taking in Durand Ridge, the head of King's Ravine, and the snow patch in the same, now nearly vanished. The second included Durand Ridge the main peak of Adams, Spaulding's Spring, Sam Adams, and Lowe's Path to the Randolph Road. The storm that struck us (Marian and myself, we do not expect my brother and sister until the 16th), found us at the head of treeline on Nowell's Ridge. Marian found a cave, into which she crept and kept dry, and I took shelter under some low spruces. We were not together when the storm came up, but duly met at 3:00 P.M., the trysting hour, just as the storm was passing away. The thunder and lightning were wonderful to watch as the great curtain of storm, first black, then pale yellow, then greenish rolled up. The wind was tremendous, the rain light where we were, but very heavy in the valleys below. We kept dry in our shelters. Only our feet became damp as we descended Lowe's Path, and as we crossed the meadow at the foot that leads over to his house, we sank to the boot tops in the marsh.

The Moose River is a flood, every waterfall is a sheet of foam, and the sound of rushing waters is everywhere to be heard. Haying cannot begin, there being no prospect of drying the wet grass. The long previous drought is being well made up for.

We have about nineteen boarders already and a crowd more expected. I hope you are feeling stronger. I am sorry to think we shall not have you at least as near as E. A. Crawford's this September. It would be much better if you were at the Mount Crescent House, we could see so much more of you, and the situation is as dry and airy as Mr. Crawford's. They have but a poor prospect for the season up at the Mount Crescent House.

One of my friends Miss E. Torrey, expects to be there by the third week in August, when the black flies will have given up.

Will you give kindest remembrances to Dr. and Mrs. Stone, and believe me,

Ever affectionately yours,
Lucia D. Pychowska

* * * * * * * * * * * *

Isabella Stone writes to Isaac Chubbuck (draft copy).

Russell House
North Woodstock, N.H.
July 17, 1885

Mr. I. Y. Chubbuck
Councillor of Improvements of AMC
Dear Sir,

Various unavoidable hindrances have arisen to prevent the completion about which I wrote you in June and now it must be postponed until later in the season when farmers are not so busy. Then, doubtless, it could be accomplished, especially as I have decided to remain here. But there is one insurmountable obstacle, that is: the continuance of my own ill health which not only prevents my usual walks and climbs, but has compelled my physician to forbid any mental effort, care, responsibility, worry or nervous excitement of any kind (even letter writing). Therefore allow me to put into your charge, to treat as you consider best, my plan for opening a route from North Woodstock to the summit of Mt. Bond. This would make a delightful excursion of eight and one-half miles from "Pollard's" by a good foot path (two and one-half miles remaining to be cut) which avoids crossing the East Branch at all (the fording of which is often very difficult) which will afford fine views of waterfalls and the cliffs of Bond as the traveller approaches them.

This is my own idea, and has been long a cherished scheme of mine, the presentation of which to the Club would have given me much pleasure. If this path be completed by the Club, I hope next summer to be able to traverse it, and to be allowed to write some account of it for *Appalachia*. Professor C. E. Fay and Mr. William Sargent agree with me that this is decidedly the best route for the continuance of the AMC path over the Twin Mountain Range in order to reach Pollards. To Mr. Pollard it would be an advantage and he has promised to give two days work.

Illness will prevent my participation in the field meeting at the Flume House much to my sorrow.

Should you conclude to undertake the above work, you will find me at Russell House, two miles south of "Pollards" until into October probably.

Will you kindly inform me on what day to expect to see you.

Very respectfully yours,

M. Isabella Stone

P.S. Will you please show this letter to Professor Fay?

* * * * * * * * * * * *

Marian Pychowska writes to Isabella Stone.

Ravine House
Randolph, N.H.
July 19, 1885

My dear Isabella,

Your mother's kind letter reached us yesterday, and my mother wishes me to send her thanks for it. I wish also to express my own thanks for the former letter addressed to me. It had been so long since we had any news of you. I expected that our correspondence would be reopened by a letter from Laconia, but I did not anticipate that it would bring such bad accounts of your health. If your friends' sympathy and interest could do you any solid good, you would soon be set up again. Meantime, I know your loving heart values every meanest little spark of human affection, how lovingly you make the most of such like little consolations which our good Lord strews along your way, so I feel sure he will not deny them to you. I cannot but feel hopeful about your health, because I have seen my mother pass through so much nervous weakness and suffering, and now year by year she is gaining in the ability to do and to endure, both physically and mentally. Formerly headaches of one kind or another were always hanging over her, ready to take possession on the least provocation and very often without any provocation at all. Sleeplessness was the source and the consequence, as with you, of many other ills. But now, headache is only an occasional visitor, she sleeps easily, though lightly, and even dares to despise the short midday rest on the bed, which used to be a necessity. Cheer yourself with her example, for I hope your patience will be crowned with a restoration as excellent.

The manuscript[3] that I send will show you what I have been doing and why I have not written before. It represents many more hours of labor from me than such a thing would require of you or another accustomed to that kind of writing. It was written with considerable enthusi-

---

[3] The manuscript mentioned here is Marian's story, "Two in the Alpine Pastures," which is an account of an excursion taken with her mother up Durand Ridge to Mount Adams. It was eventually published in *Appalachia* in December of 1888.

asm, more, perhaps than I am likely to have again, unless indeed my mercenary plans for its publication should be realized. In that event, I should be tempted to try again. As I know I am dealing with a friend who judges very kindly of my descriptive efforts, I will tell you of how far my mother went in her flattering opinion of this particular attempt. It so captured her mind, that she had a very distinct dream one night of the arrival of a check for fifteen dollars as payment for my work! I should rather say our work, for she has been so good as to make two copies, one of which has started on its fortune seeking journey, and the other I send for your perusal. You need not be in any special haste to return it. Any time before next month will do.

Perhaps I wrote you in the spring that I have undertaken to translate from the French, a little book of piety. It is a little treasure, more than two hundred years old, and the work of putting it into English is most congenial and delightful to me. The book was given me to read by a very old French priest who values it very highly. While reading it I was moved again and again with the desire to translate it, a very new desire to me. One day, in conversation with my old Father, I expressed a wish that it could be published in English, and he at once proposed that I should undertake it. You can imagine my enchantment at thus having put into my hands the very thing I was craving. I am nearly half through the book, in spite of the mania for original composition which possessed me for a short time. I am doing it for love, nevertheless I shall not be sorry if some benevolent publisher consents to give me something for my labor. It would be pleasant to think that there is a way for me to earn my bread by the sweat of my brow. What author is it who expresses so beautifully the idea (ever old and ever new) that the blessing and the curse of labor are merely two faces of the same figure? Perhaps it is my old friend Ozanam. My mother gets along well with her translating work, but is not sanguine about finding a publisher or readers at present. It may be that I have told you of my literary renaissance before, but no matter, I am not afraid of boring my old friend.

When you receive this the Apes will be let loose in your neighborhood. I wish you were better able to enjoy the advantages of this meeting which seems to have been especially arranged for your convenience. I wish this, not only for your pleasure, but for ours also, that we might have your report of all their wonderful doings. It is a most attractive programme that they have prepared, and I hope the weather will be suitable for its full carrying out. "If wishes were horses, beggars would ride", although our attendance at the meeting is so entirely out of the question, that it is almost beyond wishing for. Besides, how could anyone be so thankless as to sigh for any more mountain pleasures than we can have here in Randolph, gratis!

We have had three good days on the big mountains. I think my mother wrote of our scamper down to treeline in the face of the big Thursday storm, which prepared the new slide on Owl's Head[4]. My scamper was all the way from Spaulding's Spring, where I happened to be when I first noticed the dark west, to a cave three hectometers above treeline on Nowell's Ridge. I hardly had a minute to spare after I had crawled in, before the hail began to pelt. It would have been terrific if the storm had not divided and given us only a thin specimen of its middle. It was very grand, and the clearing off wonderfully beautiful. The most alarming thing that I encountered was the wind that followed the storm. I had to crouch and crawl down those three hectos very carefully, and was thankful to find myself still in one piece when I joined my mother under the first spruces on the path. Happily, she had not worried unreasonably about me and expected me to keep the tryst at three o'clock as, thank Providence, I was able to do.

All evening the clouds drove fiercely over the ridges of the great range. I had reason to be thankful that the storm had not caught us higher up, for we should have had a hard fight to get down through such a wind and with fog to boot. Mr. Sargent and two young men were caught near the Gateway, and they walked the whole length of Durand Ridge in all the wind, rain, and lightening, thinking it safer than to look for shelter. Mr. Watson and his man were also on the mountain in the woods, where the effects of the wind were terrible.

Our last mountain day was on Madison. My mother went to the top while I escorted Mr. Peek to "Hamilton Howk". There we were joined by Mr. Sargent and we came down "thorough brake, thorough brier" into Bumpus basin, and out by Coösauk Fall. The men were kind enough to turn over to me the fun of leading. A funny looking party, some people might say, but I for one enjoyed leading the scramble, and we saw some pretty falls and noble rocks in behind that wonderful "Blueberry Ledge".

Mr. Sargent is taking his holiday early this year, and goes back to hospital work the first of September. We are looking for Mr. Hinkley in a few days, when his attack of rheumatism (which I hear rendered him nearly blind and deaf for a time) has subsided.

My aunt and uncle came last Thursday. Their journey by Fall River, Lowell and Jefferson, a new route, was very easy, and they look well. We are planning a day's trip to Mt. Washington, not to the summit however. At least, the object in view by my mother, aunt and me is to visit the head

---

[4] On July 10, 1885, a great landslide took place on Cherry Mountain, descending the northern side of Owl's Head Peak. The debris of the slide carved a two-mile track of devastation and was mostly deposited on the farm of Oscar Stanley where it wrecked the house, killed several cattle and fatally injured one of the farm hands, Donald Walker. For quite some time to follow, the site of the slide was a popular tourist attraction.

of Huntington's Ravine and the Alpine Garden. The snow leaves that slope so late and I hope to be able to show them the June blossoms still in their prime. And then that grand view down into that deepest of deeps. Some day you will please get out near the seven-mile post and cross the col, barely a quarter of a mile, to the head of that deep.

The Tompsons are here again and the house is filling up. The Mount Crescent House has had scarcely any guests up to the end of last week, but now Mr. Leighton's prospect is good for the coming weeks. Poor man! I do hope he will learn the lesson of "slow and sure".

The Owl's Head slide seems to have made a great noise all over the country. New York and Chicago papers both had full accounts. Quite a party went from here to visit it last Tuesday and my aunt and uncle saw it of course from the train in passing. My mother and I have inspected it only from a distance. This morning as we drove to Gorham to church we met almost innumerable vehicles. All Gorham seemed on its way to the slide. We heard a rumor that Mr. Beecher[5] was to speak to the assembly, and this is probably the explanation of the concourse.

I do not know when you expect your parents to join you. When you communicate with them, please remember me to them.

My aunt sends her love and word that she will write soon to you. Miss Tompson also wishes to be remembered to you.

I had no idea I had so much to say, but now I must stop. When you are equal to writing a postal I shall be glad to see your hand.

Yours as ever,
M. M. Pychowska

* * * * * * * * * * * *

Isabella Stone writes to Marian Pychowska (draft copy).

Russell House
North Woodstock, N.H.
July 24, 1885

O Marian, you darling girl!

How shall I thank you for the letter of the 19th and for the manuscript "Two in the Alpine Pastures"? The mere sight of your writing was a pleasure. Reading the letter and glancing over the first page or two of big sheets was all I could bear at once.

---

[5] Henry Ward Beecher (1813-1887) was one of America's most noted preachers and patriot writers of the nineteenth century. He first came to the White Mountains in 1856, staying at the Crawford House. He spent many summers preaching to large congregations (most of the time under the shelter of a great canvas tent) that would gather at various mountain locales. Much of this was undertaken at the Twin Mountain House in Carroll. His sister was Harriet Beecher Stowe, the author.

Owl's Head Slide

Since then I have read the manuscript with delight, as anyone must, and lucky is the publisher who gets it. My delight was, besides a special one, for the "ways" described, are they not mine own also? "Our ways" let me say, too, won't you?, though I have never seen alpine gardens in their glory. Would that my brains were in condition fitly to characterize the radiant bird born of your enthusiasm for which the common place expressions "interesting", "beautiful", "charmingly written" are inadequate. Count me for the worse one of "the strange people for whom one single howl interchanged across the deep ravine contains as much meaning as a full chatter box." Believe in my appreciation of the many "points", the wit, the vividness, the exquisite descriptions, the strength and symmetry, etc., though it must be compressed into one "O!"

Your friendship, sympathy, and encouraging words are indeed particularly precious now. Above all, perhaps, your appreciation of my forced stationary situation. To be more than six weeks at North Woodstock without taking even a stroll of more than three-quarters of a mile and a few short rides is proof enough (to you who know me) that something serious is the matter, is it not? To miss the AMC meeting so near! And now in obedience to the physician's last letter ("mental exercise you must abstain from") to be forced to say good-bye instead of enjoying the duty and pleasure of answering your letters.

When you see Mr. Lowe give him my regards, please, and regrets that he cannot escort me up Madison or Jefferson this year. I return your manuscript with this same mail.

Excuse my using a pencil.

Yours,
Isabella

* * * * * * * * * * * *

Marian Pychowska writes to Isabella Stone.

Ravine House
Randolph, N.H.
July 30, 1885

Dear Isabella,

Your kind note and the manuscript came two days ago. It is certainly a great pleasure to me to see that my effort has pleased you, and none the less so, that I know your flattering words come rather from a heart full of friendly feeling than from the merciless critical judgement of an editor. It is this latter personage who must decide the result of my first attempt at fortune seeking. I am not optimistic, although I have had the "cheek" to send the thing to *The Atlantic*, thinking that if by any chance, they would take it, it would be by far the best place for an article of such strong New England flavor. If they do me the grace to return the manuscript I shall peddle it round in other quarters hoping that by next June it may find a resting place. You see it is greatly against me, that the season it treats of is past; magazines are made up with so much regard for the fitness of the season. Of course you shall hear the end of my adventure.

I have great reason to regret your inability to write me those long, interesting letters that have been part of my summer pleasure for so many years, but I was very glad to see your hand at all, and I hope you will favor me with an occasional postcard to let me know how you are getting along. I hope you have pleasant people in the house with you for it makes a great difference, when one is obliged to stay in or around headquarters, what the company is like. Have you no thoughts of Goodnow's in September when the place grows more quiet?

Wednesday the 22nd our Huntington's Ravine party came off. A dozen of the household, in two vehicles, were driven up the mountain. My mother, aunt, Mr. Peek, Miss Tompson and I got out just below the seven-mile post, while the rest went on to the summit. The only trouble was that we had barely two hours before we had to rejoin the wagons. This did not allow us to see nearly as much as I had hoped to show them, but at least I had the satisfaction of seeing that they were duly impressed with the superior grandeur and awfulness of the place. There were alpine flowers all over, at least the snow treasures which were the ones I specially wanted to show off.

Last Monday night there was a camp at Star Lake, just under the cliffs of John Quincy and in sight of the summit of Madison, Adams and the great shoulder of Washington. Within a few steps of camp we commanded the Great Gulf and all the grand view of the Carters, Wildcat, and as far as the Saco Valley and Moat Mountain. North and westward we had delightful glimpses of Crescent Mountain and the fogs of the Androscoggin and Dead Rivers beyond. Moonlight and dawn were superb. Our charming camp, "Camp Luna", was enclosed by three great rocks, our fire made of the "bleached horns" you wrote of. Our original intention was to put up at Madison Spring, but when we got there we found it so littered with cans, old shoes, etc., of last year's campers, that we looked for more attractive quarters. Edith, Miss Frothingham and I went up Monday morning and were joined in the evening by my uncle, Mr. Sargent and Mr. Peek.

Mail carrier arrived, so must stop. Good-bye from yours ever,

M. M. Pychowska

* * * * * * * * * * *

Isaac Chubbuck writes to Isabella Stone.

Boston, Mass.
August 3, 1885

Dear Miss Stone,

Circumstances over which I have no control (the after results of a sunstroke a few years ago) necessitated my leaving the Flume House without calling on you. But if you stay as long as you mention in your letter of July 17, I may possibly be up in cooler weather and if so, I will surely call on you and talk over Appalachian matters.

I heartily approve of your scheme for a path from North Woodstock to the cliffs of Bond and would like very much to see it carried out. Our appropriation for this kind of thing is limited. There is a chance to spend thousands of dollars among the mountains and I wish that I had it, but, as

Mail Carrier

it is, I fear that I shall not be able to carry out what has been planned already. I will see what can be done. I suppose William Sargent will carry out your other project. If so, call on me when you want the money.

Yours very truly,

Isaac Y. Chubbuck

Edith Cook writes to Isabella Stone.

Ravine House
Randolph, N.H.
August 5, 1885

My dear Miss Stone,

I have been intending to write to you almost ever since I came to Randolph, hearing how you were shut out from your active mountain enjoyments and that the hearing from your mountain friends would be to you a source of pleasure. I have put off writing from time to time, since just when I would think of it, I would find Marian had just written and it so seemed better to wait, for your greater satisfaction. Today I can tell you of wild sights we had yesterday in our peaceful valley when one long night's rain made of our quiet summer streams roaring spring torrents.

Fancy Snyder Brook a muddy river plunging down the ravine, almost making the earth shake with its boisterous strength! And Cold Brook heaping up fresh logs against the old bridge, spreading out in white waves and quiet pools over the meadow where it meets the Moose. When I looked out of my window at rising I saw that Gordon Falls—you know the one we see across the fields—was a much wider mass of white wake than usual and when the breakfast bell rang the wakes were still wider, their roar too, growing and growing. After breakfast, as we stood on the porch watching, suddenly we saw leaping white waves along the meadows, following one another like jumping sheep on the surf of the shore, while the Moose spread out its current into lakes or swept by with a deep strength in its dark brown rapids.

It was still raining hard, but Miss Tompson and I resolved to go forth into the storm in search of the wonders of the streams. We accoutered ourselves accordingly and with us went her brother Stanley, who, in India rubber boots had already made one tour of exploration. Crossing the bridge over the Moose at the path for Mt. Madison, we found a small stream had sprung into existence, through which we had to wade, after the East Branch fashion, and then of course we minded nothing in the way of wet. First, we went to see Gordon Falls that swept over one end of the logging bridge below them, and that had lost all their original form in the vast mass of turbid angry waters that seemed to fairly tumble head over heels, to speak inappropriately. Then we turned into the woods to see how Lower Salmacis Falls would look and you can imagine how the gentle summer companion of the glen seemed changed into a reckless devastating monster all along our way. Rocks that we had stood on at milder times were far out of sight, being ground by the turbulent waters. All desires of seeing how it would look in the spring were gratified and the long rock slide just above the Lower Salmacis was the very personification of a magnificent recklessness of strength.

We would like to have gone on to Upper Salmacis, but it seemed too far and so we turned back, meeting Mr. Sargent on our way. He insisted on escorting us back to the Moose as he said we could no longer cross the stream we had waded through at starting. It had risen so high that we would have to be carried over and that he and Stanley would make a chair for us. When we reached this stream we found it indeed widened and deepened and some of Mr. Watson's men were busy building a plank bridge over it, of which we were glad, indeed, to make use, and to the entertainment of some of the members of the household gathered on the safe side of the stream.

Then Mr. Sargent and Stanley turned to go on up to Upper Salmacis which they described as supremely wild and magnificent. Miss Tompson and I went on up to Cold Brook where the fall had kept more beauty of form with its added strength than the falls on Snyder Brook. It seemed strange enough to think of the mild little Moose as an enemy we didn't want to put between ourselves and home, but it did seem high enough to wash away the light log bridges on which we depended for our safe returning. In the afternoon Lillie, Marian and Mr. Peek walked up the road so as to look into the Ravine of the Cascades and see its long line of white waters foaming down the side of Mt. Adams.

This morning Miss Tompson and I walked over to Triple Falls, but of course though there was still much water, the great mass of which had subsided, as indeed it had in all the streams even yesterday afternoon. Their great rise had been very sudden and one wondered where such floods could come from.

I believe Marian has written you of our successful camping out near Star Lake and I suppose also of our expedition from the Mount Washington Carriage Road to the head of Huntington's Ravine where are those most awesome cliffs, an expedition for which our time was only too short.

This afternoon Eugene, Mr. Sargent and Mr. Peek, with Hubbard Hunt have started for Groveton from where they are going over the Pilot Range, one of Eugene's desired achievements, you know. They expect to camp out one night and we look for them back again on Friday or Saturday when Mr. Matthews, whom I think you saw here year before last, joins once more the Ravine House group. Mr. Hinkley perhaps you know, has been with us for the last ten days. And this week or next, I expect a very dear little prince from Brooklyn to be with me for a little while.

I was very sorry to hear of your illness, knowing, too, how great a loss to you is your deprivation of the active mountain pleasure you so earnestly enjoy. Of course there is much else you miss more, but here in this center of activity one is apt to think chiefly of your enthusiastic share in its whirl. I hope the rest of the hills is helping you.

Please remember me kindly to your father and mother,

Yours sincerely,

Edith W. Cook

P.S. I suppose you have read with interest as I have the account in *Appalachia* of the winter excursion into Tuckerman's Ravine.

* * * * * * * * * * * *

Charles Fay writes to Isabella Stone.

Boston, Mass.

August 15, 1885

My dear Miss Stone,

By the kindness of Mr. Henck, I am at length able to send you a copy of his early sketch map.

I was sorry not to see you as we came home from the Flume House. Our fire on Mt. Pemigewasset on that superb Saturday night may be accepted as an evidence that you were thought of by your fellow Appalachians. It was built for your special seeing.

We cordially hope that you have made a decided gain during your stay at North Woodstock and that another year may again find you joining in the pleasures of the Club excursions.

Very truly yours,

Charles E. Fay

* * * * * * * * * * * *

Marian Pychowska writes to Isabella Stone.

Ravine House

Randolph, N.H.

August 16, 1885

My dear Isabella,

We were all glad to hear of you by your late postal and to know that you can tell of a "perceptible gain". The little touch of dog day weather last week, must have caused you discomfort, if nothing worse, but I hope the exhilarating change has done away with the ill effects.

The Ravine House was in a state of great and painful excitement from last Friday evening to Saturday afternoon. A middle aged gentleman, a botanist and editor, who had been boarding here for about ten days, started out alone on Friday morning for the Pond of Safety. Mr. Peek had duly warned him of the bewitchedness of that place and given him instructions how to overcome the spell. However, evening came, and night came, and no news of the wanderer. Finally, Mr. Watson, Mr. Sargent, and Stanley Tompson set out with two lanterns to search for him. They went all the way to the Pond and all round it, blowing a horn. They found his coat (which he had left by the path on account of the heat of the day) a short distance beyond the Lookout Ledge, and his tracks and penknife cuttings about the little camp in the bog right near the pond. When they returned home, it was three o'clock Saturday morning.

After breakfast, a whole bevy of men set out to continue the search, while Miss Barstow and Mr. Matthews drove over to Stag Hollow and sent woodsmen in from that end, armed with a horn. After looking about the lake once more, the party from here divided and went off in various directions. Two men went out toward Stag Hollow and met the men who came in that way. Mr. Sargent and Thaddeus Lowe struck southeast over Randolph Mountain toward Ice Gulch and came in here about 6:30 P.M. My uncle and Hubbard Hunt took the longest but most likely route, down the Ammonoosuc.

Meanwhile the inmates of the Ravine House were more or less wrought up over the possible state of the missing man. We knew that he was without provisions, for he had not even taken a lunch with him, without a coat, and that he was nearsighted. To balance these disadvantages, we also knew that his botanical knowledge might help him to find something to sustain life, that he was a smoker and therefore was probably supplied with matches, and that he was furnished with an excellent compass (if only he did not lose his head and forget which end pointed north).

As the day wore on, conjectures were many, and about 2:30 P.M. Mr. Peek, Miss Barstow and I got ready to start for the Ledge that we might make sure that he was not lying disabled at the foot of its cliffs. Miss Barstow and I had not climbed half the pasture slope when we were called back. News had just been brought by a passing team that he was on his way up from Gorham. Our next thought was to go to the Ledge and leave a note there for the rescue party, that the lost was found. Half a mile from the house we met Mr. Watson and Rover returning from the Pond. Mr. Watson told us of the division of the rescuers, while we told him of the approach of the lost one. As there was no hope of communicating with the other parties that were out, we came back with Mr. Watson.

That same morning Mr. Nowell's party had gone over from the Mt. Adams House to go into camp on Moriah and begin work on the Moriah-Carter Trail. His wagon, on its return from Gorham, picked up our stray, borrowed a coat by the way to keep him warm, and deposited him safely here. The said stray, as you and I can easily understand, was quite as much annoyed by the commotion he had caused, as grateful for the efforts made to assist him. He said he had not suffered from cold during the night, having several times caught fire while he slept in his solitary encampment in a birch bark blanket. Berries and a cigar had kept him from hunger until he reached the clearings and got luncheon about ten or eleven Saturday morning. Evidently he wished no more sympathy wasted upon him.

My uncle and Mr. Hunt were the last to come in. They arrived at 10:30 last night, having tracked the wanderer all the way from the bewitched swamp, down the Ammonoosuc by the logging roads and bog holes noticing the place where he had camped and the inscription he left there (his initials with the word lost and date) seeing that he had rifled the berry bushes, hearing of him from the people who had furnished his luncheon and from the station master at Milan Water Station, so that they have been able to tell us as much of his doings as he imparted himself. It is fifteen miles out from the Pond to the Milan Water Station. My uncle and Mr. Hunt got a comfortable tea at the latter place, waited two hours, took train at 7:35 p.m., reached Gorham, where Mr. Watson was expecting them. Poor Mr. Watson, out all Friday night, nearly all Saturday too, at work about the farm and house in the afternoon. You may imagine how he nodded as he drove up, pitching first against Mr. Hunt and then nearly over the wheel. We had a full narrative of adventures from my uncle this morning.

As for the cause of all the hullabaloo, he quietly carried out his original plan and left here for Jefferson yesterday afternoon. I have no doubt he is very glad to be out of the way of all the talk. Perhaps it will be as well not to make the affair public, for the sake of the reputation of the Pond of Safety! Signs are now to be painted and put up at the fatal spot. It seems the wanderer did get bewildered in the usual place, not reaching the lake at all but stopping at the camp and going wrong from near there. He had evidently forgotten Mr. Peek's direction to go due south if lost for he first tried a southeasterly course and then concluded it safer to stick to the stream.

Monday

None of us have yet informed you, I think, of the completion of the Air Line route to Mt. Adams. Some of us long opposed it, out of affection for the route that leads by the Scar. But now that the thing is done, we must make the best of it, and try to do our duty by both paths.

The new route enters the woods opposite the house, instead of in the old place, and takes an almost direct course for the crest of the ridge, coming into the Scar route a short distance below the junction of the latter with the Salmacis route. The grade of the latest way is generally steeper than that of the old way, but never so steep in any one spot as is that part just below the Scar. The great gain is the saving of three-eighths of a mile in distance, bringing the whole length from here to the Mt. Adams Lawn to four miles and two hundred and twenty feet. The new path goes through beautiful forest, but I miss the companionship of Snyder Brook and the association of the old way. My mother and I went and returned by the new way once last week and concluded that our best way in the future will be to ascend the short way and come down by the easier grade of the old path.

Near the junction on the ridge Mr. Watson has built a very substantial camp[6], but it is only intended as a refuge in case of need, and consequently is placed off the path in a retired spot and is only spoken of in a whisper. We all fear that if the public are invited to it, the surroundings will become like those of Lowe's Camp or poor Madison Spring. On my way down the mountain the other day, I climbed down the Glen side of John Quincy and visited Camp Luna and Star Lake. A visit to Star Lake pays me better now than one to the summit. It is more picturesque.

Miss Frothingham, with Mr. Lowe and a large party from Jefferson Highlands went to the Gulch on Saturday, the 8th, and were much pleased. My uncle went along to show off the place and make sure they visited Peboamauk Falls—in spite of the fact that he only returned from the Pilot excursion at 10:30 the night before. He, Mr. Sargent, Mr. Peek, and Hubbard Hunt went to Groveton by train on Wednesday evening. The next day they traversed the Pilot chain to a point between its high (once fragmented) peak[7] and the great Kilkenny Peak[8] that dominates the whole group. After a comfortable night in camp, they visited the great peak and came out by way of the Lancaster neighborhood and so, round through Jefferson, home. The weather was perfect, so cool and clear. They report glorious views, but the top of Kilkenny is too big and rounding to be an entirely satisfactory viewpoint.

You see, we ladies are taking it easy this summer, and leaving the big things to the men. I find that a morning's work and a good afternoon walk make up a very satisfactory day—with an occasional all day trip to the greater heights.

The Atlantic was considerate enough to return my manuscript. Thinking it over I have come to the conclusion to wait until some time in the winter before sending it anywhere else, for June is too far off at present to offer any bait to an editor.

Miss Barstow brings from Waterville a number of sketches and the scalps (metaphorical only) of seventeen peaks visited during a month's time! She is delighted with it there. You probably know she was on the AMC camping party.

Excuse my hasty scrawl. I hope it will give you some idea of what is doing here. Believe me always,

Your sincere friend,

M. M. Pychowska

---

[6] This camp was known as Camp Placid.

[7] Mount Pilot.

[8] This peak is known today as Mount Cabot, which was originally named Mount Sebastian Cabot by William H. Peek in honor of the grand "pilot" of Henry VII.

Marian Pychowska writes to Isabella Stone.

Ravine House
Randolph, N.H.
September 18, 1885

Dear Isabella,

It seems a long time, and indeed it is nearly a month, since your postal reached me. Are you still at North Woodstock? Has the cold season braced you up, or have you suffered from it?

For several weeks past, I have given letter writing a slip, but I must not go home without giving you some account of how the Ravine House has fared since the middle of August. It has been well filled all the time, though with a varying population. Mr. Peek has persevered as usual. The Wares, mother and daughters, only left last Tuesday. Alice Tompson remained a week later than her family, but she also left us on Wednesday. Now, the household is reduced to the Cutter party[9] and our own, including in the latter Mr. Peek, Miss Barstow, and two other ladies who sit at our table.

Through a part of August our table was crowded to its utmost capacity and made very lively by the presence of Messrs. Sargent, Hinkley, Matthews and Thompson. You may imagine the volleys of puns and peals of laughter. Mr. Sargent's last exploit before going home to hospital work was a solitary expedition in search of Round Mountain by way of Safety Pond, returning by Lancaster clearings and Jefferson. My uncle had a long and amusing letter from him giving the details of his trip. As it did not prove satisfactory in regard to the mountain in question, my uncle is on the eve of renewing the attack in person and by way of Mt. Starr King. I believe I told you about their tour of the Pilot Range. It seems to me that broad wilderness will afford many a days exploring work before it is rifled of its secrets.

The "Durand Ridge Air Line" is indeed a perfect success, as even we recalcitrant conservatives must confess. Thanks to the persevering labors of Messrs. Cook, Peek and Sargent in surveying the best route and to several days of thorough axe work on the part of Mr. Watson and his men, it is now a model path, straight, broad, well cleared out and of easy grade. They have also improved the upper part along the crest of the ridge. My uncle, Mr. Peek and I remeasured it and reset the quarter-mile signs. The

---

[9] The Cutter family first summered in Randolph in 1883. The most notable (here) member of this clan was Louis Fairweather Cutter(1864-1945), who served in many capacities during his time spent in the White Mountains. As an active member of the AMC and a founding member of the Randolph Mountain Club, he successfully undertook the immense task of improving the trail systems of the region. His map of the Presidential Range, completed in 1886, is still the basis for the AMC's Presidential Range map of today.

four-mile sign which, in the day of the original path from Salmacis, stood just above the Gateway, and by the "Scar Route" was carried onward between three and four hundred feet, has now advanced again one-quarter mile and five hundred and seventy-six feet and stands three hundred seventy feet from the pole on the summit. "Camp Placid" has been used two or three times, but not, as yet, abused.

The indefatigable leaders of the "march of improvement", Messrs. Cook and Peek, have begun laying out a branch[10] from the Air Line into King's Ravine. It will diverge from near the two-mile mark and take an almost level course to the neighborhood of Moss Falls. This will be a great addition, as you see. The old round about way by Cold and Spur Brooks, has been unvisited by most of us this year, but we hear that it is very wet and grown up. The new route will be much more easily kept in order. We do not intend that the Scar shall be allowed to fall into neglect. Edith, Alice and I spent last Tuesday in that unique spot, enjoying the play of sun and shadow over the peaks, the golden and black-green tapestry of the Glen and the blue northern mountains, calling at the Upper Salmacis on our way home. The Gulch and Pond of Safety we have neglected—except that my mother has been over to the pond—but we have more than ever enjoyed the things near home. After all, nothing is more perennially satisfying than the walk around Randolph Hill, or that to the Bowman Place, always excepting the ridge.

At last I have been on "Owl's Head", a place that I thought I had missed for good, when I was unable to go there with the Ape party from the Twin Mountain House. Miss Barstow was kind enough to take me as her companion on a sketching trip thither. We put up our buggy at the base of the slide. To save time we took a very direct wood road up the mountain side and came out on the slide perhaps one-quarter mile below its apex. It is not unlike the old Tripyramid slide, though much less steep, interesting of course, but scarcely an object of beauty. With the mountain top it is otherwise. The knob of solid rock, with its picturesque low spruces, is an ideal view point, and the view is worthy of the point. What charmed me particularly was the vista through the Crawford Notch. We remained on the summit from about noon until four o'clock, Miss Barstow hard at work and I thoroughly enjoying a leisurely inspection of the whole horizon. It was the day after the heavy snow, so we had the peaks white. The same day Edith took her paints on Durand Ridge and sketched "John Quincy" with the snow on him.

I suppose you are having the same gorgeous autumn color that we are revelling in. It seems to me I never saw it so early or so brilliant.

My aunt and uncle expect to go home by way of Jefferson on Sep-

---

[10] This trail is known today as the Short Line.

tember 30, and the rest of us are to follow the next day by way of Gorham, being bound by return tickets.

My mother has gone to the Scar with a friend, or she would send love. Please send me a postal soon and believe me as ever,

Yours,

M. M. Pychowska

* * * * * * * * * * * *

Marian Pychowska writes to Isabella Stone.

Hoboken, N.J.
October 11, 1885

Dear Isabella,

Am I to think of you still as at the Bay View House? How the Apes seem to dog your steps, first in the upper Pemigewasset and now at Lake Winnepesaukee! And yet I am afraid you get no good out of them. My uncle is busy writing his report and account of the Mounts Nancy-Anderson-Lowell trip. His family gives him no help this time, but he is counting on an article from Mr. Peek upon the Pilot Range, and one from Mr. Butler on the slides about Waterville. If you have escaped taking cold, the bracing autumn weather must be doing you good. Of course you shared in the snow storm of September 23. It was an exciting week for us, and I wish my aunt had carried out her plan of writing to you then. That letter would have served as a pendant to the one she wrote you (if I remember rightly) upon the August flood. However, if we failed to write, at least we thought and spoke of you.

Monday, the 21st, was a lovely day and my mother, aunt and I availed ourselves of it to spend a day at Star Lake, visiting "Camp Luna" and "John Quincy". I confess that we used the "Air Line" both going and coming. The next day, as you know, it gathered for the storm, which was driving down the valley on Wednesday morning, first rain, then sleet, then snow, pure and unadulterated. After dinner Miss Barstow sat in the parlor window and painted the Messenger house to the east and the roadside in their wintry covering, while Edith and I went up the road and across the fields to Cold Brook Falls. The intervale was a sheet of white, the roadside bushes weighed down with snow, and it was still driving in our faces and giving a misty softness to the strange scene. Up about the bridge near the fall, the sight was wonderful, the snow with brilliant leaves and again the heaps of snow that weighed down the boughs of the large evergreens. Of course we got wet, tramping about in the snow, but we were dry enough by the next afternoon to go out again.

It had snowed some more Thursday morning, but there was a lull after noon. This time Edith and I went up to Randolph Hill. We walked under an arcade of drooping saplings, which in some places were bent so low by their burden of snow that they blocked the path completely. In some places on the Hill the drifts were two feet or more in depth (and were still to be seen from Mt. Madison on the following Saturday, marking the lines of stone walls with white). The clouds barely touched Randolph Mountain and allowed us to see up as far as the Scar on the slopes of the big mountains. The hardwood forests were in full autumn color, while the heights and ravine bottoms where the dark evergreens prevail, were covered with a thick crust of white. At the Mount Crescent House we found a huge owl, a true "snowy owl", about five feet high and very well modeled! Presently it began to rain and we continued on, round by the road, home where we found the snow much melted by the shower. I forgot to tell of the wonderful effect of the moonlight on the white fields on Wednesday evening, when we had a break in the storm.

Friday, the peaks were clear, and solid white. At noon the Bowman Place was still, in great part, covered with snow, though it had nearly gone from the fields closer to home. Edith made several charming sketches during the snowy time. I wish you could see them. For me, the grand finale of the week was an exploration of the "Howks", with my uncle. There was some snow in the lower woods, but it was really an obstacle after we left Bruin Rock. The steep path up the side of Madison was filled with it, and we sunk in it at almost every step, sometimes ankle-deep, sometimes knee-deep and once up to our waists. I was very glad to make use of my uncle's tracks, but of course my low India rubbers were small protection and my feet were soon soaked. Fortunately, it was quite a warm day overhead. After we had hauled ourselves up, tree by tree, along the slippery path, it was a relief to find that the open rocks were almost clear of snow. Reaching the top about noon, we spent some time there and then descended to the Howks, visiting those toward the Glen side, which we had omitted on our former trip three years ago. By the way, it just so happened that both times my uncle and I have gone over the Howks on the 26th of September. I see in my notebook that the 29th is the day you went with us to Durand Ridge, when the first path was opened. I anticipate writing a sketch of "The Howks" in which you will see, if you like, the details of our pleasant day. There was much wading through the snow, finding a great number of tracks (probably one of the wildcat tribe), beautiful views, and then we came down by Triple Falls Brook. When we left Randolph on October 1, the foliage surpassed anything I had ever seen before.

Since I came home, I have been working like a Turk to finish my translation. Only a few pages remain. Then for the excitement of hunting a publisher! Oh, three groans and a tiger!

Excuse my hasty letter, and let me hear once in a while how you get along with that slow work of recuperation. I wish it all good success and no drawbacks.

My mother and aunt join me in love to you and the kindest regard to Dr. and Mrs. Stone.

Always your friend,
M. M. Pychowska

1886

"I, for one, intend never to abet the making of a fire upon the scurf, even in a pouring rain, without grave cause."

Lucia Pychowska writes a postal card to Isabella Stone.

Ravine House
Randolph, N.H.
June 27, 1886

My dear Isabella,

The sight of the mountains naturally brings with it a desire to know how you and Dr. and Mrs. Stone are. Marian wrote you sometime ago, but we very readily presumed that you continued about the same and that your dear mother had little time or strength for writing to say just how you are.

You will find us here after the 8th of July. We (Marian and I) go July 1 to Mt. Washington to join the AMC party. Eugene does not come up until July 15 and Edith probably not before August 1. She goes with friends first to the seaside. Of course you will hear of the doings on the mountain top. We expect a fine botanizing time, although the high snow has nearly vanished, the season is so early. Love to all of your household, and a heap to yourself.

Truly yours,
L. D. Pychowska

Marian Pychowska writes to Isabella Stone.

Ravine House
Randolph, N.H.
July 18, 1886

Dear Isabella,

Your mother's letter, for which we thank her very much, came last week. Would that it were given us to do something more for you both than merely tell our stock of mountain gossip.

Edith's missive has already told you that our Mt. Washington plan was carried out. What is more, she was with us to help us enjoy it all. I will do what I can to give you an outline of our doings.

My parents and I reached Randolph on June 25. June 29, my mother and I climbed Durand Ridge with the object of securing certain plants, and thus lessening our prospective labor on Mt. Washington in getting specimens for the alpine books that I am now busy in putting together. When we gained the open part of the ridge, the wind blew with such great force, that my mother soon gave up the idea of getting to Star Lake. While she gathered Labrador Tea and some other things near treeline, I pushed on and found comparative calm as soon as I turned into the path through the shrub to Madison Spring. Between Star Lake and the cone of Madison the pale laurel was in perfection, and other beauties were to be had up the side of "John Quincy". While climbing the lee side of the latter, myself wholly protected from the westerly gale, it was awesome to listen to the roar of the wind along the exposed face of Madison opposite. At 2:30 P.M., I overtook my mother at the lower junction of paths and we returned in company.

A great part of the next day was spent in selecting paraphernalia for Mt. Washington, engineering so as to get the greatest possible amount of warm clothing and general comfort into the moderate sized box which was to be our trunk for the coming week. Little did I think that we should soon be too warm in our alpine nest!

On July 1, at 8:30 A.M., my mother and I said good bye to my father, and Mr. Watson, Sr. drove us over to the Glen. As we passed Dolly Copp's[1] (now Dolly Copp's no more, for the old lady has sold out and gone to live in Dummer), we spied a buggy moving along the road from Gorham, in

---

[1] Dolly Emery and Dodifer Hayes Copp were married in Bartlett, NH on November 3, 1831. Their lives as early White Mountain pioneers were quite impressive. Settling in the unincorporated township of Martins's Location, they braved the harsh elements of the unforgiving north country while farming and raising a family. For nearly forty years the Copp's home served as an inn for many a wayfarer travelling along the Pinkham Road which connected Randolph and Jackson. After fifty years of marriage, Dolly left Hayes exclaiming that was "long enough for a woman to live with any man!" So was born the expression "don't copp out."

which we soon recognized Mr. Laban Watson and Mr. Peek. Punctual to a long standing engagement, we reached the junction of roads almost at the same moment, and he and his valise were transferred to our wagon for transportation to Mt. Washington.

As you can imagine, it was a cordial meeting, and Mr. Peek had much to tell of his latest views of the Pilot region obtained in the neighborhood of Groveton and Stark, where he had stopped some days on his way to join us. It was my good pleasure to walk up the mountain, so I alighted at the toll gate.

As far as the Halfway House I kept with the team, but here I had a private scheme to carry out. Passing around the ledges after a rather blind hunt, I found the old Glen Bridle Path[2]. You may remember how plainly, from Mt. Adams, one can follow its course from the Ledge to where it strikes the road beyond the bend known as "Cape Horn". There is a real historic charm for me in these old paths, disused, in part grown up with shrub, but still betraying the past by the well worn gully amid the rocks.

It was, as I thought, a considerable saving of distance, for in spite of the time lost in finding the entrance, I emerged upon the road again just as the team came up. The breeze was now too stiff to allow me to keep up with the horses, so I took my own time, and lunched in a sheltered nook near the seven-mile post.

When I reached the Summit House I found my mother already ensconced in a comfortable east room—thanks to a thoughtful telegram from Mr. Lawrence. Mr. Peek joined us on the rocks and we topographized in the direction of Bartlett and Waterville.

The weather had been very clear, but the northerly wind was bringing down long streamers of smoke which spread and spread until at six o'clock, when the first regular detachment of Apes arrived by train, our horizon extended not much beyond Cherry Mountain and the Carters— and so it was to be with small variation for the next week. There was no sunset to distract us from our supper and pleasant meeting of acquaintances. Miss Barstow joined our Randolph coterie in the dining hall.

Whatever may be said of the aesthetic ruin of the Summit House, they did manage to make us very comfortable. Owing to the unwanted noise of engine and steam pipes, sleep was at a discount for three or four nights. The excitement of the high air may have had something to do with it too, but the last three nights we slept soundly. Although we were continually on the go, we made not a single fatiguing expedition, so that the result of the week was exceedingly healthful for all of us. The steam

[2] The Glen House Bridle Path was completed in 1852. It was cut and established primarily to serve in the hauling of building materials to the summit hotels from the north side of Mount Washington. It became obsolete after the opening of the carriage road in 1861.

heat was at first excessive, but as the weather grew warmer it was disused in the rooms. We slept with the window wide open, a thing we had not dared to do at Randolph the week before.

In the evenings we walked up and down the railroad platform, finding a light shawl an almost unnecessary wrap, while the help of the establishment went about the mountain top in the thinnest of muslin dresses. As the week wore on, the countenances of the whole fraternity deepened into a rich glow of sunburn, and there was a fine crop of peeled noses and cracked lips. It was really laughable to look around the dining hall and see the color of one's own face reflected in all the others. A generous lather of vaseline or cold cream was a very comfortable thing at night.

Thursday's party (about sixty, I believe) was in the charge of Messrs. Lawrence and Scott. The morning train on Friday brought another detachment with our worthy President and his pleasant little bride. With this party came my aunt, who had left home the day before and passed the night at Jefferson in order to speed one of her trunks on its way to Randolph. After an early dinner, Mr. Lowe escorted the newcomers down to the Lakes of the Clouds, southwest of the summit, there meeting the returning force from Mt. Pleasant[3], who had made an all-day affair of it. My mother and I marched with the latter, if my capricious skirmishing deserve so dignified a name. You know that the Crawford–Southern Presidential Range was wholly new to me.

On the way down, I bagged the Lakes of the Clouds, the two heads of Mt. Monroe and Franklin's crest. Returning to the path (which was strewn from end to end with Apes, in parties of from one to twenty or more!) I fell in with Miss Barstow and one other, keeping with them until we overtook my mother at the lovely tarn[4] (like that on Lafayette) on the col at the base of Mt. Pleasant. Here the path branched, one way leading directly up Pleasant, the other leading around its eastern slope—the throw line to Mt. Clinton[5]. My mother and I chose the latter path. It is wonderfully beautiful; the picturesque and richly hued shrub it leads through lends a fine foreground to the northward view of the cone of Washington grouped with the near heads of Monroe and the great gulfs of the Mt. Washington (Ammonoosuc) River lying below and before you.

On the southern slope of Pleasant, I stopped to chat with Mr. Peek and other stragglers, and fell in with Mr. Mann and his small party who

---

[3] Mount Pleasant is known today as Mount Eisenhower.

[4] This small stagnant body of water is known today as Red Pond.

[5] Mount Clinton's name was changed to Mount Pierce in 1913 by the State of New Hampshire to provide a memorial in honor of the fourteenth president, Franklin Pierce, who was both a "citizen and resident of New Hampshire."

had come up the old Fabyan Trail[6]. They reported it to be in excellent condition—much better, indeed, than the Crawford Path with its worn out corduroy. You see we had plenty of time to loaf and look and chat, for we had left the summit at nine o'clock, and we did not assemble on the top of Pleasant until near one o'clock. I used no wrap on this day, while my mother used hers as a protection against the sun. However, it was not over warm, and the bracing breeze kept off the black flies.

Smoke forbade distant views, but I saw enough to fill me with what lay beyond. On the way home Miss Hollingsworth (one of the best walkers) pointed out to me a patch of Rhodora, which I have never seen in bloom. I also made a side excursion to a point projecting into Oakes Gulf, whence was a good view of its depth and to a snowbank on its upper slope. Returning to the path, I was overhauled by my mother who had meanwhile picked up Edith, and we wended our way up the cone, getting in at 4:30 P.M.

In the evening we were assembled in the parlor to hear announcements from Mr. Lawrence, and a short discourse from Professor Shaler[7] upon the distribution of mountains in time and space, in which he made a special point of the fact that real mountain formation is characteristic of continents, while volcanic formation is equally characteristic of the ocean basins.

July 3 (Saturday)

Today it was Tuckerman's Ravine—the general time of starting was 10:00 A.M. in order to give a good rest to those fatigued by the long trip of the first day. As we were only too ready for an early breakfast, Mr. Peek and ourselves set out at 8:20 A.M., and had plenty of time to sketch and botanize before the crowd appeared on the scene.

The winding and somewhat dizzy path down the headwall, among the thousand streams that drain Bigelow's Lawn, was not unfamiliar. The snow arch was very fine indeed. Some of the ladies who came later went through the entire length (one hundred to two hundred feet I should think), but we were content to climb in a short distance from below, and look up the dim arched cavern to the cascade falling in the light at the upper end. It was very beautiful and quite easy to pass between the streams that drip from every point of the roof. Alongside of the snow, we found two rare but rather unattractive plants. Edith and I scrambled up the ravine side toward the small arch and sat under the grateful shade of the crag and looked over the edge of the steep white slope, down which Edith longed to coast! This was a fine point of vantage whence to view the long line of Apes descending the slide opposite us. You have no idea how pictur-

---

[6] The Fabyan Bridle Path (originally the first Crawford Path) was made passable to horses by Horace Fabyan soon after 1840. The path, which had become overgrown, was reopened in 1886 and in passing years, was abandoned once again.

[7] N. S. Shaler of Cambridge, MA, was a founding member of the AMC.

Mount Adams from Mount Clay

esque they were and how much they added to one's ability to realize size and distance on these big barren mountains.

After lunch there was a dispersion. A large party went down to the Hermit Lakes and returned. A few, including Miss Hollingsworth (and Miss Frothingham, I think) went out by the Raymond Path to the carriage road, making a good day's work in such warm weather. My mother returned leisurely to the summit, while Edith and I went round the headwall to the Lion's Head Crag, which gives a good view of the ravine and lakes. Returning across the Alpine Gardens we were screened by the mountains from the breeze, and the heat of the sun really suggested the idea of sunstroke. The long climb up the cone was not wholly exhilarating.

In the evening Dr. Farlow[8] displayed specimens of plants found during the day, and furnished botanical information to all inquirers. It was a most agreeable diversion.

Sunday, July 4

It is still warm and very smoky with the sun rising and setting a mere red ball, the chief interest being to watch the cone of shadow cast by our mountain on the adjacent ranges. This uninteresting aspect of the

---

[8] Dr. William G. Farlow of the Boston Society of Natural History was an expert on mountain flora.

Tip-Top House, Mount Washington

weather was counterbalanced by its entire safety from fog and dangerous wind. Sunday afternoon Edith and I strolled down the carriage road to the head of the Great Gulf, enjoyed the view and found new plants.

Monday, July 5

This was the warmest day of all, taking from me at least all desire for great deeds. A large party took the seven o'clock train as far as Gulf Station[9], and proceeded, some to Jefferson, some to Adams, a very few to Madison. Mr. Lawrence expressed himself much pleased with "our parish", which he then visited for the first time. One lady and one man joined our late starting party at 8:30 A.M. We skirted the Great Gulf, Edith and I visiting each projecting rock and looking down each gully, loafing in fact, all the way over to Mt. Clay. I circumnavigated the mountain and came back over

---

[9] The Gulf Station House was located below the summit cone of Mount Washington to the northwest where the Cog Railroad traverses the top of the Great Gulf.

the top until we found a lovely camping ground[10], lacking only one thing, namely water, which we were deprived of all day long. For two hours or more, we three with a new acquaintance, Miss Baker, lay on the soft, dry moss, under the shade of a great rock, and looked over a rich alpine pasture, gay with deep yellow geums, to the mountain and levels of Jefferson bathed in summer heat and smoke—yet beautiful. On the return, Edith and I climbed the cone the back way, and came in past the poor old Tip-Top House[11]—which, by the way, is going to utter ruin for lack of little care. This evening Mr. Scott's party, which had gone to the Castles, did not get in till toward nine o'clock, causing uneasiness to a few.

Here I will stop and give you a rest for some days, when I hope to finish my long tale, and also impart to you the details of a very sad disaster which has befallen our dear Durand. Tomorrow weather permitting, we go to view the destruction.

Good-night, and God bless you with something better than my nonsense. With kindest regards to Dr. and Mrs. Stone.

Most sincerely yours,
M. Pychowska

* * * * * * * * * * *

Marian Pychowska writes to Isabella Stone.

Ravine House
Randolph, N.H.
July 25, 1886

Dear Isabella,

It was a great pleasure to read your familiar hand on the postal that came last night, and to be so heartily reassured of your interest. I speak for my mother as well as for myself.

I see that the editorial stratagem wherewith I closed my last letter, has had the effect intended. Now I do not mean to risk the rest of the Mt. Washington story by postponing for its sake the satisfaction of your desire to know the fate of Durand. I will proceed to the latter at once, "as

---

[10] It is here where Edith Cook painted one of the mountain landscapes included among the illustrations of *Mountain Summers*.

[11] During the early summer of 1853, Samuel Fitch Spaulding of Lancaster, NH, along with Abraham Bedell and Anson Stillings of Jefferson, built the Tip-Top House on the summit of Mount Washington. By the end of July that same year, this precarious mountain-top hostel was opened to guests and it remained in operation until 1872. From 1872 until 1877, it housed summit employees and from 1877 to 1884, it served as headquarters and printing office for the newspaper, *Among the Clouds*. The Tip-top House has been reworked and renovated many times over the years (most recently by the AMC) and is the only one of the early stone structures on the mountain that remains today.

one who speaks and weeps", metaphorically.

In plain English the fact is, that on Wednesday the 14th of July at 1:30 P.M., a thin line of smoke was seen rising from the floor of King's Ravine. In an hour's time the fire had increased fearfully. From my post of observation opposite the ravine, I could see flames leaping and swaying under the blast of wind driving, as usual, up the ravine as through a flue, and meeting, above, the strong east wind. These conflicting currents made an eddy which soon filled the ravine with smoke, so that we could no longer judge of the fire's progress, except by the increasing volume of deep yellow, angry looking smoke that poured up the great chimney and rolled westward, and by the occasional bursts of flame which showed that the fire had climbed Durand Ridge and was eating—I may say, gobbling—its way into the wind and toward us. For half an hour it was fearful to watch, the power and speed were so, to all appearance, irresistible. However, contrary winds, or other blessed circumstances favored us, and about three o'clock it began to abate slowly. O, how anxiously we scanned the weather, and hoped the moon would spare the precious clouds that were gathering over the Carters. After dark, there was an occasional lurid glow from the ridge, and, from any viewpoint down the road, sparks of flame were seen dotting the crest, showing that the fire was working among the shrub on the Salmacis slope. Meanwhile my uncle arrived to share in our mourning.

The next day a curtain of low cloud shut in the wounded mountain, and soon we had rain, rain in abundance, scotching the destroyer completely. We cannot be duly thankful—"The mercy of God is as a cloud of rain in the time of drought".

It is an ugly piece of work as it stands. The ravine is burnt from side to side all the way from the lowest boulders just beyond Moss Fall, up to the open place where we lunched together—black, naked, contorted trees, the earth so burnt that the path was often hard to trace. The floor proper is only partially injured, the center being untouched, Nowell's Ridge is intact, but Durand Ridge is badly hurt. The fire ran up the gullies, from the Gateway gully exclusive, all the way along that side, including a broad tract of the dense spruce forest, down as far as to a line connecting Moss Fall with the upper junction of the paths on the ridge. Happily the fire rarely reached the crest on this lower part of the ridge, so that the "Air Line" is uninjured up to within a few feet of treeline. At this point the fire swept across the path fifty feet or more, and from here on to near the Gateway, path, crag, shrub, and alpine growth are cruelly scarred. My uncle assures me that the fire nowhere extended more than seventy-five feet down the Salmacis side.

Last Monday, he and my mother and I went up into the Ravine to measure the new "Short Line" path which diverges from the "Air Line", and to "view the scenes of disaster". Thundershowers came on before the measurement was finished, so that when we gained the view point, the mists were drifting up, first hiding, then revealing the ghastly black side of Durand. The measuring tape and I were well adorned with charcoal in solution. Having wiped the aforesaid tape and wound it up, I crawled under my mother's sheltering rock and we ate a somewhat cheerless lunch. I persuaded my mother not to go on with my uncle up the ravine and down the ridge, as we had intended, but to return home the way we had come. On the way out, I reconnoitered among the lower boulders, regardless of smut. The best we can say is that the fire has opened some impressive views, and that time will change the raw coat of black, first to red, and then to bleached bones, lending perhaps more than the former grandeur to the crag of Durand. But the beautiful mossy path through the lower boulders is, I fear me, spoiled for age.

Now the question comes; who did the deed? It is not certainly known who did it, yet I am convinced that I myself had a hand, yea, two hands in it. I feel that I can safely trust the confession to you—that you will not betray me nor my accomplices—however you may share Mr. Lowe's indignation against us. We did not go to do it, and we are very sorry if we did it. I, for one, intend never to abet the making of a fire upon the scurf, even in a pouring rain, without grave cause. But, to the point.

Saturday July 10, Professor Fay and two ladies who had come from Mt. Washington to make a stay at the Mount Crescent House, went into King's Ravine, I accompanying them to dispense the hospitalities of the new path completed that very day. It began to rain soon after we set out, but we pushed on in spite of the ever increasing wet. The ladies were not fast walkers, so that when one o'clock came we had not yet reached the viewpoint. As we neared it, we met Mr. Scott with a small party who had camped on Mt. Adams after their walk from Washington the previous day. They had gone down into the ravine and lunched there. When we met them they were bound for Mr. Lowe's, whence a wagon was to carry them to the Twin Mountain House. You will laugh when you hear how they were unwittingly drawn into the vortex of the Ravine House. Mr. Lowe had visited their camp the evening before, and instructed them to use "Chicago Avenue" as a short cut to the ravine. This they did, but in going out, having picked up their packs where they had left them, at the junction of Chicago Avenue and Ravine Path, they did not find the continuation of the latter path, and so took Spur Brook Avenue[12], coming out at Cold Brook Falls. This brought Mr. Watson a job in conveying them up to Lowe's. The blame of this mistake is with the Club. It ought to make it worthwhile for Mr. Lowe to keep his path open.

After some conversation, we parted from the outgoing party, Mr. Scott telling us that if we were quick we might be able to rekindle the fire

---

[12] Spur Brook Avenue is today the upper section of the Amphibrach Trail.

they had just left. When we reached the viewpoint, wet and chilly as we were, the fog shutting from us all but the surrounding shrub and boulders, I soon found the fireplace. There were no brands, no coals, but the mossy scurf upon which the fire had been, was smoldering, and our efforts soon aroused a small but comforting blaze. One of the ladies wondered how fire could burn where everything was so soaking wet. But, alas, burn it did.

We did not linger long after lunch. One of our gentlemen did his best to tramp out the remains of the fire, and we turned our backs without a suspicion, upon the seeds of destruction. Perhaps I judge rashly, _perhaps_ it was not _our_ fire that broke out suddenly four days later. _Perhaps_ not, but then whose was it? There are no other claimants.

Monday the 12th the same party, with the addition of my mother, Mr. Lowe, and others, went up the Air Line, along the ridge and up Mt. Madison. I had not a thought of our Saturday's fire, but I looked down as usual and made out the view point in the ravine. If there had been smoke from a smoldering fire, should we not have noticed it? And yet, when we made our post mortem last Monday it seemed to me pretty clear that a fire might smoulder in the scurf during four days time until it gained the shrub with a favorable wind, and _our_ fireplace did seem to be the starting point.

And so the matter stands. Professor Fay thinks my theory incredible, in view of the rain and the length of time that elapsed before the outbreak. At all events, it is a lesson I hope never to forget, against fires on the scurf.

I shall have to leave the rest of the Mt. Washington story for my next writing. Meanwhile I will answer a question contained in your mother's letter. No, Mrs. and Miss Howler[13] have not appeared in public, though a kind friend has tried to find an audience for them in at least one magazine.

As ever yours,
M. M. Pychowska

---

[13] Mrs. and Miss Howler are the two characters in Marian's story "Two in the Alpine Pastures."

Marian Pychowska writes to Isabella Stone.

Ravine House
Randolph, N.H.
July 30, 1886

Dear Isabella,

If I remember rightly, the Mt. Washington chronicle was completed up to Tuesday, July 6.

In order to give a resting time to those who had taken the long tramp of Monday to Jefferson and Adams, there was no general excursion on Tuesday morning. We three with Mr. Peek walked down the carriage road one mile and crossed the plateau between Chandler's Ridge and Nelson's Crag to the head of Huntington's Ravine. You may remember my telling you about a very fine projecting crag that juts into the ravine, which Miss Barstow and I happened on when we made our first visit two years ago. I wished to revisit the place and see if my first impression would be justified. To reach the head of this projection it is necessary to descend two or three hundred feet of a very steep broken rock slide. This deterred my mother from following us. It is a dizzy, awesome place, so that even Mr. Peek and my aunt were not willing to investigate it thoroughly, but I found my remembrance of its impressiveness was not exaggerated.

When we returned to dinner at the Summit House, we learned that the general afternoon walk was to be across the Alpine Garden, from the top of Huntington to the Lion's Head crag above Tuckerman. Mr. Edmands asked me to show them the projection of which I had previously spoken to him and Mr. Lowe. So in effect, I had the satisfaction of introducing our crag officially to the President of the AMC. Mr. Edmands did not think it a safe place to invite the party to follow, consequently Messrs. Lowe, Lawrence, Nowell and one other were the only ones to venture down the slide. I was surprised to find that the spot was new to all of them, as well as flattered by the enthusiastic interest they showed in viewing the great crag from all sides. Mr. Lowe was so impressed as to spout verse, and his enthusiasm, as you may well think, pleased me more than anything else.

The crag is a jutting ridge of rock, extending down the ravine wall five hundred feet or more, and showing a superb cleavage, with great smooth surfaces and bold angles. One can easily walk out to the point of the promontory and look down the abyss. From under the slide which leads down to the crag, flows an icy cold streamlet which first gladdens a little garden of alpine moss and flowers, and then leaps down the clean rocky trough formed by the underside of the long crag. One of the best ways of seeing the place is to creep out into the little mossy garden slope and look down into the ravine. The gentle murmur of the sliding streamlet is in strange contrast to the feeling one has of fear lest one should slide after it into the awful depths.

In the evening we had an informal discourse from Dr. Farlow upon alpine floras.

On Wednesday the 7th we went with the general excursion to Boott's Spur. Following the Crawford Path down to the plateau, we struck the old Davis Path. Mr. Lowe bade me observe how, in some places, the only remaining sign of the path was the more abundant growth of a special kind of grass. There were other places where it wound around the spur, where the rocks had been displaced and set in order so as to favor the horses footing, forming a very picturesque roadway reminding one of foreign parts, such as the Alps or the Pyrenees. At the crest of Boott's Spur, we left this attractive path and coasted the edge of Tuckerman's Ravine, getting superb views down between the noble crags to the lakelets. This was by far the most beautiful day we yet had as to weather. The atmosphere was somewhat clearer, and the play of color, light and shadow produced by the swift driven cloud masses added beauty and impressiveness to all. The cone of Washington is singularly imposing as seen from this side and across the ravine. A few of us wandered beyond the main party, down the eastward buttress, crossing it to gain a fine view into the Gulf of Slides. Here again I enjoyed Mr. Lowe's society, and together we found the tiny Alpine Eyebright.

After lunching with the main party, I skirmished about among the crags lying between The Gulf of Slides and Oakes Gulf. I soon fell in with Messrs. Lawrence and Carpenter[14], who were doing the same thing and we formed a party to visit the southern end of the spur and get a view into the Slide Gulf from its farther wall. To accomplish the latter project we had to cross a small belt of prime shrub. Mr. Lowe hesitated, doubting whether it would pay, but on my saying it was only an affair of ten minutes, we plunged in and made the crossing in seven minutes. Such a bout with the tough dwarfs is exhilarating, and we were paid for it besides by getting the best view of the gulf.

It was well named, very broad in the upper basin and narrow toward the outlet. The whole of the upper basin is seamed with slides of loose sandy character, which have swept away almost all evergreen growth, and have themselves been overgrown with deciduous growth of birches and alders. Thus the whole ravine is striped, sides and bottom with the yellow of fresh slides and the pale green of old overgrown ones making it very different from the somber boulder strewn depths of the more northern ravines. One small tract the sweeping slides have spared. Raised somewhat above the general level of the floor, the primeval growth was here saved and in the midst of this bit of quiet dark forest, lies a pale green

---

[14] Frank O. Carpenter of Boston, MA, served as Councillor of Exploration for the AMC in 1887.

deer pasture of mossy swamp with the stream winding through it. We were directly above it and I looked down into it somewhat covetously. This gulf had another peculiarity. We have, both of us, sat time and again on a crag above some deep ravine and been delighted by some bird song coming up to us from below. But here the depths seemed full of birds, White Throated Sparrows, Swainson Thrushes, and Winter Wrens by the scores, singing madly, in spite of the high wind that raked the ravine from end to end.

Our return through the shrub took fifteen minutes, owing to our trying a more roundabout way, and also to the fact that we were taking the growth against the grain, so to speak; that is to say, we had to fight up against the direction of its long arms as determined by the prevailing winds. On the crest of the ridge we again struck the Davis Path, and followed it down nearly to where it enters the forest. The Montalban Ridge leading away to Giant Stairs, Resolution and Crawford was most alluring. Returning along the path, we met the full force of the wind as it swept across Oakes' Gulf. Happily it came at right angles to our course, and so was not too fierce to spoil our fun.

Earlier in the day we had noticed the smoke that rose from behind Mt. Franklin. Now it had filled Crawford Notch and drifted way round to Conway, while great yellow-brown volumes rolled up from the increasing fire, making the southern landscape all lurid, the air about us being still clear. The clouds began to come down as we neared the summit, and we sat some time to watch the strange passing gleams of light cross from the Lakes of the Clouds to Tuckerman's Ravine, and the sweeping fringes of the cloud that was soon to wrap us in.

I believe I have already told you of the official gaieties of this last evening, of the songs from the Chairman and the Virginia reel for which the President played.

Next morning the old mountain gave us a royal send-off in the shape of a sunrise—the only one of the week. When our weather broke and fled, it let in the view of a world of mountains scarce seen for the past week, some standing clear and blue, and others wrapped in fleece. The cloud masses that formed over Monroe and the whole Crawford Range were wonderful.

After breakfast there was a general dispersion of the AMC. Some opted to take the morning train. Miss Barstow went down with the party taking the Fabyan Path and Mr. Lowe took charge of those Jefferson bound, among whom were Messrs. Ladd and Nowell, Miss Frothingham, Miss Clark, Professor Fay, etc. and this party went by the Castles. My mother and Mr. Peek also started early down the carriage road, not wishing to be hurried in keeping the appointment with Mr. Watson at the Glen at four o'clock. My aunt and I spent the whole morning enjoying the clear view and loafing from one point to another.

We dined at twelve and by one were saddled and bridled and off in pursuit of my mother and Mr. Peek. The last dinner was sad, for the atmosphere of the AMC had departed from the dining hall and the ordinary palefaced tourist just up from Fabyan's was once more supreme. I had quite a homesick pang at turning my back on the scene of such a pleasant week. As we strode past the Halfway House, a jovial looking man came out and hailed us, requiring toll. We paid, saying we had not known whether the toll was taken here or at the foot. The man asked us to wait until he should give us a pass for the Glen tollgate, and when he came back with it he laughingly apologized for having called after us in the first instance, as at the moment of our passing he was sitting for his photograph and could not move. Our amusement over this episode was greatly increased when I read the pass. It ran as follows: "July 8, Pass two footers, J.C.". Footers is good is it not? We stepped on the Glen piazza just as Mr. Watson's team drove up, containing my father who had come to greet us.

And now, I believe, I have done my long story, my last letter having told you about the unhappy ruin made in our ravine!

The Ice Gulch is no longer a mysterious and inaccessible haunt. Hubbard Hunt has cut out the Peboamauk Trail[15], which traverses the burnt district—very direct, but not beautiful like the old way[16] along the mountain ridge. Mrs. Fay with her two little girls, respectively seven and eight-years-old, walked over to Peboamauk Falls and up as far as the second chamber of the Gulch—the cleverest little climbers you ever saw! Two gentlemen have made the whole trip including the entire length of the Gulch between dinner and supper. However, I do not set great store by our refrigerator. It is a first rate curiosity, and beautiful too, but I enjoyed a day on Randolph Mountain much more. On the latter day, my uncle, mother and I cleared out the old path and opened a clearer view at the north viewpoint.

Mr. Sargent is here now, and Mr. Hinkley expected this evening. Miss Susie Stearns, to whom he has recently become engaged, came last Saturday and is under the nominal charge of my mother.

I must positively stop scrawling, hoping that your imagination and memory will suffice to reconstruct a little pleasure out of my account.

Lovingly yours,

M. M. Pychowska

---

[15] Known today as the Ice Gulch Path.
[16] The Cook Path. This trail, as one might imagine, was later named in honor of Eugene and his family.

Edith Cook writes to Isabella Stone.

Ravine House
Randolph, N.H.
August 1, 1886

My dear Miss Stone,
    Since you have said that any mountain news would be welcome to
you—even the putting on of a new pair of canvas shoes— I will write out
for you this afternoon a little picture that it would have given you pleasure to see; and that I shall not soon forget, and of which I am able to
speak to very few lest the spirit of enterprise and desire should lead someone to try to break the game laws of New Hampshire. Not that devotion
to the laws is uppermost in my mind, but rather a consideration for the
peace of the beautiful creatures that stood so long gazing at me up on the
Bowman Place.
    Yesterday Lillie and Dovie[17] started forth, for the day, to pay visits
along the road from here to the Mt. Adams House. I walked with them as
far as the end of the Bowman Place where I wanted to gather some of the
fringed orchids that grow there so profusely, for a nosegay, to give to a
guest, expected that evening to be under Lillie's charge. It is a wet little
meadow generally, at this end, but this year it is very dry. I can walk there
dry shod where once we only escaped wet feet by very rapid jumping
from tuft to tuft. I wandered in on it in search of my orchids and seeing
some finer ones on the edge of the wood, I went for them. On the little
meadow the grass had been lately cut and was standing heaped in little
cocks; about one of these I saw something move. At first I thought it was
a man mowing, then I saw it was a four-legged animal of red color. I
dreamed deer and reasoned calf, and went out into the meadow to make
sure. There, on the edge of the wood through which you have passed to
go to the Castles, stood two beautiful red deer, their heads up as listening,
their broad ears on the alert, and their graceful forms set in relation to one
another as if an artist had posed them for modelling—their immediate
background a civilized haycock, but their farther background the dark
green forests.
    I never had seen wild deer so near before and as I walked softly
toward them one of them turned away and then returned, looking stead-
fastly at me as I looked at them. I could hardly believe that I was truly
looking at these wild creatures of the woods. We gazed for some minutes
at one another, as if we were both equally rapt in admiration and specula-
tion, and then the larger animal of the two, the buck, I suppose (they were
both quite small), turned and galloped off into the woods, setting his tail

---

[17] Dovie was a nickname for Marian that was occasionally used by members of
her family.

up and flinging his heels out in a wild way. After the noise of crackling twigs was lost, I heard a kind of barking from the retreating creatures after whom I observed with the kind of feeling that I should never look on their like again. But you can imagine the graceful beauty of the picture, the two delicate creatures with the green mossy meadow under their feet, the fresh green haycock beside them, sunny green bushes about them, and shadowy green forests behind them, and their upright listening attitude. I suppose those two creatures will always fill for me that corner of the Bowman Meadow. How I wished for someone to see them with me!

Thanks for your postal card. It came while I was about on a week's visit to Jefferson Hill when I went to stay with a friend whom I am now expecting to come and stay with me. Mr. Sargent has now joined us from Mt. Katahdin which he has climbed. Mr. Hinkley is booked for tomorrow —we have already under our charge the young lady to whom he is engaged. But perhaps Marian has already written you of the very positive personality of our household and I only meant to tell you of the bit of animal beauty at the Bowman Place.

With kind regards to your mother and father,

Yours sincerely,

Edith W. Cook

* * * * * * * * * * * *

Marian Pychowska writes to Isabella Stone.

Ravine House
Randolph, N.H.
September 19, 1886

Dear Isabella,

I realize that another season is well nigh over, when I consider that I am sending the last bulletin thereof to you.

This cold storm is a seasonable occasion for penmanship indoors, while outdoors it is doing its work upon the foliage. There is much less brilliant color than at this time last year, but every day, yea, every hour, shows an advance in the change. Owing to the dry time, the birches and ashes have turned before the maples, so there is a preponderance of yellow. The zone of birches just below treeline is very bright, looking like a rainbow lying across the mountain sides and filling the ravines. We womenfolk enjoy these things very cheaply, from our porch, from the Hill, or from the Bowman Place. I have come to derive as much pleasure from these saunterings as from the explorations of old.

My mother, aunt and I have had a day on Mt. Crescent. (We have given way to Mr. Peek and to local usage and no longer call it Randolph Mountain. The summit east of the Gulch is now distinguished as "Black

Crescent", for the old local name was "Black Mountain".) Logging and burning have scarred the way to our Randolph-Crescent, so that it is not the lovely wood-path that you climbed, but the outlooks north and south are beautiful as ever. In spite of the heat of the day, we were glad to find a sunny spot at that chilly northern outlook.

Another all-day jaunt was taken last Monday, the 13th, by my aunt, Mr. Sargent and myself. It was Pine Mountain this time. Edith tried to fix the date of our Pine excursion of three years ago. Was it not September 13? It was a most beautiful day; not soft and hazy as we saw it of old, but cold, clear and strong. Mt. Madison was dark and grand under the cloud masses, Washington veiled halfway down in mist, and brilliant sunshine and showers chased one another across Carter Notch and the adjacent mountains. We had our shower on the way down, making our skirts heavy with wet, but this did not detract from the pleasure of the day.

Yes, the Pilot Range has really been done. Last Wednesday morning, the trio, Cook, Peek, and Sargent, set forth. Cook and Peek picked up Messrs. Lowe and Hunt, and drove round to Lancaster Gore, whence they attacked the Bunnell Notch, which lies between a shoulder of the Grand Pilot ("Mt. Sebastian Cabot", as Mr. Peek names it) and "Terrace Mountain" (an interjection between the Pilots and the Plinys). Mr. Sargent was determined to test his woodcraft, and so he set forth solus to meet the others across the Pond of Safety wilderness. By dint of pistol shots and shouts, he did manage to join them, and all camped in the notch.

Wednesday was very fine as regards weather, but Thursday was stormy. My uncle and Mr. Lowe left the others in camp, while they went up to the Grand Pilot in the fog and set up a sign bearing the new name favored by Mr. Peek. This little entertainment of giving names is very innocent, when one considers in what out-of-the-way places it is practiced! It will hardly influence "public opinion"!

After another night in camp, they visited "the Bulge" and "the Horn", two summits that lie to the eastward of "Sebastian Cabot", and which are well seen from the north viewpoint of Randolph-Crescent. The clouds cleared away when they reached "the Horn", so they had a good view thence. Heavy showers in the afternoon drenched them, but they were true to their appointment with the team, and all got home safely before ten that night. They seem much relieved in mind since the deed is done at last.

When this storm is past, we hope to visit the Castles, that my aunt may take a pencil drawing or so.

We have followed the fashion of late, in regard to balsam pillows. Picking has been the business of numbers of the Raviners. I discovered that I could combine my picking with the daily walk, by fastening my botanical box to my waist. So if you were to meet me strolling along the road to Lowe's, you would find a girl with some branches of fir under her arm, a tin box open in front of her, and fingers busy stripping the needles, while feet and eyes wander at will.

I know not yet the date of our departure, but October 1 will probably find us at home. My mother and I are in our usual health once more.

Hoping to hear good news of you soon, and with love in which my mother joins me, I am always,

Your friend,

M. M. Pychowska

* * * * * * * * * * * *

Marian Pychowska writes to Isabella Stone.

Hoboken, N.J.

October 24, 1886

Dear Isabella,

You are a faithful friend indeed to keep in mind my birthday and write me a letter thereupon. Not a word do you say of how you are and what you are doing. Is that to come out in the sequel?

My "last bulletin" from Randolph proved rather premature. Not that we did anything very worthy of record, but that the change of season seemed this year more wonderful than ever. The preparations were so slow, and then all of a sudden it burst into full glory and was in perfection when we left, October 1. During a pause in the storm, on September 21, my aunt and I climbed the "Air Line" as far as timber limit. Winter in person forbade our going further. Already, below the junction of the old Scar Path, we found patches of snow lying on the brilliant moss. Higher up, the tree tops were all frosty. In general the clouds were sweeping as far down as the Gateway, but, as we crossed the first viewpoint, they lifted, letting us see all of Madison, John Quincy, and all but the peak of Adams. I never saw our old friends so stern, for they were not merely rock-bound, but ice-bound, ice and snow plastering the faces of cliffs and setting off their angles. A fitting foreground for the bleak scene that was made by the burnt scrub, the naked black stems all cased in shining ice. And such a breeze as greeted us when we reached the bare ridge! It took away all thought of further progress, and made us realize the risks run by the party who had come over the peaks from Mt. Washington two days previous. Edith and I did not linger long on the ridge, but retreated to the Scar to lunch.

My aunt and uncle left Randolph one day earlier than the rest of us. Mr. Peek was to have gone that same day, but, finding the trains would allow him to stay over, he concluded to take me to visit a spot of which he had just heard, known to the neighbors as the Devil's Den, but better deserving Edith's name of "Moose Cave". He, provided with the stable lantern, and I with a hammer in my belt, set forth to inspect the unknown.

You well know the Moose River Road by which we go to Pine Mountain. This we followed as far as the first crossing. Finding the stream swollen, we decided to keep the right bank, knowing the cave to be on that side. The woods and shore were beautiful and pathless. In about one-third of a mile we reached the place where the river makes its sharp bend toward Gorham. Here the bank rises into a cliff. Climbing a slope carpeted with the most luxuriant trailing arbutus, we circumvented the cliff and came out upon its brow. There was no expansive view—only the peak of Madison and its Howks rising over the tall hemlock and spruce, a stretch of the stream below us lined with splendid autumn color, the fairest of skies, and the most golden of September sunshine—but it was enough to enthuse over. Yet, truth to tell, I spent most of my time cracking open the debris lying about the small cavern which we duly found at the foot of our cliff by the stream-side. It was not extensive enough to make our lantern of any use.

Another of our late finds was a beautiful wood path connecting the Moose River Road with a lonely farm on the side of Randolph Hill. I think this path, so plain and unobstructed, must be the regular route from the Hill to the cave.

October 31

As to your question about the East Branch of the Pemigewasset, that broad rushing stream so impressed us who crossed it at Pollard's, that we often speak of some difficulty that arises as being "nothing to the East Branch".

Now I will explain why I have let a week pass over my unfinished letter. The day after we reached home, our friend Professor Leeds asked me to take the place in his laboratory left vacant by the excellent lady assistant who had been with him for two years or more. I was greatly pleased at this speedy entrance into what promises to be interesting and lucrative work, for the winter at least. My three weeks trial last winter was not enough to make me feel really at home among the delicate chemical operations, and I have gone through a few small agonies of mind over my unfitness for such accurate work. But Dr. Leeds is willing to train me and his good sub-assistant, Christian Strauss, does all he can to make my way easy. My work is from 8:45 A.M. to 1:45 P.M. on every day but Saturday, when I come home at one o'clock. The Institute is about one-half of a mile from home, so I enjoy the exercise. As Dr. Leeds is Analyst to the New Jersey State Board of Health, beside having much to do with the analysis of the water supply of several towns, the work is of serious importance. This gives it a certain zest for me, which I would not feel at all if I were dabbling in chemistry for its own sake. It is not agreeable to determine with critical palate the exact flavor of a half dozen samples of vile butter or oloe-margarine, but it is a great satisfaction to think that when the said samples have been officially denounced, the less fortunate, who suffer by these wretched cheats, may be spared the infliction of such stuff for food.

You may wonder why I have taken my handwriting so aback. I find it convenient in the laboratory, as being more rapid and close. I hope it may acquire <u>beauty</u> in time...

Ever yours,
M. M. Pychowska

SELECTED BIBLIOGRAPHY

AMC White Mountain Guide, 25th ed. Boston: Appalachian Mountain Club, 1992.

Appalachia. Boston: Appalachian Mountain Club. Volume 1, Number 1 - Volume 49, Number 4.

Belcher, C. Francis. *Logging Railroads of the White Mountains*. Boston: The Appalachian Mountain Club, 1980.

Bent, Allen H. *A Bibliography of the White Mountains*. Boston: Appalachian Mountain Club, 1911.

Burt, F. Allen. *The Story of Mount Washington*. Hanover, NH: Dartmouth Publications, 1960.

Campbell, Catherine H. *New Hampshire Scenery: A Dictionary of Nineteenth Century Artists of New Hampshire Mountain Landscapes*. Canaan, NH: Phoenix Publishing, 1985.

Cross, George N. *Randolph Old and New*. Randolph, NH: The Town of Randolph, 1924.

Drake, Samuel Adams. *The Heart of the White Mountains: Their Legend and Scenery*. New York: Harper & Brothers, 1882.

Evans, George C. *History of the Town of Jefferson, New Hampshire 1773-1927*. Manchester, NH: The Granite State Press, 1927.

Hixon, Robert and Mary Hixon. *The Place Names of the White Mountains*. Camden, ME: Down East Books, 1980.

Kilbourne, Frederick W. *Chronicles of the White Mountains*. Boston: Houghton Mifflin Company, 1916.

Manning, Robert E. *Mountain Passages: An Appalachia Anthology*. Boston: Appalachian Mountain Club, 1982.

McAvoy, George E. *And Then There Was One: A History of the Hotels of the Summit and the West Side of Mt. Washington*. Littleton, NH: The Crawford Press, 1988.

Mudge, John T. B. *The White Mountains: Names, Places & Legends*. Etna, NH: The Durand Press, 1992.

Randolph Mountain Club. *Randolph Paths*. Randolph, NH: 1917.

Town of Randolph Sesquicentennial Committee. *Randolph, N.H. 150 Years*. Randolph, NH: 1974.

Washburn, Henry Bradford, Jr. *The Trails and Peaks of the Presidential Range of the White Mountains*. Worchester, MA: 1926.

Waterman, Laura and Guy Waterman. *Forest and Crag: A History of Hiking, Trail Blazing and Adventure in the Northeast Mountains*. Boston: The Appalachian Mountain Club, 1989.

Wight, D. B. *The Androscoggin River Valley*. Rutland, VT: Charles E. Tuttle Company, 1967.

INDEX

Note: Trails, mountains, and other scenic features are generally listed under their modern names (e.g. Mt. Garfield, not Mt. Hooket). Excluded are trivial passing references to mountains and other phenomena. Also excluded are references to the four principal correspondents (Edith Cook, Lucia and Marian Pychowska, Isabella Stone), as their presence pervades the letters on almost every page.

ABOUT THE EDITORS:

June Hammond Rowan is a geographer and city planner. She has worked in the White Mountain National Forest for the U.S. Forest Service and the Appalachian Mountain Club's Research Department. Peter Rowan is a White Mountain historian and collector of books on the subject. He has served for several years on the Board of Directors of the Randolph Mountain Club and was one of the principal builders of both Gray Knob and Crag Camp on Mount Adams. The Rowans are avid hikers and have explored much of the White Mountains.

Editors' Note: Any changes to the text were made strictly for the sake of clarity. Grammar, including punctuation, capitalization and quotation, has, for the most part, been left as in the original form.